today's isms

WORKS BY WILLIAM EBENSTEIN

Today's Isms: Communism, Fascism, Capitalism, Socialism
  (Sixth Edition)
Totalitarianism: New Perspectives
Two Ways of Life: The Communist Challenge to Democracy
  (Second Edition)
Communism in Theory and Practice
Great Political Thinkers: Plato to the Present (Fourth Edition)
Modern Political Thought: The Great Issues (Second Edition)
Man and the State: Modern Political Ideas
The Nazi State
The German Record: A Political Portrait
Introduction to Political Philosophy
Political Thought in Perspective
Fascist Italy
Church and State in Franco Spain
The Pure Theory of Law
The Law of Public Housing
American Democracy in World Perspective (co-author)
American Government in the Twentieth Century (co-author)

WILLIAM EBENSTEIN

today's isms

communism · fascism
capitalism · socialism

sixth edition

PRENTICE-HALL, INC.
englewood cliffs, new jersey

P–13–924423–9
C–13–924431–X

Library of Congress Catalog Card Number 79–106000
Printed in the United States of America
Current printing (last number):
10 9 8 7 6 5 4 3 2 1

PRENTICE-HALL INTERNATIONAL, INC., London
PRENTICE-HALL OF AUSTRALIA, PTY. LTD., Sydney
PRENTICE-HALL OF CANADA, LTD., Toronto
PRENTICE-HALL OF INDIA PRIVATE LIMITED, New Delhi
PRENTICE-HALL OF JAPAN, INC., Tokyo

TO THE MEMORY OF JOY

contents

part two   **the democratic way of life**

preface

The major conflict of our age is between totalitarianism and democracy. Not long ago the chief threat to liberty was fascism; today it is communism. Despite the defeat of the fascist powers in World War II, fascism has by no means disappeared, and some see the main threat of fascism not in formerly fascist states such as Germany or Italy, but in leading democratic nations, such as the United States, that are beset with grave social ills—urban decay, racial conflicts, crime, and civil disorder. As for communism, three decades of Stalinist terror were followed by relative liberalization under Khrushchev. Yet after his fall, his successors returned to harsher methods of government in a gradual process of re-Stalinization. The liberal impulses of Polish "national communism" have been increasingly repressed in both domestic and foreign affairs, and the "spring of freedom" in Czechoslovakia was forcibly ended by the Soviet invasion and occupation in August 1968. Communist China, too, has progressed further toward radical totalitarianism as a result of the Great Proletarian Cultural Revolution in the late 1960's. Like other systems, communism is constantly changing, but such changes do not necessarily weaken its basic totalitarian structure and ideology.

This book is a discussion of the main representatives of each side —communism and fascism on the totalitarian side, capitalism and socialism on the democratic. In a short book, it has seemed advisable to concentrate on the isms that shape the fate of the world rather than to discuss in detail the numerous other isms that are important, but have not been decisive, in the struggle for men's minds. These lesser isms, whether philosophical, political, social, or economic, are therefore dealt within this book only to the extent that they are related to the four major isms. The psychological roots of totalitarianism and democracy are given particularly close attention, since it is difficult to understand either system without understanding both the personality traits and psychological motivations to which each system appeals.

The key approach in this book is through the *way of life* concept rather than through one particular aspect, such as government or economics. Totalitarianism and democracy are more than specific social, political, or economic systems: they are two ways of life, with contradicting beliefs and values, based on distinct conceptions of the nature of man. The scope and gravity of the present world crisis can therefore be fully grasped only by perceiving it not merely as the result of conflicting political or economic ideas and practices, but as of two ways of thought and action encompassing the totality of social life.

William Ebenstein

University of California,
Santa Barbara

the totalitarian way of life

part one

totalitarian communism

chapter one

THE ECONOMIC
INTERPRETATION OF HISTORY

Before Marx, history was interpreted in several typical fashions. Some interpreters sought the key to history in the working of divine providence and conceived of human development as but part of the unfolding of God's design of the whole universe. The main difficulties of this *religious* interpretation of history are that God's will is unknown and unknowable to man's direct experience and that whereas there is only one God, there are many contrasting human conceptions of God and his plans for mankind.

A second dominant pre-Marxist approach to the understanding of human history was *political:* great emperors, kings, legislators, and soldiers were viewed as the decisive forces in history; and historical writing was largely the record of kings, parliaments, wars, and peace treaties.

This political emphasis in human affairs has one main shortcoming: it tends to exaggerate the relative role that most people assign to government and politics in the total setting of their lives. It is natural that statesmen, politicians, and political philosophers consider politics the most important single element in human relations, and political remedies the most important answer to human troubles. But human nature and human problems are more intricate than politics; politics is only one approach—and not always the most penetrating one—among many others.

A third major approach, the *hero interpretation of history* (popularized in modern times by Carlyle), is closely related to the political one, inasmuch as most heroes in world history are conventionally chosen from great kings, emperors, generals, legislators, founders of new states, pioneering reformers, and revolutionaries. The main weakness of the hero interpretation is that it overstresses the role of individuals at the expense of larger cultural, religious, social, and economic circumstances that form the background without which there can be no meaningful exercise of leadership. Although it is undoubtedly true that leaders mold events, it is no less true that events mold leaders.

The fourth pre-Marxist approach to the understanding of history was through the impact of *ideas:* ideas were conceived (by Hegel, for example) to be the principal causes of the historical process, and the material conditions (social, economic, technological, military) of society were thought of as essentially derived from, and caused by, the great motivating ideas. This emphasis on ideas often also implied that history was progressively evolving toward the realization of key ideas, such as freedom and democracy.

While this theory, like other interpretations, undoubtedly contains much that is valid, the exclusive emphasis on ideas as the main driving force in history overlooks the fact that ideas not only generate events but also reflect them. Therefore, to isolate ideas as the chief agent of human action is to neglect the framework of circumstances; circumstances, after all, make some ideas possible and others not, and it is circumstances from which ideas derive their vitality and practical impact.

The study of history may also be focused on *war:* the phenomenon of conflict is present in all phases of human development, and the birth, rise, and decline of states are often directly connected with warfare. The shortcoming of the military interpretation of history lies in its failure to recognize war as the result, rather than the cause, of events. There is no doubt that war often marks a turning point in the life of nations and civilizations; yet the dramatic swiftness and decisiveness of war should not draw our attention from the multitude of psychological, ideological, and material factors that lead to war and contribute to its complexity.

Marx's analysis of society was set forth through his *economic interpretation of history:* the production of the goods and services that support human life, and the exchange of those goods and services, are the bases of all social processes and institutions. Marx does not claim that the economic factor is the only one that goes into the making of history; he does claim that it is the most important one, the *foundation* upon which is erected the *superstructure* of culture, law, and government, buttressed by corresponding political, social, religious, literary, and artistic ideologies.

In a general way, Marx describes the relations between men's material conditions of life and their ideas by saying that "*it is not the consciousness of men which determines their existence, but, on the contrary, it is their social existence which determines their consciousness."*

In a nomadic society, for example, horses might be considered the principal means of acquiring and accumulating wealth. From Marx's viewpoint, this foundation of nomadic life is the clue to its superstructure of law, government, and dominant ideas. Thus, Marx would say that those who are the owners of the greatest number of horses in such a nomadic society would also be the political chieftains who make and interpret the law; they are also likely to receive the highest respect and deference from the tribe's members who own no horses. In the realm of ideas, the predominant social and cultural concepts would reflect the dominant economic position of the owners of horses. Even in religion the impact would not be missing: God might be represented in the image of a swift and powerful rider, and the concept of divine justice and rule would be, in a sense, an extension and magnification of human justice as determined by the horse-owning chiefs.

In a settled agricultural society, the ownership of land would provide the clue to the political, social, legal, and cultural institutions and conceptions. In such a society, according to Marx, the landowning class is the real ruler of state and society, even if another formal organization of authority exists. Similarly, the landowning class would also set the predominant social standards and values.

Finally, according to Marx, *in the modern industrial society of the last two hundred years the ownership of the means of industrial production is the master key:* the capitalists not only determine the economic destiny of society, but also rule it politically (regardless of formal and legal façades to the contrary) and set its social standards and values. The ultimate purpose of the law, education, the press, and artistic and literary creation is to maintain an ideology that is imbued with the sanctity and justice of capitalist property ownership.

Our understanding of history has gained immensely from Marx's economic interpretation. It is virtually impossible to write history today without some attention at least to the relation of economic forces and conflicts to political, military, and international issues.

In pointing out Marx's overemphasis on economics, however, one must not go to the other extreme of denying that economic interests play an important part in human affairs. The Marxian theory reduces man to an earthbound beast with no spark of the lofty and divine; some anti-Marxian theories, on the other hand, have raised man to the level of an angelic being, having no contact with the earth, nearly divine in his goodness. Men are only too often inclined to dress up their selfish and material aims and actions in high-sounding moral or religious phrases.

Marx's economic interpretation suffers from the same defect which afflicts all theories that pretend to supply the master key to history: *excessive generalization and simplification.* Whenever a single factor (be it the hero, war, religion, climate, race, geography, and so forth ad infinitum) is required to do the work of explanation and illumination that can only be properly done by several factors, its burden proves too heavy. No single factor has been predominant throughout history, and which factor is the most important in a particular situation is a question of empirical inquiry.

In any event or series of events there is always a complicated pattern of many factors, and it is none too easy to disentangle them. It is difficult enough to identify precisely the component motivations of an action of one person, because these actions are often mutually contradictory and logically inconsistent. It is even more difficult to isolate the determinant components in a single action of a small group; and it is virtually impossible to generalize about large-scale collective actions and processes throughout the whole of history.

To take one practical illustration: the Marxist interpretation holds that *imperialism* is caused primarily by economic interests and rivalries and that war in the capitalist era is the culmination of such imperialist rivalries. There have undoubtedly been manifestations of imperialism in history, ancient as well as modern, whose origins can be traced to economic factors—some of the classical imperialist expansion of advanced capitalist nations like the Netherlands, England, and France in the eighteenth and early nineteenth centuries can be attributed chiefly to economic forces. It is also possible to set forth examples of minor wars, in antiquity as in more recent times, that have been primarily motivated by economic interests and conflicts.

The economic interpretation, nevertheless, misses the core of the great and vital conflicts of history.

The Greeks who fought the Persians 2,500 years ago did so not primarily to protect Athenian investments and trade interests in Asia Minor, but because they knew that the victory of Persia would mean the end of Greek civilization. Persian victory would undoubtedly have entailed serious economic and financial losses for the Greeks, but the main effect would have been the destruction of the Greek way of life, its devotion to the search for truth and its appreciation of human values.

To take more recent illustrations, the core of the conflict in the two world wars was not the protection of British investments in Africa or of American loans to Britain and France, but the more fundamental issue of whether freedom—religious, intellectual, political, racial—was to survive, or whether totalitarian militarism was to rule the world. Again, there is no doubt that a German victory in either war would have entailed profound economic losses for the vanquished, but the economic effects would have been relatively minor compared with the effects of forced reversion to a way of life based on a denial of the Western tradition.

Finally, communist imperialism cannot be explained in Marxian economic terms, according to which imperialism is the last phase of an advanced and mature economy with an abundance of capital that it seeks to invest in less developed areas. From the economic viewpoint, the Soviet Union and communist China are hungry for capital, suffering from its scarcity rather than abundance. Their imperialism is motivated by noneconomic drives of national interest and political expansionism.

The Hungarian Revolution of 1956 and the short-lived Czech "socialism with a human face" in 1968 clearly showed that Soviet imperialism can ultimately rely only on tanks and guns, and not on economic or ideological penetration. The repression of the Tibetan rebellion by China in 1959 and her conquest of Indian border areas in 1959–1962 showed that China, too, ultimately relies on force as the primary instrument of imperialist expansion. Finally, the growing incidence of armed clashes between China and Russia and the rising threat of all-out war between the two main communist states shows that conflict between rival imperialisms is not confined to a particular economic system such as capitalism but may occur under any system.

What the Marxist-communist interpretation misses in the analyses of major conflicts, is, first, the element of *power* (which is often the cause rather than the effect of economic advantage) and, second, the clash of *value systems,* which are frequently more important to people than economic interests, whether the values concerned are specifically political, religious, intellectual, or—in a wider sense— the symbolic expression of a whole way of life.

In fact, where conflicts of interest are primarily economic, com- promise will usually be relatively easy. It is where more deeply felt values are at stake, such as individual liberty, freedom of religion, or national independence, that compromise becomes more difficult.

DYNAMICS
OF SOCIAL CHANGE

Before Marx, basic social change was thought to be the result of the work of great political leaders, legislators, and pioneering reformers. Marx rejects the traditional emphasis on the force of personality as the principal agent of important social change and looks for an explanation in impersonal economic causes. The two key concepts that he uses in approaching the problem of basic social change are, first, the *forces of production* and, second, the *relations of production.* The clash between these two is the deeper cause of basic social change, as expressed by Marx in his *Critique of Political Economy* (1859):

At a certain stage of their development the material productive forces of society come into contradiction with the existing productive relation- ships, or, what is but a legal expression for these, with the property rela- tionships within which they have moved before. From forms of develop- ment of the productive forces these relationships are transformed into their fetters. Then an epoch of social revolution opens. With the change in the economic foundation the whole vast superstructure is more or less rapidly transformed.

The Marxist conception of the *forces of production* expresses *man's relation to nature* and is essentially what we would call today technological and scientific know-how. Marx's notion of the *relations of production* expresses *man's relation to man* and encompasses all that we would include today under the term *social institutions.* Seen in these more modern terms, what Marx roughly suggests is that in every social-economic system there is at first a balance between knowledge and social organization, but gradually a disequilibrium or lag develops between available scientific knowledge and existent social institutions. *Our scientific knowledge grows faster than our social wisdom.*

This lag is the more modern, and broader, version of Marx's more specific lag between the forces of production and the relations of production. Since the economic aspects of society are for Marx its chief determining factor, it is not surprising that he reduces the general phenomenon of the lag between knowledge and wisdom to the more specific lag between forces of production and relations of production.

Thus, to provide an illustration in line with the Marxist pattern, when new productive forces developed within the productive relations of the feudal system, social revolution was, according to Marx, inevitable because the productive relations of feudalism (property relations, market controls, internal customs and tariffs, monetary instability) did not permit the utilization of the newly developing productive forces of industrial capitalism.

The capitalist system, having run its cycle, now shows the same tendency to rigidity, Marx holds, and it is due to meet the same fate when its productive forces (the capacity to produce) have outstripped its productive relations (law of private property, production for private profit). Like the social systems preceding it, capitalism thus will eventually stand in the way of scientific knowledge and will not permit technological resources to be fully employed.

What has doomed all historically known forms of economic organization, according to Marx, is the fact that when new productive forces develop, the existing productive relations—that is, the existing social institutions—stand in the way of their proper utilization.

Each system thus eventually becomes wasteful in terms of the creative potentialities that have developed in its womb but are not permitted to be born and to grow. Only public ownership of the means of production can, according to Marx, bring into existence a new system of productive relations based on production for common use rather than for private profit that will match the tremendous forces of production actually or potentially known to man. In other words, man's capacity to produce will find full expression only in a social system in which production is limited by scarce resources and incomplete knowledge, and not by such faulty social institutions as production for private profit based on the private ownership of the means of production.

Marx's insight that man's knowledge of physical nature ("forces of production") grows faster than his wisdom in creating social institutions ("relations of production") is highly important in understanding a vital source of tension and conflict both between and within nations. In international affairs, our capacity to produce hydrogen bombs is way ahead of our institutional arrangements for harnessing nuclear energy for peaceful purposes. Within advanced industrial nations, poverty testifies to the fact that our capacity to produce goods and services surpasses our wisdom to create institutions through which wealth can be more equitably distributed.

What distinguishes Marx from non-Marxists is his insistence that *basic social change*—caused by the excessive lag between advanced scientific knowledge and retrograde social institutions—can be brought about *only by revolution;* whereas non-Marxists affirm that the necessary changes can be effected by peaceful means.

REVOLUTION
THE ONLY WAY OUT

In the *Communist Manifesto*, Marx explains why revolution is the only method of basic social transformation. When technological know-how ("forces of production") begins to outstrip the existing social, legal, and political institutions ("relations of production"), the owners of the means of production do not politely step aside to allow history to run its inevitable course. Since the ideology of the ruling class reflects the existing economic system, the owners of the means of production sincerely believe that the existing system is economically the most efficient, socially the most equitable, and philosophically the most harmonious with the laws of nature and the will of whatever god they venerate.

Marx penetratingly denies that the individual feudal landowner or industrial capitalist obstructs social change out of selfish greed: the resistance of the ruling class to change is so obstinate—making revolution finally inevitable—precisely because it identifies its own values with universally valid ones. The ruling class will, therefore, mobilize all the instruments of the legal, political, and ideological superstructure to block the growth of the forces that represent the potentially more progressive economic system. For this reason, Marx states early in the *Communist Manifesto,* the "history of all hitherto existing society is the history of class struggles."

Marx could find no instance in history in which a major social and economic system freely abdicated to its successor. On the assumption that the future will resemble the past, the communists, as the *Communist Manifesto* says, "openly declare that their ends can be attained only by the forcible overthrow of all existing social conditions."

This is the crucial tenet of Marxism-Leninism and is the one that most clearly and irreconcilably distinguishes it from democracy.

Marx had no clear-cut notion how the political transformation from capitalism to communism would come about. Though in the *Communist Manifesto,* as throughout most of his other statements on the problem, he believed in the need for revolution, he was occasionally less dogmatic. Speaking in 1872 at a public meeting in Amsterdam following the Congress of the International, Marx conceded that the working class can travel on different roads in its quest for power: "We know that we must take into consideration the institutions, the habits and customs of different regions, and we do not deny that there are countries like America, England, and— if I knew your institutions better I would perhaps add Holland— where the workers can attain their objective by peaceful means. But such is not the case in all other countries."

Marx never fully pursued the implications of this distinction, and the orthodox opinion of Marxism-communism has remained that fundamental social and economic change is impossible except by class war, violence, and revolution.

In the early 1830's there occurred two major revolutions that Marx failed to appraise properly. In 1832, the passage of the Reform Act in England meant that the government of the nation would thenceforth be shared by the aristocracy and the middle classes, with the weight constantly shifting in favor of the latter.

At about the same time, the Jacksonian revolution in the United States effected a similar peaceful shift in class power by bringing the men from the backwoods into American politics and successfully challenging the supremacy of the gentlemen from Virginia and New England who had treated the government of the United States as their God-given preserve.

These changes in Britain and the United States were more than just political victories: they inaugurated a permanent shift in the distribution of social and economic power in both nations, the kind of basic change that Marx had in mind. When revolution swept over Europe in 1848, England was spared because the aims of the revolution of 1848—winning for the middle class its proper share of social and political power—had already been peacefully obtained by the British middle class in 1832.

If Marx had given the political factor its due weight, if he had fully grasped the importance of the Reform Act in England and the Jacksonian revolution in the United States, he might have realized that socialism, too, might be accomplished without violence in countries that possessed democratic traditions strong enough to absorb far-reaching social and economic changes without resorting to civil war. A recognition of the cultural and political factors in the equation of social change would have amounted, however, to a virtual abandonment of the central position of Marx: history is the history of class wars, and ruling classes always defend their positions to the bitter end.

When Marx allowed, occasionally, that in countries like England, the United States, or the Netherlands violent revolution would be unnecessary in transforming capitalism into the classless proletarian society, it was obvious that what the three countries had in common was *political democracy*, providing the means for peaceful social change. Whether the range of Marx's exceptions should now be enlarged or not thus depends on whether democracy has spread in the world since his death.

In any case, Marx's concession that in a few politically advanced countries revolution might be unnecessary has always caused the communists a good deal of headache. Lenin took up the question in *State and Revolution* (1918), his best known and most influential political tract, claiming that by 1917 "this exception made by Marx is no longer valid" because England and the United States had developed bureaucratic institutions "to which everything is subordinated and which trample everything under foot." Between 1872 and 1917, both England and the United States broadened the suffrage and moved steadily in the direction of more political and social reform. In 1884, only one year after Marx's death, a British Liberal leader, Sir William Harcourt, said, "We are all socialists now," indicating that all parties accepted basic social and economic reform.

Since the historical record of the years 1872–1917 seemed plainly to contradict Lenin's dogma, it was necessary to rewrite history. Far from admitting that England and the United States had moved toward more political and social democracy since 1872, Lenin maintained that both countries had become more repressive, authoritarian, and plutocratic.

Since 1917 the United States has seen the peaceful revolution of social reform, which started early in the century with Theodore Roosevelt's Square Deal, was continued by Woodrow Wilson's New Freedom, and culminated in Franklin D. Roosevelt's New Deal.

In Britain, Lloyd George's "People's Budget" of 1909 gave the propertied classes a taste of things to come. In 1945, the victory of the Labour party at the polls was more than a mere electoral triumph. Just as 1832 meant the incorporation of the middle classes into the government of the nation, 1945 meant the same thing for the working classes in Britain. Whether the Labour party is henceforth in office or in opposition, the British working class will remain an active partner in the business of governing the nation.

The relentless communist insistence on revolution as the only way of basic social change violates Marxist doctrine at one central point. According to Marx, the conditions of man's existence determine his consciousness, and social change is, therefore, not the product of mere will and free choice. Where the conditions of society permit peaceful change from private to public ownership of the means of production, the use of force and subversion is, in a deeply Marxian sense, un-Marxian.

The communist dogma of universal revolution and dictatorship is in harmony with Marx's theory of consciousness only in societies in which the conditions of social and political life have created a general distrust in the possibility of peaceful change; it is out of harmony in nations whose democratic consciousness is the result not of paper constitutions but of the conditions of their existence. By insisting on universal revolution and dictatorship as the one and only method of change, communists in fact proclaim the un-Marxian doctrine that, regardless of historical, cultural, social, economic, and political conditions, a uniform consciousness—the creed of communism—can be imposed everywhere by sheer force.

There is a similar, reverse dogmatism maintained by anticommunist adherents of free enterprise who would like to see it practiced in the whole world. They, too, violate elementary common sense and historical experience. Whether a society is likely to operate a capitalist economy is not a matter of pure logic and choice, but the result of historical environment, cultural heritage, social institutions, and political ideologies. Thus, in 1900 it would have been easy to predict that basic changes in Britain or the United States would occur without revolution and that such changes would be accompanied by violence and revolution in countries like Russia or China.

At present, it is often possible to predict whether change will be possible with or without violence. Yet there are countries, such as Brazil or India, where prediction is difficult because the balance of democratic versus undemocratic habits and traditions is not easy to define. Clearly, in view of the fact that such borderline countries exist, no general prediction based on dogma—be it communist or anticommunist dogma—is likely to be accurate. Every prediction is a question of investigating each particular situation rather than of applying preconceived universal laws of development.

MARX'S HUMANISM
AND THE CONCEPT OF ALIENATION

Marx's emphasis on class struggle and violent revolution as the conditions of basic social change has in recent years proved a liability to the spread of Marxism in both communist and noncommunist countries. In communist countries, the experience of Stalinist totalitarianism has shown more sensitive people, particularly in the younger generation, that a doctrine of hatred easily leads to the practice of brutality, and that no true community can be founded on the perpetuation of hostility and violence. In noncommunist countries, the experience of far-reaching social change in the direction of the welfare state has convinced many that Marxian class war and revolution are not only morally questionable but also practically unnecessary, and that therefore the desired changes of capitalism can be accomplished better through gradual amelioration based on social cooperation than through sudden, fundamental changes based on revolutionary violence and class struggle.

In their search for a humanist basis of Marxian communism, liberal-minded writers in both communist and noncommunist countries have concentrated on Marx's early thought, particularly his *Economic and Philosophical Manuscripts,* written in 1844 when he was twenty-six. Interest in this early writing by Marx has been greatly stimulated by the fact that it focuses on the concept of "alienation" (or estrangement), a concept which has become extremely fashionable in contemporary thought as a result of highly popular works of social psychologists and existentialist philosophers. The concept of alienation has many roots. In its Judeo-Christian origin, alienation signifies the separation of man from God through sin. In early nineteenth-century German philosophy, Hegel formulated a more secular version of alienation which, though still tinged with religion, emphasized man's separation from his essence, spirit, the absolute. Marx rejected the concept of alienation as developed by the religious tradition, particularly in its Protestant Calvinist version, as well as in Hegel's metaphysical version, since both approaches seemed to him too abstract, too divorced from man in his concrete reality.

Finally, the romantic doctrine of alienation greatly influenced the young Marx. Although in the early nineteenth century romanticism was primarily a worldwide literary movement, its manifestation in Germany also had strong social and philosophical elements. In its social outlook, romanticism was basically a protest against the spread of industrial civilization. The romantics felt that industrialism was destroying the natural and organic bonds of life that characterized pre-industrial, medieval Europe. They lamented that man in industrial society was becoming estranged or "alienated" from nature, from his fellow men, from family and nation, and—most important of all—from himself. In despair, some romantics felt that the only escape from the evils of industrial civilization was the return to agrarian life—a highly impractical proposal.

In his *Economic and Philosophical Manuscripts,* Marx shared the romantics' concern about alienation, but he arrived at a different conclusion because he saw the problem of alienation in a different perspective. Marx had the genius to see that industrialism was here to stay, and that it should be welcomed as the only hope of liberating mankind from the ills of material want, ignorance, and disease. Whereas the romantics saw the evil in industrialism, Marx perceived alienation as the result of *capitalist* industrialism. Under capitalism, Marx said in the *Manuscripts,* man is alienated from his work, the things he produces, his employers, his fellow workers, and himself. The worker does not work, Marx writes, in order to fulfil himself and his creative potential, for his work "is not voluntary but imposed, *forced* labor." His work does not satisfy the worker's needs, but is merely a means of satisfying the needs of others—the capitalist employers who use him as an instrument for making profits. Capitalism thus dehumanizes the worker, who "sinks to the level of a commodity," and produces palaces for the rich, but hovels for the poor. The worker is alienated from the employer, who appropriates the products of his labor and enjoys pleasures and freedoms denied the worker. He is also alienated from his fellow workers, with whom he competes for employment and favors bestowed by the employer. Money is the most visible symbol and expression of alienation under capitalism, the "visible deity" that transforms all human relations—including love and friendship—into monetary relations. Marx specifically affirms the need for a society in which love cannot be bought, but can "only be exchanged for love."

Marx shows in his *Manuscripts* that man's predicament included ethical and psychological as well as economic elements. Postulating communism as the only solution to the human alienation engendered by capitalism, Marx defines communism in the *Manuscripts* without reference to hatred or class war: "Communism is the *positive* abolition of *private property,* of *human self-alienation,* and thus the real *appropriation* of *human* nature by and for man. It is, therefore, the return of man himself as a *social*, that is, really human, being, a complete and conscious return which assimilates all the wealth of previous development. Communism as a fully developed naturalism is humanism and as a fully developed humanism is naturalism." In ambitious language born of youthful confidence, Marx also says that communism "is the solution to the riddle of history and knows itself to be this solution."

Yet this phase of Marx's humanistic and ethical concerns did not last long. In a crucial change of outlook, influenced perhaps by his growing familiarity with the living conditions and struggles of the working class, he quickly abandoned the humanistic and ethical elements in his conception of communism. In *The German Ideology*, written jointly with Frederick Engels in 1846, the ethical socialists were attacked for talking of "human nature, of Man in general" rather than of man as a member of the proletariat, the working class. The individualistic leanings of the *Manuscripts* were increasingly replaced by the concept of *class*, and the ideal of love and fellowship was replaced by that of class struggle.

In the *Communist Manifesto* of 1848, Marx specifically ridicules the philosophical socialists who talk about "alienation of humanity" or about the "philosophical foundations of socialism," conveniently forgetting that he himself had defined communism in the *Manuscripts* as "the true solution of the conflict between existence and essence, between objectification and self-affirmation, between freedom and necessity"—all terms taken directly from Hegel's philosophical vocabulary. In the *Communist Manifesto* Marx also attacks the ethical socialists as "utopians," because they reject revolutionary action and "wish to attain their ends by peaceful means, and endeavor, by small experiments necessarily doomed to failure and by the force of example, to pave the way for the new social gospel."

Marx was aware that in his *Manuscripts* of 1844 he had expressed ideas which were similar to those of the ethical and philosophical socialists. He therefore decided not to publish what he later considered an insignificant juvenile aberration. In fact, the *Manuscripts* were not published during Marx's life, and after his death his literary executor, Frederick Engels, also refrained from publishing the *Manuscripts*. They were finally published in German in 1932;

an English translation appeared nearly three decades later. Since then, the *Manuscripts,* particularly because of their focus on the fashionable concept of "human alienation," have been used for diverse purposes. In communist countries, particularly among more liberal Marxists, the *Manuscripts* have served as a weapon to discredit totalitarian attitudes of orthodox communists. While more liberally oriented thinkers in eastern Europe cannot explicitly propagate "liberalism" by name, they can advocate some of its substance under the protective cover of the "young Marx." Some Yugoslav Marxists have argued, for example, that the replacement of a capitalist economy with a state-run economy does not in itself solve the problem of alienation, and that state property should therefore be transferred to groups of workers on the basis of self-management, that is, by more democratic participation in the decision-making process. Without using words like "liberalism" or "democracy," such liberally oriented Marxists affirm the basic principle that no socialism or communism deserves that name unless it has the political element of democratic self-government.

In noncommunist countries, the *Manuscripts* have served the goal of making *Marxism* respectable, since Marx is then presented as a humanistic socialist and liberal individualist primarily concerned with man's self-realization through love and free cooperation in a classless society without force and oppression. Such interpreters of Marx stress his humanistic goals, particularly as expressed in his early writings, and treat less the means for basic social change he advocated from the *Communist Manifesto* to the end of his life— class struggle, revolution, and the dictatorship of the proletariat. By focusing on Marx's ultimately humanistic goals, these Western interpreters seek to make him the descendant of the humanistic ideals of Jefferson rather than the ancestor of Lenin's dictatorial methods.

Whatever the merits of these two *political* efforts in communist and noncommunist countries—to make liberalism respectable in the former and Marxism in the latter—from the purely analytical and historical viewpoint Marx cannot be transformed into a basically liberal humanist, since from *The German Ideology* (1846) on, he saw in the humanistic, ethical, and liberal socialists the most dangerous enemies of communism. Most of Marx's polemical writings were directed not against avowed opponents of communist doctrines, but against socialists who happened to disagree with him on what socialism meant and how it was to be achieved. This attitude of Marx was later repeated faithfully by Lenin and other communists, and to this day communists consider democratic socialists of the British Labour party type as more dangerous and damaging to the cause of communism than the conservative parties of a capitalist society.

ECONOMIC CONTRADICTIONS
OF CAPITALISM

The end of capitalism will be brought about, Marx argues, not by "subversive conspiracies" of professional revolutionaries, but by the same inexorable laws of social development and change that destroyed previous systems. Marx uses, first, the "grave-digger" theory: the more capitalism succeeds, the more capitalist enterprise is organized in *large-scale* units. As a result, large numbers of workers are in constant and close association and mutually reinforce their status as proletarians. Big Labor inevitably follows Big Business.

The capitalist class has no way of escaping the dilemma of rearing its own destroyer as it goes along: the *law of the falling profit rate* (which is not to be confused with the absolute amount of profit) makes such escape impossible. Marx's prediction of the declining profit rate was based on the assumption that, under the capitalist system of production, the entrepreneurial class would steadily accumulate more and more capital; the greater abundance of capital would inevitably be reflected in the decline of the price (interest) and return (profit) of capital.

There can be no disagreement—because the facts speak too plainly—that the absolute amount of profits has risen immensely since Marx and is constantly rising.

What about Marx's prediction that the *rate* of profit (and of interest) would go down because capital would become more abundant?

Here, too, the prediction has not come true. During the depression of the 1930's, the rates of profit and interest were low and seemed to confirm Marx's forecast. Yet in the 1950's and 1960's, as in earlier periods of prosperity, the rates of interest and profit again reached new highs, thus disproving Marx.

The facts of economic history do not support Marx's "law of the falling profit rate." Marx's prediction was erroneous because he looked primarily at the *supply* side of capital: more and more capital is constantly created and accumulated in the capitalist system, and increased supply of a commodity (i.e., capital) leads to a lower price—provided the demand remains the same. Yet this is exactly what did not happen. The reason for the high interest rates (price of capital) in the 1950's and 1960's, the highest in a century, is that, despite an all-time abundance in the supply of capital, the *demand for capital has grown even faster* since too many companies simultaneously want fresh capital for the improvement, expansion, and building of productive facilities.

The price of capital (interest) or return of capital (profit) are subject to supply and demand and not to any Marxian law of predetermined, constant decline. Whenever the demand for capital outruns the supply, the rate of interest goes up, and the price of capital behaves like any other price.

The reason Marx overlooked the importance of the demand side in the capital market was his expectation (and hope) that the capitalist system would gradually lose its vitality and growth, thus requiring less new capital for investment. This, however, has not happened.

Finally, Marx underestimated the role of technological progress. Capitalism constantly produces not only more capital, but *more efficient capital*. More available capital need not lead to lower rates of profit if the capital is more efficient.

In a stationary economy in which there is little or no technological innovation, more capital might automatically lead to lower rates of profit and interest. In a progressive economy in which the productivity of capital is constantly raised, profits and the rate of profit may go up although the absolute amount of available capital is also rising.

Moreover, technological innovation strengthens the demand side in the capital market because new technologies require large capital investments, thus counterbalancing the effects of increased capital on the supply side. The current capital investment needed to create a new job in the average American industry is well over $20,000, and it is much higher in electronics, chemicals, and petroleum. Therefore, as long as capitalism continues to progress technologically, the effects of increased capital resources will not, as Marx assumed, depress either the absolute volume of profit or the rate of profit.

Marx's main objection to capitalism was its inefficiency as well as its injustice. Here again, experience has contradicted his forecasts. Per capita consumption in western Europe is more than double that in the Soviet Union, and in the United States it is three to four times greater. As to technological innovation, the capitalist countries still are in most cases the creators, and the communist countries, except in space science and technology, the borrowers and imitators.

Marx also stated that capitalists would seek to stem the impact of the law of the falling profit rate in two ways: first, they would constantly seek to "rationalize" industry, or make it technologically more efficient. This would eliminate the less efficient enterprises and would lead to concentration of economic power, large-scale industrial organization, and increasing proletarianization. Second, they would invest capital in underdeveloped countries, where the return for capital (profit) is still very high. This device, Marx points out, only delays, but does not avert, the inevitable doom. In the colonial country, too, capital becomes increasingly more abundant, a native capitalist class develops, threatened by its own proletariat, and the law of the falling profit rate makes the imperialist solution of the capitalist dilemma at home unfeasible.

Contrary to Marx, the flow of private investments from industrially advanced nations has not been guided only by the economic consideration of profits, but by the political consideration of safety and stability. In 1969, American investments abroad were over $60 billion. The western hemisphere, in which American capital has traditionally felt safest, accounts for about one half, and western Europe accounts for over one quarter. In Asia and the Pacific, the trend of American investments has been toward Australia, Japan, and the Philippines rather than toward less developed and less stable nations like India and Indonesia. This is a typical illustration of Marx's underestimation of the political factor in economics.

Another source of tension that undermines the vitality of the capitalist system, according to Marx, is *unemployment*. In Marx's own time, industry expanded at an enormous rate, and there was a chronic shortage of labor. Yet Marx foresaw that the maldistribution of wealth and income under capitalism would lead to periodic crises of unemployment. The depression decade of 1929–1939 seemed to confirm his prediction; there was severe unemployment right up to 1939, when the preparation for war gradually eliminated it.

After World War II, the growth of welfare-state policies in the major capitalist countries led to the recognition of full employment as a primary social objective. Among the major Western economies, only the United States has had a serious unemployment problem, averaging about six percent in the decade of 1954–1963 but dropping to considerably lower levels in more recent years. Other Western nations, such as France, West Germany, Sweden, and Switzerland, have for years had a labor shortage and have brought in large numbers of workers from Italy, Spain, Greece, and Turkey. In 1969, ten percent of the French labor force and six percent of the German were foreign workers. Oddly—and contrary to Marx's predictions—communist states like Poland and Yugoslavia have suffered from chronic unemployment for many years, and since the middle 1960's even the Soviet Union has admitted the existence of unemployment.

Marx also predicted that two other developments would disintegrate the capitalist system: the *concentration of economic power* and, as a direct result, the *increasing proletarianization* of society. There is little doubt that, compared with earlier stages of industrial development, the contemporary capitalist economy shows impressive features of concentration. Yet it is doubtful that the tendency toward concentration in the capitalist system keeps on forever; at a later stage of industrial development the forces of competition begin to catch up with excessive concentration. Also, antimonopolistic public policies play an important part in strengthening competition.

Marx did not foresee that in highly advanced capitalist nations concentration of management might be mitigated by important counterforces: the spreading ownership of industry among large numbers of persons through the holding of shares of corporate businesses and the growing control of business managements by government, public opinion, and labor unions.

THE ROLE
OF THE SALARIAT

Marx's prediction of the inevitable proletarianization of society in a capitalist economy has been very largely disproved by events.

In the initial phases of industrial development, under capitalism or any other system, the industrial working class, Marx's "proletariat," constantly increases at the expense of artisans, landless peasants, and other social groups whose members seek employment in the expanding factories and mines. In a later and more advanced phase of industrial development, however, the industrial working class begins to decline in proportion to the total population, though it still continues to increase in absolute numbers. What Marx did not foresee was the enormous growth in an advanced economy that would create employment, but not of the proletarian type.

In the United States, for example, the volume of industrial production and the number of persons employed in industry have increased tremendously since 1900, yet the proportion of the industrial working class in the total work force has consistently declined, for two reasons.

First, within industry itself, there has been an increasing shift of employment from production or blue-collar workers (Marx's "proletariat") to white-collar workers (or "salariat"). Between 1947 and 1967, total employment in manufacturing increased by about 25 percent. Yet, whereas the number of production workers in manufacturing increased by only ten percent, the number of white-collar workers ("nonproduction workers") rose by 100 percent. Although the number of blue-collar workers in manufacturing remained almost stable during the period 1947–1967, output more than doubled. Both technological progress and automation have reduced the number of blue-collar workers needed to produce a given quantity of goods, such as steel, coal, or automobiles.

The second, and more important, reason for the relative increase in white-collar workers is the rapid growth of employment in enterprises that produce services rather than physical goods. Between

OCCUPATIONAL SHIFTS IN CIVILIAN EMPLOYMENT

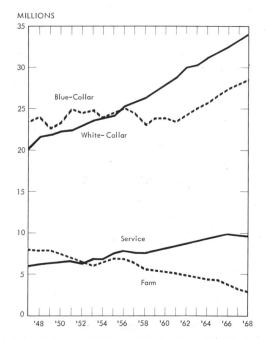

Data from First National City Bank of New York, Monthly Economic
Letter (October 1966) and Bureau of the Census

1947 and 1967, total employment in the United States rose from
about 57 million to 74 million. Nearly all of this increase was due
to the services-producing sector of the economy (schools, hospitals,
banks, communications media, entertainment, retail stores, government). In the goods-producing sector of the economy, there was a
slight increase of employment in manufacturing and construction,
but this increase was offset by a reduction of employment in agriculture and mining. As a result of the massive shift from producing
goods to producing services in the American economy, there has
been a corresponding shift in the profile of employment. In 1947,
less than half the labor force was employed in white-collar or
service jobs. In 1967, 60 percent were employed in such jobs: 47
percent as white-collar workers (professional and technical workers,
managers, clerical workers, salesworkers), and 13 percent as service

workers (repair services, waiters, household workers). Whereas in 1947 blue-collar workers outnumbered white-collar workers, in 1967 the latter outnumbered the former by four to three.

The year 1956 was a milestone in economic history. For the first time in American history, or in that of any nation, *the number of persons engaged in producing goods was smaller than the number of persons performing services.* In recent years the same changes have occurred in the Swedish and British economies, where more people now produce services than goods.

This new type of economy is called *service economy* to distinguish it from the industrial economy that preceded it. Marx foresaw the transition from the agrarian to the industrial economy, but in all his writings there is not an inkling of the service economy that follows the industrial economy.

In 1870, about 75 percent of all American workers were in industries producing goods. This percentage has gone down steadily over the years, until in 1967 only about 33 percent were employed in goods-producing industries (manufacturing, agriculture, mining, and construction). In 1967, by contrast, 66 percent of the Soviet labor force were employed in the goods-producing sector of the economy—close to the relative composition of the American labor force in 1870. Yet the same trend operates in the Soviet Union, too, and as her economy progresses, the proportion of persons employed in the service industries is rising.

Farm workers and service workers are neither white- nor blue-collar workers. These two groups are numerically not as important as blue-collar and white-collar workers, but they show the same overall trend from goods-producing to service-producing employment as living standards rise. In 1953, service workers for the first time exceeded the number of farm workers and are consistently increasing in relative and absolute strength, whereas farm workers have gone down in both absolute and relative strength.

The following figures illustrate the growth of the salariat and other changes in the composition of the American labor force in the years 1910–1967. Most striking are the proportionate growth of clerical and sales persons from 10 percent of the total labor force in 1910 to 23 percent in 1967, the sharp drop of the combined total of farm laborers and unskilled industrial laborers from 29 percent to 9 percent, and the increase of the proportion of semiskilled and skilled workers from 26 percent to 32 percent. Politically, the latter is very important because the skilled workers and the foremen generally look upon themselves as middle class and tend to be more conservative in their political outlook.

What is politically important in this development is that *the salaried person tends to identify himself with the middle and upper classes rather than with the working class,* even if his income is below that of the worker. This is wholly contrary to Marx's expectations and predictions. Marx assumed—necessarily, from his interpretation of human action—that the transformation of the independent middle class into a dependent salaried class would automatically change the outlook of the old middle class from bourgeois to proletarian. Yet the new middle class of the salariat has generally refused to join the ranks of organized labor. Whereas about one-half of workers in goods-producing industries are in labor unions, only seven percent of white-collar and service employees are unionized. This difference also shows up regularly in elections. Salaried persons, more often than not, vote Republican, whereas blue-collar workers typically vote Democratic.

This attitude has been particularly marked in societies with rigid class lines; but even in the United States, with its more fluid class lines, the salaried man or woman who earns $600 a month is genererally politically more conservative than the wage-earner who receives $200 or more a week. Because salary-earners have failed to identify themselves psychologically with the working class, they have very largely remained outside the ranks of organized labor. In the United States, the labor movement has been able to organize the workers in industry and to a lesser extent in agriculture but has found it more difficult to organize teachers, clerks, civil servants, and other groups of white-collar employees.

The political problems posed by the rise of the salariat are not confined to industrial development under capitalism; they also appear under communism. In its first phase of industrialization, Russia witnessed a tremendous growth of her industrial proletariat. But as the Soviet Union entered a second phase of industrialization, a new salariat began to develop, with a way of life of its own and with its own ideas, different from those of the working class.

Despite communist denials, class lines are beginning to crystallize in communist Russia and the other communist states. One important line of differentiation is that between white-collar and factory worker, a distinction not necessarily based on differences of income. The influence of the white-collar group—"intelligentsia" in Russia —is constantly rising at the expense of the working class, as can be seen in the changing social composition of Soviet political bodies, university students, and other key groups of social importance.

As long as the Soviet leaders adhere to Marxist-Leninist fundamentalism, they will find that time works against them and that the slogans of Marxism-Leninism will not fit a society in which the white-collar class rather than the proletariat sets the style of life and thought. Thus, a class struggle along orthodox lines is beginning to take shape in communist societies undergoing industrialization, and —as in capitalist countries—proletariat and salariat do not generally find themselves on the same side of the barricades.

LENIN'S CONTRIBUTION TO THE THEORY OF COMMUNISM

The nature and deeper meaning of philosophical ideas can frequently be inferred from their appeal and impact. In the countries of western Europe and the United States, the inevitability of revolution as Karl Marx preached it has had comparatively little impact; the liberal tradition in those countries keeps the door open for peaceful change. Although many social reformers have agreed with some of Marx's indictments of capitalism, they have refused to embrace a philosophy of class hatred and war to remedy social injustices.

In only two major countries did the ideas of Marx take root in the nineteenth century: Germany and Russia. Despite the façade of representative institutions, imperial Germany was in fact an autocracy that did not permit genuine government by the people. The Germans followed the philosophy of Hegel (although Marx claimed that he had turned Hegel upside down). Hegel had asserted that the *state* was an objective reality and that its laws, like those of nature, could be *understood*, but not *changed*, by man. Marx followed the cast of Hegel's thought by claiming that the laws of *society*, in respect to its nature and evolution, have the same scientific validity that Hegel had claimed for those of the state.

By contrast, the liberal philosophical tradition of the West rejects the Hegel-Marx conception that human reason can only understand the laws of the state and society and affirms the possibility of rational control and creative change of social and political institutions. The experience of free government is the psychological background for this affirmative, activist philosophy, whereas the experience of autocratic government in Germany provided the psychological background for the determinism of Hegel and Marx.

In nineteenth-century Russia, conditions for the acceptance of Marxian ideas were even more favorable than in imperial Germany. Whereas Germany paid homage to virtue by at least adopting the forms and formalities of representative institutions, Russian tsarism long recoiled from such hypocrisy on the ground that pretenses, if practiced long enough, might easily turn into second nature.

Of all the major states in Europe, Russia was first in illiteracy, economic backwardness, religious obscurantism, oppression of minorities, political despotism, and social inequality. Marx's prophecy, clothed in the language of scientific magic, of the eventual liberation of man from bondage and oppression through revolutionary action made a strong impression on Russian radicals. *Das Kapital*, Marx's magnum opus, was translated into Russian before any other language; oddly enough, the tsarist censorship permitted the publication of the work on the ground that it would not be read by many because of its difficult style.

Among the Russian followers of Marx, Lenin (1870–1924) was both the leading theoretician and the most agile and effective practical politician.

Lenin's most important contribution to the theory of communism, perhaps the only one he made, is to be found in his pamphlet *What Is To Be Done?* (1902): the concept of the *professional revolutionary*.

Marx, reflecting the nineteenth-century's respect for man's capacity to think for himself, had assumed that the working class would *spontaneously* develop its class-consciousness in the daily struggle for economic existence and that its leadership would largely come

Drawing by Alan Dunn; Copr. © 1949 The New Yorker Magazine, Inc.

"FELLOW-COMRADES AND UNDERCOVER AGENTS OF THE F.B.I. . . ."

from its own ranks. Lenin had much less confidence in man, even if he belonged to the proletariat. Communist activity, said Lenin, is to be carried on along two lines. First, workers are to form labor organizations with primarily economic objectives, operating openly, legally, and as publicly as conditions allow. Side by side with such organizations, there are to be small groups of professional revolutionaries, patterned after the army and the police, highly select and entirely secret. Lenin did not care whether the professional revolutionary was of proletarian origin or not, as long as he did his job well. The organizations of the professional revolutionaries must be highly centralized, he went on, and must constantly guide and supervise the open, communist-led economic associations—the labor unions, the cooperatives, and the rest.

In particular, Lenin advised the professional revolutionaries to *infiltrate* and form cells in all existing social, political, educational, and economic bodies in society, be they schools, churches, labor unions, or political parties. Above all, he advised infiltration of the *armed forces*, the *police*, and the *government*.

Lenin also made it perfectly clear that communists should engage in *illegal* work even where legal Communist parties are permitted. He thought that legal opportunities should be utilized to the fullest extent, but he specifically advised communist activists to work through *front organizations*, constantly changing names and officers of organizations and always keeping the ultimate objective in mind: revolutionary seizure of power.

In particular, the secret nucleus of professional revolutionaries is responsible for the recruitment and training of spies, saboteurs, and agents for all other activities relating to intelligence, foreign and domestic. From the testimony of former communist agents it is evident that one of the first things a recruit into the inner ring of communist leaders has to do is break all connection with overt Communist party or front groups, stop reading the party press, and lead the life of a solid, respectable bourgeois. There are bridges between the legal Communist parties and the inner rings of spies and agents of the professional revolutionaries since necessity often compels the choice of such agents from party ranks; ideally, however, the two sets of organizations are to be kept separate.

FROM MARX TO LENIN

Lenin always thought of himself as a faithful follower of Marx. Yet, as a man of action operating in Russia rather than in western Europe, he was bound to modify Marxism in its practical revolutionary application. In his concept of the professional revolutionary Lenin consciously introduced a new approach to class war and communist organizational strategy that has permanently changed the nature of Marxism as understood by Communist parties. Other modifications by Lenin have created a body of ideas and attitudes, Marxism-Leninism, which combine some original ideas of Marx with their reformulations by Lenin. Communist thinkers are convinced that the Marxian inspiration and its Leninist modification are always

perfectly harmonious. Noncommunist thinkers feel that some Leninist positions contradict Marx in spirit if not in letter.

In comparing Lenin with Marx, one is struck by the differences
of temperament, background, and outlook. Marx was above all the
scholar and polemicist, whereas Lenin was primarily the master organizer and practical politician and leader. Marx sought to change
the whole world by his ideas, whereas Lenin had one fixed, and
more limited, goal: to seize power in his own country, Russia, and
to reshape it according to communist principles. Yet the most important difference between the two men is not to be found in explicit
fundamental doctrine, but in the different inarticulate and implicit
premises of their times. Marx was the product of the nineteenth century, and though he tried to envision, and help create, the society of
the future, he always retained a world view typical of the nineteenth century. By contrast, Lenin, though born in the nineteenth
century, developed to maturity and stature in the twentieth century,
and his deepest attitudes were typical of the twentieth century.

Marx's belief in the *primacy of economics over politics* not
only resulted from his economic interpretation of history, but also
reflected a typically nineteenth-century bias. The prevailing view
in the nineteenth century was one of almost unlimited faith in economic forces as the main engines of social and economic progress.
Thus, liberals in the nineteenth century confidently expected that
the right economic policies would ensure domestic stability and
progress, solve the problem of poverty, and lead to universal peace.
Laissez-faire economic policies within nations and free trade between nations made up the magic formula that would lead to a
world without force and oppression. Marx's formula was different
from that of his liberal contemporaries, but it was nevertheless an
economic formula.

By contrast, Lenin, in typically twentieth-century style, believed
in the *primacy of politics over economics*, although in terms of explicit doctrine he always considered himself a faithful follower of
Marx's economic interpretation of history. Because of his deep commitment to the overriding importance of politics, Lenin spent most
of his revolutionary energy in building up an organizational apparatus in tsarist Russia. Although, before the revolution, he spent
seventeen years abroad, mostly in Switzerland, he kept in close

touch with the day-to-day activities of the Bolshevik group which he led. His ability to maintain his leadership and the discipline of his revolutionary movement from afar for so many years testified to his political acumen and dynamic personality as a leader and organizer.

Because Marx was so committed to nineteenth-century economic thinking, he expected that the first communist revolutions would occur in western Europe, with its advanced capitalist economies. Marx shared the general conviction of his century that the laws of economic development could not be interfered with, and that each country had to go through the various stages of capitalism before it became ripe for communist revolution. By contrast, Lenin looked at the problem from a more political viewpoint. The task of communist leadership and the professional revolutionaries, Lenin thought, was to attack and destroy the existing social and political system where it was weakest—in the economically less developed areas of Europe, Asia, Africa, and Latin America. Lenin agreed with Marx that communist revolution was inevitable, but he asked: Why wait until capitalism has matured? Why not smash it where it is politically and organizationally weakest—that is, in economically retarded Russia and in Asian and African areas?

As a Russian, Lenin had a profound understanding of the weak social cohesion and low organizational energy that mark economically underdeveloped societies. In such countries, the mass of the population consists of poor peasants living in isolated villages, with inadequate means of communication. There are few or no independent labor unions and practically no middle class—the backbone of anticommunist resistance in economically more advanced countries. In his own country, Russia, Lenin noticed that a comparatively small force of army and police could keep control over a vast—but unorganized—mass of people. Lenin therefore believed that with a relatively small but highly disciplined and well organized counterforce, power could be wrested from the apparatus of the existing system, and the success of his revolution in November 1917 proved him right.

Lenin also had a deep understanding of the importance of the underdeveloped areas in the balance of world power. Marx shared the typical nineteenth-century prejudice that Europe was the center of the world and that underdeveloped areas were merely colonial appendages of leading European powers. As a Russian, with one foot also in Asia, Lenin was free from this European conceit. He was the first important political figure early in this century who saw that the world was more than Europe, and that, above all, the underdeveloped areas would increasingly become a major factor in world politics. Many people in the West still do not grasp the crucial role of underdeveloped areas; Lenin—with his genius for political analysis and organizational strategy—understood at such an early date that communism would first be established in underdeveloped countries before the hard core of anticommunist resistance—western Europe and North America—could be tackled. A master strategist, Lenin hoped that, once the "soft underbelly" of world capitalism had been conquered by communism, western Europe and North America would not put up too much resistance.

Both Marx and Lenin believed in the inevitable victory of communism throughout the world. Yet this common belief was marked by significant differences. Marx expected that a communist revolution would lead to the *dictatorship of the proletariat*, an essentially economic entity, *over the bourgeoisie*, also a basically economic category. Marx even hoped that in such a temporary dictatorship of the proletariat there would be a variety of parties and groups, all united in the common goal of destroying the last remnants of capitalism but differing on lesser issues. By contrast, Lenin's concept of dictatorship meant, in more political terms, the *dictatorship of the Communist party over the proletariat,* since he had little faith that the working class had the political understanding or spontaneous organizational ability to secure the existence and expansion of a communist state.

Marx believed that communism in a particular country would be preceded by internal economic crises, and that each country would develop its own revolutionary movements when conditions were "objectively ripe." By contrast, Lenin took a more activist and worldwide view, combining ideological universality with Russian national interests. Particularly after the success of the November Revolution, he saw that Russia would become the base and nerve center from which communist revolutions in other countries could be engineered.

Finally, Marx and Lenin viewed international politics in different perspectives. In nineteenth-century fashion, Marx took comparatively little interest in international politics, since economic forces and tendencies were presumed to determine world affairs. By contrast, Lenin saw every problem in its global perspective, both before and after he seized power in Russia. Even while Russia was still reeling under the devastating impact of military defeat, revolution, and civil war, while millions of Russians were starving, Lenin devoted much of his thought and political effort to organizing centers of communist activity throughout the world, particularly in Asia, which he correctly sensed would be the most fruitful target for communist expansion in the near future.

COMMUNIST DOCTRINE AND POLICY TODAY

Since Lenin's death in 1924, there has been no new addition or modification of basic Marxist-Leninist thought. Stalin and Khrushchev, who ruled Russia from 1924 to 1964, were stronger in practical administration than in theorizing. Most of the post-Leninist communist writings are but a rehash of Marx and Lenin, adapted to the momentary needs of the dictatorship. The core of communist long-term strategy, largely followed by the communist leaders today, consists in the concept of the *four basic tensions* underlying our present-day world:

1. The tension between capitalists and proletarians everywhere
2. The tension between imperialist states and colonies
3. The tension between rival imperialist states
4. The tension between communist states and capitalist states

This conception of the four basic tensions, far from being a mere exercise in semantic classification, provides a clear blueprint for communist strategy and tactics. It is virtually impossible to open a newspaper without seeing some evidence of communist application of these concepts to practical issues and policies.

1. The *tension between capitalists and proletarians* is the classical conception of Marxism and goes back to Marx's belief in the contradiction between forces of production and relations of production.

Capitalism today represents in communist thought the forces of production, the technological and scientific know-how, which cannot be fully utilized under the capitalist system of production for profit. The proletariat represents symbolically the relations of production, a new set of social institutions to be fully established after the overthrow of capitalism, allowing for the fullest use of all available knowledge and resources in a communist economic system, in which social institutions will aid, and not hamper, the productive process.

The great depression of 1929–1939 convinced the communists that capitalism is in a state of hopeless decay and that the tension between actual production under capitalism and productive capacity under a communist organization of the economy must ultimately lead to a revolutionary solution. When after World War II a major economic crisis failed to materialize in the capitalist world, communists began to doctor facts and figures to prove that the prevailing prosperity was actually a depression and that a really big depression was around the corner.

Communists have been even more disappointed by the phenomenal economic expansion of some leading capitalist countries, such as West Germany and Japan, that, in the 1950's and 1960's, grew faster than both the Soviet Union and the United States. Communist hostility to the unification of western Europe is based not only on politics and diplomacy but also on economics; the Common Market countries (France, Germany, Italy, Belgium, the Netherlands, and Luxembourg) have shown that rapid economic progress can be reconciled with individual liberty and international cooperation—a contagious example to the peoples in eastern Europe. COMECON, the Council of Mutual Economic Aid of the Soviet Union and the east European communist states, cannot match the Common Market for economic and political reasons. Economically, COMECON was intended from the beginning to be an instrument of centralized planning primarily for the benefit of the Soviet Union. The old Marxist description of capitalistic imperialism—"trade follows the flag"—also fits communist imperialism. Where Soviet political influence is strongest in COMECON countries, Soviet commercial dominance is also strongest. Thus, 15 percent of all Soviet trade—considering both communist and noncommunist countries— is with East Germany alone, and more than 40 percent of all East

German trade is with the Soviet Union. Neither goods nor people can circulate freely within COMECON. Goods are exchanged through bilateral barter arrangements among governments, and citizens of COMECON countries cannot freely move in the area. By contrast, the 185 million citizens of Common Market countries can, since 1968, travel freely as well as settle down and accept employment in the member states, and goods, too, circulate freely, without any tariffs or restrictions.

The communists' main concern with the tension between capitalists and workers is *political* rather than *economic*.

Thus, in formulating a policy for a strike, a communist will ask himself one primary question: Will it aid the cause of the communist revolution? The welfare of the particular group of workers involved is secondary to the overall objective of serving communism.

When Russia was a friendly nonbelligerent on the side of Nazi Germany in 1939–1941, the communists fomented strikes in Britain and the United States, not to help British or American workers, but to paralyze production in Britain and the United States, the two main opponents of Nazi Germany. The moment Russia was drawn into World War II by the German attack on June 22, 1941, communists everywhere opposed strikes as treason, exhorted workers to work 60, 70, and 80 hours a week, and called everybody a fascist who sought to protect the rights of the workers against demands for all-out production.

The concern with political issues of communist elements in Western labor unions, particularly foreign policy issues, has continued in the post-World War II period. NATO and American foreign policy have been among the favorite targets. More recently, revolutionary elements of the New Left have sought to infiltrate labor unions in the United States and western Europe, and the overriding goal has again been political: destruction of the existing political and economic system at home, combined with support of communist revolutionary movements and guerrilla activities abroad, particularly in the developing nations.

2. The *tension between imperialist states and colonies,* although mentioned by Marx, was more clearly elaborated by Lenin, who lived in an age of colonial rebellion. Whereas Marx predicted the proletarian revolution in the most advanced industrial nations of the

West, Lenin concentrated on the backward areas of the world as the most fertile soil for communist propaganda and eventual takeover.

When communists speak of colonies, they refer not only to territories legally dependent upon another state—the number of such dependencies has in any case approached the vanishing point by now—but also to small, weak states that are in fact in the sphere of influence of the leading Western states. From the communist viewpoint, most states in Latin America or Africa are colonial although they are legally independent and sovereign. The communist strategy is always to help the colonial or weaker state against the West.

All over the globe, communists take up the cause of anti-imperialism, as long as the imperialists are British, French, or American rather than Russian or Chinese. Thus, Cuba under Fidel Castro has been hailed by Moscow and Peking as being truly independent because on both domestic and international issues the Castro regime rapidly moved into the communist camp. When the Belgian Congo became independent in 1960, the Soviet Union tried unsuccessfully to turn it into a communist satellite. The suppression of a major communist rebellion in Indonesia in 1965 and the ouster of the procommunist dictator of Ghana, Nkrumah, in 1966 was particularly unpleasant news to Moscow and Peking.

Moreover, communists approach colonial tensions from a long-range viewpoint rather than in the light of the immediate interests of local Communist parties. Thus, in Iran the ultranationalist dictatorship of Mossadegh was supported by Moscow until his downfall in 1953, despite his anticommunism, because he sought to oust Britain and the United States from any sphere of influence in that oil-rich country. In Argentina, the fascist dictatorship of General Perón was also endorsed by the Kremlin until his overthrow in 1955 because he was anti-British and anti-American. The Soviet Union has showered President Nasser of Egypt with arms and all forms of diplomatic support although the Communist party is outlawed in Egypt. This is a minor consideration to the Soviet government, compared with the fact that Nasser is bent on wiping out Western influence not only in Egypt but in the whole Near and Middle East.

The Soviet government has also consistently supported anticommunist Pakistan to obtain a foothold in an area involving India and, above all, China. Even the extremely anticommunist regime of Indonesia, set up in 1965, has received friendly treatment as a means of neutralizing Western influence and, more importantly, of isolating China. In recent years, the Soviet Union has also flirted with Franco's Spain, the most anticommunist regime in western Europe, in order to strengthen the Soviet position in the Mediterranean and to undermine American influence there.

The communist line in all these cases is simple: whatever hurts the influence or prestige of the Western powers is good for world communism although local communists may have to take this long-term view from prison cells. An ultranationalist, anticommunist regime in a developing or weak state is looked upon by Moscow as but a prelude to communization, provided American or British influence can be kept out of the picture. Communist support for anticommunist regimes in weak states makes perfect sense in the light of long-range communist objectives.

India and China now lead the struggle for Asia, and indirectly for all developing countries. China is following the communist totalitarian system, whereas India is trying to combine political democracy with a program of rapid economic development.

If India succeeds, world communism will lose a decisive battle. If India bogs down in a quagmire of lassitude, corruption, and economic stagnation, the field may well be clear for communism to sweep from India to the rest of Asia. During the 1950's, China's economy grew by an average annual rate of eight percent, as compared with India's average annual growth rate of 3.7 percent during the same period. In the 1960's, both nations have been unable to sustain impressive growth records. The catastrophic effects of the Great Leap Forward of 1959–1961 substantially slowed up China's economic progress in the early 1960's, but since then she has again shown remarkable economic and technological progress—without receiving economic aid from either the United States or the Soviet Union.

By contrast, India's economy has been comparatively stagnant throughout the 1960's. She suffered from near-famine conditions in 1964–1966 and was saved only by massive economic aid by the

United States and other Western nations. During the period 1948–1968, the United States alone gave or loaned about nine billion dollars to India, the largest single recipient of American economic aid. Yet in spite of this economic aid—in addition to military aid which she receives from both the United States and the Soviet Union—India has been barely able to keep her output in line with her annual population increase of about 12 million. If over the next 20 or 30 years India should only hold her own while continuing to receive large foreign economic aid, whereas China is able to move ahead by her own effort in economic, technological, and scientific development, India can hardly hope to do well in her race with China for leadership in Asia.

If India, with a population of about 550 million, should ever become communist, the balance of world power might gradually shift to communism. In the general elections of 1952, the Indian Communist party polled only 3.3 percent of the popular vote; in later elections this figure rose to about 10 percent, and the Communist party was able to take over control of several state governments in alliances with other leftist groups.

3. The *tension between rival imperialist states* goes back to Marx's theory of the decay of capitalism. When the rate of profit falls because of large accumulation of capital relative to the labor force, the capitalist looks for profitable employment of capital outside his own country and finds such opportunities in newly developing countries, countries in which capital is very scarce and labor abundantly available. However, as time goes on, investment opportunities in backward areas constantly shrink, and capitalists then look to their governments for aid. According to the Marxist-communist doctrine, the capitalist state is but the executive committee of the propertied classes, and therefore the flag willingly and eagerly follows trade. As capitalists from several countries collide in the same zone of influence and expansion, their governments become involved in a struggle for power.

War under capitalism is thus viewed by communists as a clash between rival imperialist forces motivated by the quest for economic expansion. World Wars I and II are interpreted by communists in this fashion, although the communists have never explained why, if England was so anxious to preserve her commercial position in 1914, she did not go to war with the United States, which by 1914 had attained first place in industrial—and inevitably political and military—power. In 1939, despite a decade of depression, American supremacy in industry and finance, and the resulting ability to wage war, had become even more obvious, and communists again find it difficult to explain on Marxist grounds why England and France fought Germany rather than the United States.

The 1961 Program of the Communist Party of the Soviet Union states that "the contradictions between the principal imperialist powers are growing deeper," and then specifies what the main sources of conflict in the noncommunist world are: "The Anglo-American, Franco-American, Franco-West German, American-West German, Japanese-American, and other contradictions are becoming especially acute. Fresh contradictions will inevitably arise and grow in the imperialist camp."

Because they do not believe that capitalist states can work together peacefully and amicably, communists exploit existing tensions and create new tensions between capitalist states. Thus in Britain the main communist propaganda slogan is that America will fight to the last Englishman. In France, the communists have managed to exploit the issue of wine versus Coca-Cola as one of French national independence versus American imperialism.

The successful creation of NATO (North Atlantic Treaty Organization) in 1949 was a blow against communism not only because of its military value against aggression but also because the very existence of NATO belies the communist myth that capitalist states cannot collaborate for common objectives. By contrast, disunity among the United States, Britain, and France over major issues in the Middle East contributed to the growth of Soviet influence in the area. In 1956, when Egypt seized the Suez Canal, the United States on one side and France and Britain on the other found themselves in opposite camps. During and after the six-day war between Israel and the Arab states in June 1967, the United States supported Israel, Britain stood aloof, and France under de Gaulle sided with the Arab states. This Western disunity enabled Russia to become firmly entrenched in the Middle East for the first time in its history.

The Soviet government was immensely pleased in 1963 and 1967 when France twice vetoed the entry of Great Britain into the Common Market. While General de Gaulle was staunchly anticommunist, his opposition to British entry removed a major source of anxiety in the Soviet leadership for the time being. With Britain in, the Common Market nations would surpass the Soviet Union in population and economic strength, not to speak of the dynamic psychological effects of such a community based on freedom. Without Britain, a united western Europe is a source of constant concern, but not a fatal blow, to communist goals.

In 1966, the Soviet government felt greatly relieved when the French government ordered NATO headquarters to leave France and for all practical purposes withdrew from any military participation in NATO. General de Gaulle based this policy on his concept —or dream—of a closely cooperating Europe from the Channel to the Urals, in which France and Russia would be the two leaders, with Britain and the United States being excluded from the Continent. The Soviet invasion and occupation of Czechoslovakia in 1968 shattered de Gaulle's concept beyond repair. President Georges Pompidou, who succeeded de Gaulle in 1969, has returned to more realistic policies in line with France's strength and resources, and French attitudes toward NATO have become friendlier under his leadership.

4. The *tension between communist and capitalist states* is increasingly recognized by communists to be the most important of all four tensions. Marx had never given much thought to the question of the coexistence of capitalist and communist states. He thought of conflict as the vehicle of social development, but his concept of conflict related to domestic class struggles. Being steeped in nineteenth-century economic optimism, Marx may have hoped that tensions between states would eventually be resolved through economic means. Lenin and his successors, however, faced with the realities of governing the first communist state and spearheading what they considered to be a world revolution, gave a great deal of thought to the question how communist and capitalist states can get along in one world.

As far back as 1924, when Russia was still on the defensive and struggling for her very existence, communist leaders developed a doctrine that was not taken seriously in the West but that accurately anticipated future policies. In his *Foundations of Leninism* (1924), Stalin wrote that the world is divided into two hostile camps, "the world front of imperialism" and the "common front of the revolutionary movement in all countries." In particular, he considered the Soviet Union the "base for the overthrow of imperialism in all countries," and this idea of the *Soviet Union as the first phase of the inevitable communization of the world* has since then guided Soviet long-term strategy.

With a slight dash of humor, Stalin held out one hope for the capitalist states. War is not inevitable if the capitalist countries are willing to surrender voluntarily without resisting communization. Stalin wrote that communism may spread to so many countries that the remaining capitalist states will realize the hopelessness of resistance, and this "encirclement" by communist states will make voluntary surrender "expedient."

Before World War II was over, the Soviet government violated every pledge it had made to establish democracy in eastern and southeastern Europe. With the help of the Soviet army, communist regimes were set up in Romania, Bulgaria, Hungary, Poland, and East Germany. Leaders of proven democratic background and loyalty were imprisoned, exiled, or killed. In China and Indochina, communist revolutions were supported, with complete success in the former and with partial success in the latter. In Greece, the communists started a civil war in December 1944 which ended in communist defeat after Yugoslavia broke with Moscow in 1948. In Malaya and the Philippines, communist guerrilla forces fought for years against the established regimes, causing much bloodshed and devastation. In France and Italy, the communists tried to stage general strikes on several occasions, presumably with the ultimate intent of transforming industrial strife into revolution.

In the Balkans and eastern Europe, the communists argued that political democracy had never existed there and that the real choice lay between fascist totalitarianism and communist dictatorship. If such argumentation did have an effect on noncommunists for a time, its value was completely destroyed in Czechoslovakia in February 1948. Although the Soviet Union used the Czechoslovakian Communist party as its tool, this was the first case of the subjugation of a truly democratic nation to communist dictatorship by armed force, represented by the Soviet army standing on the borders of Czechoslovakia ready to intervene. The communist seizure of Czechoslovakia gave the prime impulse to the formation of the North Atlantic Treaty Organization and speeded up tremendously the rate of rearmament in the Western nations, particularly in the United States. It was partly because of the Czechoslovakian experience that the United States, joined by many other members of the United Nations, determined to resist armed communist aggression in Korea in 1950.

After the death of Stalin in 1953, Nikita Khrushchev gradually emerged as Stalin's successor. In a major address before the Twentieth Congress of the Soviet Communist Party on February 14, 1956, Khrushchev stated that Soviet foreign policy was guided by the following five principles: peaceful coexistence; nonaggression; noninterference in internal affairs of other nations; mutual respect for territorial integrity and sovereignty; and equality and mutual benefit. In addition, Khrushchev declared that communization of noncommunist nations need not always be carried out by force, particularly where it could be accomplished by parliamentary majorities. Significantly, no nation has ever gone communist as a result of free elections.

Soviet acceptance of the principle of peaceful coexistence suggested to many that communism had abandoned its objective of world revolution, and that post-Stalin communism would be different from Stalin's foreign policy. Some optimists in the West went even so far as to hail the "dawn of liberalism" in the Soviet Union. Yet only nine months later, in October and November 1956, the dawn of Soviet liberalism turned into the nightmare of the Hungarian tragedy.

Immediately after the Hungarian Revolution was suppressed, Khrushchev had this to say to a group of Western diplomats at a diplomatic reception in Moscow on November 18, 1956: "Whether you like it or not, history is on our side. *We will bury you.*"

In spite of the official acceptance of the principle of coexistence by Stalin's successors—Khrushchev, Brezhnev, and Kosygin—Soviet foreign policy has been more daring and ambitious than in Stalin's days. Stalin, following the tradition of the tsars, concentrated on the expansion of Soviet power in areas in which Soviet land armies could be the decisive factor. His successors have discarded such limitations. In 1956, following Egypt's seizure of the Suez Canal, Soviet influence was firmly established in the Near and Middle East. Between 1955 and 1966, Egypt received over a billion dollars in Soviet military aid, or nearly one-third of all Soviet foreign military aid. In addition, Egypt received about a billion dollars in economic aid, or one-fifth of all Soviet foreign economic aid during the period. The military equipment included the most modern tanks, jets, submarines, and missiles. After his visit to Egypt in 1966, Premier Kosygin referred to Egypt as an "important stronghold of national liberation and progressive development throughout the vast area of the Near East and Africa" (June 10, 1966).

Encouraged by Soviet advice, Egypt in 1967 ejected the United Nations peace force in the Gaza Strip and blockaded the Gulf of Aqaba to Israeli shipping, thus seeking to strangle Israel into submission, since the gulf is Israel's waterway to her only southern port, Elath, and from there to the Red Sea and the Indian Ocean. The blockade of the Gulf of Aqaba by Egypt triggered the six-day war of June 1967. Israel captured much of the military equipment given to the Arab states by the Soviet Union, and a considerable proportion of the captured matériel, estimated at several hundred millions of dollars, had hardly been used by the defeated Arab forces.

Immediately after the fighting was over, the Soviet Union intensified its military effort in the Arab states, particularly in Egypt. In the two years following the 1967 war, Soviet arms given to Arab states were estimated at two to three billion dollars, and much of the replenishment was carried out by Soviet airlifts. Before the 1967 war, there were between 500 and 700 Soviet military advisers in Egypt. In 1969, estimates ran to 4,000–7,000, and the Soviet advisers now operate down to the battalion level. Soviet pilots fly with the Egyptian air force, and Soviet advisers and technicians operate more sophisticated equipment, such as submarines, radar, and missiles. The port of Alexandria has become, for all practical purposes, a home port for the Soviet navy, which also uses facilities in Syria and Algeria. According to Western intelligence sources, there has also been "a substantial flow of Soviet funds to editors, party leaders, teachers, and key military personnel" (*New York Times,* July 16, 1968).

Under its present leadership, the Soviet Union has acquired more diplomatic, military, ideological, and economic influence in the Middle East than ever before. The economic benefits of the vast Soviet investment in the Middle East are far from negligible. Trade is increasingly oriented toward the Soviet Union and eastern Europe, but the main prize is oil. The Soviet Union is currently self-sufficient in oil, but a Soviet foothold in the Middle East is insurance against a future in which the expanding Soviet economy will depend on outside sources of oil. As a result of the closer ties between the Soviet Union and the Arab states, Soviet exploration teams have been drilling for oil in Syria, Iraq, and Algeria.

Soviet influence in the Middle East was substantially extended to east Africa in 1969. In May of that year, the government of Sudan was overthrown by a military coup, and the new government included a number of communists. One of the first acts of the new government was to outlaw all political parties with the exception of the Communist party, and to invite Soviet arms experts to negotiate the sending of Soviet arms and military technicians. Northern Sudan is culturally part of the Arab world, and the Soviet Union can thus intensify its influence on Egypt, which borders Sudan to the north. Southern Sudan is part of black Africa, and through it Soviet pressure can be exercised on nearby Ethiopia, the only major center of pro-Western sympathies in the area.

Since 1959, Soviet power has also become firmly entrenched in the western hemisphere through the establishment of Fidel Castro's communist regime. Cuba has been the number one center of propaganda, infiltration, sabotage, and subversion in the western hemisphere. Emboldened by the inaction of the United States, the Soviets introduced large numbers of aircraft capable of carrying atomic bombs as well as large quantities of missiles into Cuba in 1962. On October 22, 1962, the President of the United States announced that Cuba would be subjected to a blockade and that the Soviet missiles would have to be removed from Cuba—or else. After first denying that there were any Soviet missiles in Cuba, the Soviet government realized that the United States meant business. As a result, the missiles were shipped back to Russia, but thousands of Soviet "technicians" were left behind in Cuba, as well as large quantities of Soviet weapons other than missiles.

The Soviet defeat in the Cuban missile crisis was probably one of the factors that contributed to Khrushchev's ouster in 1964. Subsequently, the new Soviet leadership intensified Soviet economic and political links with Cuba. Guerrillas trained in Cuba were sent to various Latin American countries to foment revolution and civil war; such activities assumed alarming proportions in Guatemala, Venezuela, Colombia, and Peru. In 1966, the first "Tricontinental Conference" was held in Havana, attended by representatives of 83 communist organizations in Africa, Asia, and Latin America. The conference, a direct outgrowth of the Afro-Asian Solidarity Conference held in Cairo in 1957, established a permanent organization, the Afro-Asian-Latin American Peoples' Solidarity Organization, headquartered in Havana. Behind the long name of this organization lies a short goal: to communize Africa, Asia, and Latin America through "wars of national liberation."

The communist concept of "coexistence" differs markedly from the Western understanding of that term. In the West, coexistence is the application of the principle of pluralism to the international community. Just as different ideological and economic groups are expected to tolerate each other in the national state, nations with different economic and political systems are expected to accept each other's differences peacefully.

By contrast, the Soviet concept of coexistence is much more limited and more dynamic. It recognizes the possibility of agreements between communist and noncommunist countries in limited practical areas that are ideologically neutral, as in the limited test-ban treaty between the Soviet Union, the United States, and Great Britain in 1963. But such specific agreements do not, in the Soviet view, alter the basic ideological conflict between communist and noncommunist states. Peaceful coexistence is viewed by Soviet leaders as a means not of reducing ideological tension in the world but of exploiting it. In the words of the December Declaration of 1960, issued by the leaders of 81 Communist parties in Moscow on December 6, 1960, peaceful coexistence provides "favorable opportunities for the development of the class struggle in the capitalist countries and the national-liberation movements of the colonial and dependent countries." This view sees coexistence as a one-way street in which communist ideology can move into noncommunist countries, but which does not permit traffic in the other direction, that is, the movement of noncommunist ideologies into areas of communist control.

In his address to the 23rd Congress of the Soviet Communist party on March 29, 1966, Leonid I. Brezhnev, its general secretary and the top Soviet leader, clearly showed the continuity of communist thought and policy. First, Brezhnev expressed the orthodox communist conviction that "the doom of capitalism" is "becoming more and more obvious." However, he warned that the capitalists, unmindful of the historical law of their doom, "will never give up their domination by their own free will. It is only through tenacious class battles that the working class and the rest of the working people will achieve victory." Brezhnev also promised that the Communist party of the Soviet Union "will do everything in its power for the world socialist system to become ever mightier and to advance from victory to victory." With respect to the issue of spreading communism in developing countries, Brezhnev fully stood by the policy objectives of the 1961 Program of the Communist Party of the Soviet Union. He stated that the CPSU "regards it as its internationalist duty to continue to do everything to support the struggle of the peoples for final liberation from colonial and neo-colonial oppression."

The Soviet concept of permanent ideological hostility between communist and noncommunist states was expressed even more clearly by Brezhnev on March 29, 1968, in Moscow: "Our party has always warned that in the ideological field there can be no peaceful coexistence, just as there can be no class peace between the proletariat and the bourgeoisie." In their reading of modern history since Marx, communist leaders have developed great faith in the power of Marxist-Leninist ideology of undermining existing social and political systems. Brezhnev's concept of limited coexistence and permanent ideological hostility thus implies, in the words of a seasoned observer of international affairs, "an intention to do other societies in, even if the goal is accomplished by nonwarlike means" (C. L. Sulzberger, *New York Times*, October 27, 1968).

SOCIAL-ECONOMIC
CHANGES UNDER COMMUNISM

The first major attack in this century against the established social order occurred in Russia toward the end of World War I. The tsarist regime was overthrown in a bloodless revolution in March 1917, and it seemed that Russia would have the opportunity to develop democratic institutions for the first time in her history.

The majority of Russians wanted political liberty as well as fundamental social change. Inexperienced in the conduct of public affairs, however, and failing to understand the true nature and goals of communism, the new, democratic government of Alexander Kerensky allowed the Bolsheviks, led by Lenin and Trotsky, to subvert and quickly destroy the new democratic state.

Between March and November 1917, the Bolsheviks (the party was not known as the Communist party until 1919) used three classical methods of gaining power, methods they were to repeat later in almost identical fashion in other countries.

First, they presented themselves in their propaganda as a people's party dedicated to liberty, democracy, and social justice and opposed to all forms of reaction and social injustice. In an agrarian country like Russia, the communists emphasized the need for agrarian land reform and encouraged the seizure of land by the peasants even before they were in control of the government. A generation later the Chinese communists proclaimed themselves (and were believed by many to be) no more than *agrarian reformers*, thus following the pattern of propaganda established by the Russian communists in 1917.

The second technique the Bolsheviks employed was *infiltration* of other political parties, trade unions, soldiers' councils, and local government authorities. In particular, the communists managed to infiltrate and gradually disrupt the Social Revolutionaries, the largest party in Russia, dedicated to social reform and especially concerned with the question of the peasants. This technique of infiltration was again employed by the communists during and after World War II when they tried to take over socialist parties in a number of countries.

The third method used by the Bolsheviks in their revolution was *force*. In free elections in the summer and fall of 1917, the Bolsheviks polled about one-quarter of the total vote. Though this represented a far from negligible proportion, the Bolsheviks accepted the fact that in a free election they could not hope to win. In November 1917, therefore, the Bolsheviks seized the key positions of power in Petrograd and Moscow, and from there the revolution quickly spread all over Russia. Opposition to communist revolution sprang up in various parts of the country, and a civil war ensued that lasted until 1921.

The ravages of World War I, followed by the devastations of the civil war, made immediate social reform impractical. Lenin was realistic enough to see that the Russian people would starve to death if communist principles were imposed at that time. As a result, he inaugurated in 1921 the New Economic Policy, which permitted limited private ownership; this policy's main objective was to maintain and increase production on the farms and in the workshops and factories by retaining the old capitalist incentives of efficiency and profit. The application of the NEP for some seven years gave Russia a breathing spell, allowing the communist rulers to consolidate their power more effectively and giving the Russian people the temporary illusion that the bark of communism was worse than its bite.

But in 1928 Stalin decided that the time had come to put communist principles into practice, and he withdrew the temporary concessions earlier made by Lenin (who died in 1924). The first five-year plan, starting in 1928, aimed primarily at the rapid industrialization of Russia and secondarily at the collectivization of farming. In 1917 many peasants had sympathized with Bolshevism, not for reasons of theory or ideology, but because the Bolsheviks promised them the land they and their ancestors had tilled and coveted for centuries.

The reasons that motivated Stalin to force collectivization on the peasants were manifold. First, the communist rulers felt that agricultural production would be increased by mechanization and that this could be more easily effected on large-scale, collectivized farms than on small, individually owned ones. Second, individual ownership and operation of farms denied a key principle of communism, namely, that all means of production be transferred to public ownership. Collectivization would bring agriculture in line with industry, which was developed from the start on the basis of state ownership and operation. Third, the communist rulers saw in continued individual farm ownership a direct political and psychological threat to the acceptance of totalitarian political direction from the center.

The independent peasant had to be transformed into a dependent agricultural proletarian; as a member of a collective farm, the peasant was constantly working with others, talking to others, eating with others, and could thus be more easily supervised and regimented.

Another reason behind collectivization was the need for labor for the newly developing industries in the cities. The required labor force could be obtained only by mechanizing agriculture and thus saving human labor. Finally, collectivization had an important military objective: in case of war, the collectives were to provide the nucleus for organized resistance behind the lines. In World War II, these military expectations were largely fulfilled: the Germans were never completely able to suppress Russian guerrilla activities behind their lines.

The cost of fundamental social and economic change in Russia was heavy. In the process of collectivizing the farms in the years 1929–1933 between four and five million peasants lost their lives or were uprooted from their homes and deported to slave labor camps in Siberia or the Arctic. To show their resistance to collectivization, the peasants slaughtered as much livestock as they could for their own use, so that by the time collectivization was accomplished, the number of livestock had greatly decreased. The number of cattle in the Soviet Union was 67 million in 1928, 34 million in 1934, 58 million in 1950, and 97 million in 1967. Cows numbered 33 million in 1928, 19 million in 1934, 25 million in 1950, and 41 million in 1967. During the same period the Soviet population increased by 85 million, from 150 to 235 million. The human population thus increased at a much faster rate than the number of cattle and cows.

By contrast with Soviet figures for livestock, there were 57 million cattle in the United States in 1928, and 109 million in 1967; there were 31 million cows in 1928, and 50 million in 1967. During the same period the population of the United States increased from 121 to 198 million, or by 77 million. Cattle and cows thus increased faster than the human population. The rate of increase of cattle and cows in the United States could have been much greater still—but the problem here is one of overproduction, not of scarcity, as in the Soviet Union.

As the accompanying table shows, the Soviet diet still emphasizes starches—cereal products and potatoes—whereas the diet of most Americans is mainly vegetables, fruits, and foods of animal origin. Cereals and potatoes make up well over half the Soviet diet, but only about one-quarter of the American diet. What is even more remarkable is that the Soviet diet of 1967 is below the quality of the American diet of 1909–1913.

The only realistic way to compute the cost of a family's food budget is to ascertain the number of working hours it takes to buy a given quantity of food. Seen in such a comparative perspective, the cost of Soviet food in terms of working time is considerably higher than in Western countries. As the table on page 52 shows, the cost in terms of working hours of a weekly basket of staple foods for a

SOVIET AND AMERICAN DIETS BY MAJOR FOOD GROUPS

(calories per person per day)

	Soviet Union 1967	United States 1909–1913	United States 1967
Grain products, potatoes, and pulses	1,717	1,560	827
Fats and oils, including butter	369	408	528
Sugar	354	408	518
Meat and fish	217	555	626
Milk and milk products, excluding butter	347	328	391
Vegetables, fruit, eggs, and other foods	196	231	290
Total	3,200	3,490	3,180

Source: Joint Economic Committee, Congress of the United States, *Soviet Economic Performance: 1966–1967* (1968)

INTERNATIONAL MEDIAN FOOD BASKET FOR A FAMILY OF FOUR

Wheat flour	2 kg	Margarine	1 kg
White bread	3 kg	Milk	10 l
Macaroni	1 kg	Cheese (gouda)	500 gm
Beef	1 kg	Eggs	24
Pork	1 kg	Potatoes	5 kg
Chicken	1 kg	Apples	1 kg
Cooked ham	500 gm	Oranges	1 kg
Sugar	1 kg	Bananas	1 kg
Cocoa	100 gm	Tea	100 gm
Butter	500 gm	Coffee (ground)	500 gm

Cost in Working Hours (1967)

New York	7.3
Moscow	59.2
London	13.9
Paris	32.1
Munich	21.0

Source: Joint Economic Committee, Congress of the United States, *Soviet Economic Performance: 1966–1967* (1968)

family of four in Moscow in 1967 was eight times higher than in New York, and two to four times higher than in other Western cities.

These comparisons do not allow for differences of quality. An observer who speaks from first-hand experience remarks, for example, that "the fresh fruit and vegetables available in a Moscow retail store would not be offered for sale in a New York supermarket" (Joint Economic Committee, *Soviet Economic Performance: 1966–1967*, 1968, pp. 265–66). Apart from the question of quality, the average Soviet family spends more than one-half its income on food, whereas the average American family spends only about one-sixth of its income on food.

Looking at some selected goods and services, measured in terms of working time, the comparison between prices in Moscow and those in Western cities suggests how far the Soviet consumer is still behind the Western consumer.

Looking at the farm picture as a whole, one discovers that the contrast between Soviet and American agriculture is the most striking of all segments of the two economies. In the United States,

SELECTED GOODS AND SERVICES
IN TERMS OF MINUTES OF WORKING TIME (1967)

	New York	Moscow	London	Paris	Munich
Toilet soap (small bar)	2	16	7	17	11
Razor blades (10)	21	55	23	34	42
Aspirin (100 tablets)	14	71	7	65	84
Nylon stockings (1 pr.)	14	367	21	28	42
White bread (unwrapped)	13	56	13	16	31
Chicken (1 kg)	21	294	45	127	84
White sugar (1 kg)	6	116	11	24	17
Plain chocolate (100-gm)	7	89	7	9	9
Eggs (cheapest, 12)	9	144	21	40	27
Tea (100 gm)	10	67	10	56	24
Ground coffee (1 kg)	42	500	113	185	141
Bus fare (for 2 mi.)	5	6	5	6	7
Dry cleaning of man's overcoat	30	306	67	168	155
Laundering of shirt	6	24	15	26	17
Electricity (1 kwh)	1	4	1	7	2
Medium-priced car (months)	4.1	47.3	7.3	12.9	6.4

Source: Data from Joint Economic Committee, Congress of the United States, *Soviet Economic Performance: 1966–1967* (1968)

about 5 percent of the labor force is currently employed in agriculture. In the Soviet Union, the percentage is well over 30, the ratio that existed in the United States sixty years ago. In the United States, therefore, one person employed in agriculture feeds himself and nineteen other workers and their families on the highest standard in the world, and vast surpluses still accumulate which are given away or sold to the rest of the world. In the Soviet Union, one-third of the population depending on agriculture for a living can barely feed itself and the other two-thirds of the people. Items like coffee and chocolate, part of the ordinary diet of workers in Western countries, are still luxuries in the Soviet Union. Before 1914 Russia was one of the world's leading exporters of farm products; the collectivization of agriculture has often turned her into an importer. In 1963–1966, the Soviet Union bought more than seven million tons of grain annually, and in 1966 she contracted to buy nine million tons of wheat from Canada in the following three years. One reason for such advance purchases of food by the Soviet Union was the fact that communist China also has been unable to feed its people and has therefore been competing with Russia for available food surpluses in capitalist nations.

In the early years of Soviet collectivization of farming, government-imposed low prices induced many peasants to grow as little as possible and to slaughter much of the livestock for their own consumption. As a result, there was widespread famine in the early 1930's, particularly in the Ukraine, where peasant resistance was strengthened by the force of nationalism.

After World War II, the Soviet government decided to intensify collectivization. Between 1950 and 1967, the 250,000 collective farms were amalgamated into 36,000. The objective was to increase production and at the same time reduce the individuality of the peasant. In addition to these 36,000 collective farms (*kolkhozy*), there are 12,000 state farms (*sovkhozy*) in which the peasant works on a wage basis, just as in a Soviet factory. The peasant in the collective farm still has some share in the success or failure of the whole farm.

The absolute numbers of collective farms and state farms do not give an accurate picture of Soviet farming, for the average state farm employs almost twice as many workers as the collective farm, has four times as much land, and has a crop area about three times as large as on the average collective farm. From the viewpoint of communist ideology, the state farms represent the highest possible form of agricultural organization and production because the peasant has been completely turned into a proletarian dependent on the state for his wage. Communist leaders hope that someday all collective farms will be transformed into state farms, and under Khrushchev's administration state farms were clearly favored over collective farms. His successors have been more realistic, and the new Collective Farm Charter of 1969 specifically recognized the collective farm as a basic Soviet institution.

After more than thirty years of farm collectivism, the Russian peasant is still deeply opposed to communism in agriculture. Peasant pressure has forced the government to allow the member of the collective farm to devote part of his time to a small plot of

Photograph by Robert S. Ebenstein

**THE AUTHOR IN LINE TO BUY FRESH FRUIT
IN THE CENTER OF MOSCOW**

land under his own personal management; he may then sell the
products of his own effort on the open market at higher prices than
are paid by the government (which is able to buy farm products
at artificially low prices bearing little relation to the natural forces
of supply and demand).

Although the peasant's own piece of land amounts to only an
acre or so, it supplies him with nearly half of his income, and these
dwarf holdings, amounting to only three percent of all Soviet farm
land, account for about one-half of all Soviet potatoes, meat, vegetables, and eggs. The peasants sell their personal produce in the
regular "farmers' markets" found in most Soviet cities. It is not un-
common, however, to see individual peasants, often women, arrive
in the center of Leningrad or Moscow with a basket of fresh toma-
toes or fruit and sell the produce in a few minutes to an eager crowd
of buyers who are always on the lookout for items that are scarce
or of inferior quality in government retail stores.

Since 1967, the incentive principle combined with profit-sharing
for farmers has been experimentally introduced into both state and
collective farms. Soviet critics of state farms have attacked their

main weakness: "A state farm is given what it asks for and therefore it is virtually indifferent to the prices of materials or equipment, just as it is indifferent to the prices paid for the products it delivers to the state" (reported in the *New York Times*, March 28, 1967). From 1967 on, therefore, a number of state farms which were already making a good profit were given the right to keep about one-third of their profit to be used as bonuses for farm workers and for improved housing and production facilities. In the collective farm sector, the Brezhnev-Kosygin administration in 1967 adopted two reforms to raise farm productivity. First, collective farms were allowed to set up their own workshops and small factories and to sell their products—processed foods, handicrafts—for profit. The second reform went even further. Under it, several groups of collective farmers were given land and monthly advances to be reimbursed at harvest time. The farmers were given no instructions or supervision, but let loose with the goal of making the best of their opportunity. Yields were 10–15 percent higher than in the rest of the same collective farms, and the Soviet farm specialist who reported on the experiments expressed the main point of his argument in favor of these experiments in writing that "the land must have a master, not a wage earner" (The Economist Intelligence Unit, *Quarterly Economic Reviews: USSR*, March 1968, p. 5). Time will tell to what extent these experimental reforms will make Soviet farming—the Achilles' heel of the whole Soviet economy—more productive and provide the Soviet consumer with low-cost food of high quality. For the time being, it appears that Soviet farming will continue to be, in the near and intermediate future, "the most expensive food producer in the world" (Joint Economic Committee, *New Directions in the Soviet Economy*, 1966, Part II–B, p. 429).

Psychologically, the Russian peasant has not been transformed into the proletarian that the communist rulers planned him to be. In the years after World War II, thousands of Russian peasants who had been sent to Germany as forced laborers during the war refused to go back home after having seen life outside the Soviet Union. Almost to a man, these peasants are opposed to collectivization and hope to own their own farms after communism is gone.

This sentiment of the peasants has been confirmed by events in Yugoslavia and Poland. After his break with Moscow in 1948, Tito allowed the peasants to decide whether they wanted to continue farm collectives or return to individual farming. The farm collectives rapidly disappeared, and Yugoslav farm output has more than doubled since 1952. In Poland, the Gomulka brand of national communism, brought into power by the October Revolution of 1956, also allowed the peasants to choose between individual and collective farming. Less than one percent of arable land is held by collective farms, 12 percent by state farms, and 87 percent by private peasants. The small number of collective and state farms have done poorly, whereas private farming has prospered since 1956.

Yet all these peasants—whether in the Soviet Union or in other communist states—are not fanatical individualists. While irreconcilably opposed to collective farms, they eagerly accept cooperative farm institutions, such as Canadian, Danish, and New Zealand farmers have developed. There is a world of difference between collectivism and cooperation: the purpose of *collectivism* is to *destroy the individuality* of the farmer; the aim of *cooperation* is to *strengthen the individual farm.*

Interestingly enough, workers and professional people who have escaped from Russia have indicated in interviews that they wish to maintain public ownership in only the key industries after communism is gone, but want to return to private ownership in light industry, retailing, and some of the professions. Where economic activity—as in agriculture, light industry, and retailing—can be performed in the classical pattern of the individual owner-manager-worker, what little uncensored Russian opinion we have is opposed to the economic changes of communism. Only where ownership, work, and management are technologically not feasible in one individual unit—as in heavy industry and some public services—does public ownership meet with approval.

In the field of industrialization, progress under Soviet communism has been immense, as was first proved by Russia's ability to withstand the onslaught of Germany in World War II. Though Russia received some strategic supplies from the United States during the war, the bulk of the industrial production needed to defeat Germany came from Russian workshops and factories. Russian industrialization, from the first five-year plan, has been oriented primarily toward the power of the state. For this reason, the government con-

PROPORTION OF SOVIET INDUSTRIAL INVESTMENT IN PRODUCER
GOODS AND CONSUMER GOODS INDUSTRIES

	1918–1958	1959–1964	1966–1970 (Plan)
Producer goods	88.3%	86.9%	88.1%
Consumer goods	11.7	13.1	11.9

Source: Foreign Affairs, July 1966

sistently emphasized heavy industry as especially vital to the production of armaments and showed less concern for the development of
consumer goods industries.

Until the middle 1950's, appliances common in the American
home were generally unknown in the Soviet Union. Since then, as
the accompanying table shows, the Soviet economy has made great
strides in meeting consumer demand for basic appliances. However,
the supply of such appliances is still way behind other advanced
industrial nations, and the gap in durable consumer goods between
the Soviet Union and the United States, for example, is widening,
since *current* annual American production of consumer appliances
(apart from large imports) is still considerably surpassing Soviet

SOVIET UNION AND UNITED STATES: HOUSEHOLD STOCKS
OF SELECTED DURABLES

(units per thousand persons)

	Soviet Union 1955	1960	1966	United States 1966	Soviet Union as percent of United States in 1966
Sewing machines	31	92	151	136	112
Refrigerators	4	7	40	293	14
Washing machines	1	10	77	259	30
Radios	66	130	171	1,300	13
Television sets	4	22	82	376	22
Automobiles	2	3	5	308	1

Source: Joint Economic Committee, Congress of the United States, *Soviet Economic Performance: 1966–1967* (1968)

production. Telephones, not listed in the table, are perennially in short supply. In 1967, there were 7.9 million telephones in the Soviet Union, as compared with 104 million in the United States—more than one-half of the world's total. The gap is increasing year by year, since currently five million new telephones are installed annually in the United States as compared with a few hundred thousand in the Soviet Union. Telephone directories, too, are hard to find—and use—in the Soviet Union. In 1969, the latest telephone directory in Moscow had been printed in 1961, and there were no plans to publish a new one.

Recent polls by Soviet researchers reveal that most Soviet citizens put refrigerators and cars first on the list of consumer durables they wanted to buy once they became available. The researchers found that the previously "negative and ascetic" view of Soviet ideology on consumer desires had given way to a more relaxed attitude, and that with the growing supply of consumer goods most people had developed a "fetish" for some items, particularly cars and refrigerators. Although the production of refrigerators rose from half a million in 1960 to more than three million in 1968, the waiting period for buying a refrigerator in 1969 could still be as long as two years (*New York Times,* July 1, 1969).

The waiting period for a car ranges from four to seven years. In the 1950's, annual Soviet production of automobiles hovered around 100,000, stepped up in the late 1960's to over 200,000. (In the same period U.S. automobile production reached nine million a year.) The Soviet Union—see the table on page 60—is the only advanced industrial nation in the world to have remained outside the automobile age. Both Stalin and Khrushchev looked upon the automobile as a typical expression of capitalist frivolity and unrestrained individualism. The decision, therefore, of the new leadership after Khrushchev to bring Russia into the automobile age is one of the most important turning points in the history of Soviet communism since 1917. In 1966, the Soviet government contracted with Italy's Fiat automobile company to build a huge plant in the Soviet Union which will eventually produce about 500,000 cars a year. In the same year, the Soviets also made an agreement with France's biggest automobile company, Renault, to enlarge existing facilities of

Russia's leading automobile plant in Moscow, in order to increase its annual production of cars from 80,000 to about 300,000. The announced goal was total Soviet production of about 800,000 cars by 1970, but in 1969 it was officially recognized that full production would not be reached before the mid-1970's. The goal of Soviet automobile production for the 1970's will still be less than a tenth of American production in the 1960's, but it is an important beginning.

The fetish of the automobile is not confined to would-be Soviet buyers but has also gripped Soviet authorities, as is evident in the following report by a British correspondent in Moscow:

The authorities, rather pathetically, would have you believe that Moscow is clogged with cars and faces traffic problems like any other great city. To prove the point, they sometimes hold up vehicles on the city's main highways for as much as half an hour, and then release the stream—while a movie cameraman films the resulting "traffic jam." There is something peculiarly sad about a society prepared to go to such lengths to imitate the excesses of the West (Anthony Carthew, "Moscow Report," *New York Times Magazine*, May 18, 1969, p. 118).

THE AUTOMOBILE IN RUSSIA AND THE UNITED STATES

	Russia	United States
Cars in use	900,000	71 million
Cars relative to population	1 per 260 persons	1 per 3 persons
Auto production	200,000	9.3 million
Bus and truck production	420,000	1.8 million
Car models available	4	More than 360
Paved highways	71,000 miles in area of 8.7 million square miles	2.3 million miles in area of 3.6 million square miles
Gasoline stations	1,250	212,000
Price of auto	$6,000 for medium-sized sedan—about 5 years' pay for average worker	$2,500 for comparable car—about 5 months' pay for average factory worker

Source: Adapted from *U.S. News and World Report,* June 6, 1966

Reflecting rising living standards and the growing pressure of consumer demand, the new leadership under Brezhnev and Kosygin has since the mid-1960's experimented with a measure of broadened consumer choice. Until that time, central planners determined what each plant had to produce, how much labor had to be employed, and at what prices the goods were to be sold. Gradually, after the worst shortages of consumer goods abated, the Soviet government found that an increasing number of items (cameras, bicycles, lamp shades, sewing machines) remained unsold on store shelves and in warehouses, because they were overpriced, defective, poorly designed, or had been produced in unrealistically large quantities. The reforms began on a small scale before Khrushchev's ouster but were vigorously pushed by Kosygin from 1965 on. Consumer goods industries were the first affected by the "Kosygin reforms." This was done on the basis of the traditional low concern for consumer goods, so that if the reforms did not work out, Soviet production of heavy machinery and military hardware would not be disrupted. After the consumer industries, the Kosygin reforms were gradually applied to light and heavy industries, and by late 1969 70 percent of all Soviet industry was covered.

As the reforms have been applied to consumer industries, performance in sales rather than in gross output has become the main criterion of enterprise efficiency and profitability. Management now contracts directly with suppliers for materials and sells directly to wholesale and retail outlets. The size and composition of the labor force are now determined primarily by management rather than by central planners. However, central planners still determine the volume of sales to be met as well as the rate of profit in terms of invested capital. If management can fulfill or exceed the planned sales volume, plant managers may receive bonuses of up to 50 percent of basic salary, and production workers, too, receive bonuses. Profits of individual enterprises will thus be substantially determined by the orders they receive from stores, and their orders will in turn be largely determined by the preferences of consumers.

While these reforms will give the consumer more choice than in the past, they should not be exaggerated as a recognition of the free market and of consumer sovereignty or as a return to capitalism. In the capitalist market economy, the consumer determines not only

Drawing by Herbert Goldberg, © 1967 by Saturday Review, Inc.

**"I SUPPOSE WE'LL INHERIT THE CAPITALIST HEADACHES
—MORTGAGES, CRABGRASS, BUYING ON CREDIT. . . ."**

which make of car he will buy but also *how many* cars will be produced. In the Soviet Union, the government will continue to determine how much of capital and labor resources will be allocated to automobile production. Similarly, the volume of construction in the capitalist market economy is determined by relative consumer preferences in relation to residential buildings, supermarkets and shopping centers (both virtually nonexistent in the Soviet Union), restaurants, and hotels and motels. In the Soviet Union, the government will continue to determine how much of available materials and manpower will be allocated to construction of heavy industry or military installations rather than of restaurants and supermarkets.

The main effect of the Kosygin reforms—and by no means an unimportant one—is thus likely to be the reduction of waste through stronger incentives for increased efficiency and profitability rather than the abandonment of the key principle of communist economics. For the government will continue to decide how, for what purposes, and in what relative proportions available capital resources and manpower are to be allocated.

Of all the segments of the Soviet economy, services and housing have been the most neglected. Complaints in the Soviet press reveal that it takes three to four months to have shoes repaired, even longer to have a radio or television set repaired, and that it is next to impossible to get any laundering or drycleaning done. Perpetual shortages of restaurant and hotel facilities not only limit domestic Soviet tourism but also deprive the government of the eagerly sought hard currencies of foreign tourists. Shops and stores of all types are in conspicuously short supply. "Why are there queues in our food stores?" *Pravda* asked (January 23, 1966)—as if it didn't know. The Soviet shopper has to stand in line three times. In the first line, he finds out whether the item is in stock and what it costs. In the second line, he pays the cashier and gets a receipt. In the third line he exchanges the receipt for the merchandise. A few supermarkets and self-service stores have been opened in the late 1960's, and more are planned for the future, but there is no indication that the traditional methods of retailing will disappear very soon.

The Soviet record in housing is even more unimpressive. In the precommunist Russia of 1914, available per capita living space for the urban population was seven square meters (one square meter is equal to 10.76 square feet). In 1940, after a decade of communist industrialization and planning, per capita living space had dropped sharply to 4.34 square meters. Until 1957, the figure still stood under five square meters. From 1958 on, the Soviet government made a determined effort to improve housing conditions, and by the end of 1967 urban per capita living space finally reached seven square meters again—the level of 1914.

The Soviet government defines nine square meters per person as the minimum "health norm," but at the rate of recent building this minimum standard is unlikely to be reached for many years to come. Current living space per person in the Soviet Union is less than half the space available per person in Austria and West Germany, and less than one-fourth the per capita space in the United States.

Since housing is perpetually scarce and most available housing is state-owned, the government allocates available space on the basis of social criteria as it perceives them. Thus, the primary consideration is not need but the contribution a person makes to society, as expressed in this manner by a Soviet writer: "We consider it just to provide housing in the first instance to those who do excellent work" (*Problems of Communism*, May–June 1969, p. 7). Outstanding scientists, scholars, artists, high-ranking party and government officials, and military personnel with the rank of colonel and above receive extra space in recognition of their status and work. Need is recognized only in the case of persons with certain types of illnesses who require some additional living space.

The main benefit for the Soviet citizen in state-owned housing is the low rent: in 1968, the average office or factory worker earned about $125 a month, and out of this income only about five percent went into paying the rent.

Since the government has been unable to supply sufficient housing, the occupancy of one apartment by several families—each family living in one room and sharing the kitchen and toilet or bathroom facilities—has been one of the most vexing problems. However, by the late 1960's, only about one-third to one-half of urban families shared kitchens and bathrooms, and the long-term goal is to have each family enjoy the privilege of having its own kitchen and bathroom.

Soviet citizens with more money, initiative, and connections can find two ways of escaping state-owned housing: through private housing or cooperative housing. If a citizen wishes to build his own house, he must first obtain permission from the government to use a plot of land, since all land belongs to the state. Next, he must obtain construction materials, either legally or through the black market. The maximum size of the house is limited by law to 60 square meters, or the equivalent of five small to medium-sized rooms. Finally, the law generally forbids private building in major urban areas so that most private home ownership is in smaller towns or rural areas. Until recently, close to one-third of urban housing has been privately owned, but the Soviet government is persistently trying to reduce the proportion of privately owned housing, particularly in the urban sector.

The second method of escaping state housing is cooperative housing. In larger cities, a minimum of 60 members is required, made up generally of fellow workers in a plant or families in a neighborhood who want better housing. In general, cooperative housing—accounting for 10 to 15 percent of new urban housing in recent years—is used mainly by the more affluent groups in Soviet society, since membership requires a large down payment for construction costs and monthly payments that are several times higher than rents charged for smaller and less desirable accommodations in state-owned housing.

As in the United States and other Western nations, living in a cooperative apartment house in the Soviet Union is a status symbol of upwardly mobile executives, engineers, and members of the better-paid professions. Yet the Soviet government favors cooperative housing over private housing, since cooperatives fit the communist ideology of collectivism better than private home ownership, considered an unfortunate remnant of bourgeois ideology that is tolerated only for practical reasons and for the time being. Also, the higher-ups in the party and government who determine what the correct ideology is happen to be among the more affluent elements in society who prefer the comforts of the better-designed cooperative housing to the austerities of the smaller and mass produced accommodations in state-owned housing.

The persistent housing shortage in the Soviet Union is recognized by Soviet law. No one is allowed to live in Soviet cities without registering with the police, and the police often reject a request for residence in large cities because housing is not available. Violating the law on this point is no trifle. In 1968, a young Soviet writer was sentenced to one year of labor camp on the charge of having lived in Moscow without permission of the police (*New York Times,* August 28, 1969).

The Soviet emphasis on production rather than welfare or consumption is also illustrated by the attitudes toward the unemployed, the aged, and women in the total setting of the economy. The Soviet policy on unemployment maintains that a person who loses a job can always find work if he is willing to take any job at any wage; therefore, there is no unemployment relief. The Soviets do not worry about the loss of pride and emotional disequilibrium a person might suffer if he has to take a lower-paying job of less prestige in an entirely different part of the country. Similarly, the pension for the aged is so low that many old people keep on working as long as they are able. This is in sharp contrast to the outlook in the United States and other capitalist countries that penalize the recipients of old-age pensions if their earnings exceed relatively moderate amounts.

The puritanical Soviet attitude toward work has both practical and ideological roots. From a practical viewpoint, an expanding and modernizing economy has an insatiable need for productive workers. A planned economy like the Soviet is always geared to the maximum utilization of all available resources, including manpower (and womanpower). Ideologically, the Soviet attitude is also strongly influenced by Marx's treatment of the problem of work. Marx looked upon work as man's most creative and noblest form of personal self-fulfillment. His quarrel with English classical economic theory and capitalist practice was not that they, too, encouraged a positive attitude toward work, but that under capitalism work becomes a mechanism of exploitation, degrading the worker to a soulless robot, enslaved to the "fetishism of commodities."

In Marx's thought, the classless society of the future would by no means abolish the duty to work. The first stage of communism, Marx said, would be guided by the principle of "from each according to his ability, to each according to his work." In the second, and higher, phase of communism, the principle of "from each according to his ability, to each according to his needs" would prevail. Thus, even in the higher phase of communism, Marx held, work is still "the primary necessity of life." Soviet doctrine and policy fully concur with the positive Marxian attitude toward work and have no use for the Western idea of letting able-bodied adults live off public welfare or even unemployment relief. The emphasis must be, as a Soviet writer sees it, on "undeviating adherence to the principle of 'he who does not work, neither shall he eat,' and against loafers and the remnants of parasitic elements who wish to live at the expense of society, giving it nothing and avoiding participation in socially useful labor" (G. M. Shtraks, *Soviet Review*, Fall 1963, p. 7). The Soviet attitude toward work is also reflected in the criminal code. Under Soviet law, a person who does not work or refuses to work commits the crime of "parasitism" or "hooliganism" and can be sentenced to several years of forced labor to acquire a more positive attitude toward work. Thus, in 1964 a young poet, Iosif Brosky, was sentenced to five years of forced labor in the far north for changing jobs too often and failing to produce "material wealth." His claim that he considered writing poetry work was not recognized, since he was suspected of oppositionist leanings.

Soviet use of womanpower has been one of the greatest successes in the economic development of the Soviet Union. Before Stalin embarked on his five-year plans for the industrialization of the country, women accounted for 24 percent of the labor force. Currently, fully one-half of the labor force is female, as compared, for example, with 40 percent in the United States. Soviet women are encouraged to enter all types of employment and to receive training in the professions and sciences, including medicine and such "hard" sciences as engineering and physics. Although top positions are generally held by men, talented women nevertheless have career opportunities which are matched in only a few other countries. Side by side with this equality of opportunity in higher-education and higher-income careers, the Soviet woman has also had to accept equality in more menial types of work. For example, women make up 28 percent of the labor force in construction, as compared with a negligible percentage in such work in Western countries. The visitor to the Soviet Union is struck by the large number of women that can be seen digging ditches, repairing roads and railroad tracks, and doing other types of heavy manual work that in most other countries is reserved for men. In many cases, one can see entire gangs of road workers made up of women.

The Soviet worker is subject to decisive managerial authority such as has not been known in most capitalist countries for more than two generations. The communist promise to liberate the worker from capitalist oppression has been partially fulfilled: the capitalist has been eliminated, but this has not led to the freedom of the worker, since the place of the capitalist has been taken by the state.

The main function of Soviet labor unions—as of labor unions in other communist countries—is to promote maximum production as determined by state planners. In pursuing the goal of maximum production, the Soviet labor union enforces labor discipline within the plant and organizes competitions to increase output. Basic conditions of work—wages and hours—are set by the government and cannot be significantly changed by union pressure, since party members are expected to ensure that labor unions adhere to government policies. In addition to its role as an agent of government policy, the labor union has administrative and social welfare functions: unions help to enforce safety laws, administer the social insurance system, provide housing for workers, and supervise educational, cultural, and propaganda activities. The character of the Soviet labor unions as "company unions" is underlined by the fact that they include managerial personnel, since the managers directly represent the employer, the government.

During the first 15 years of the Soviet regime, an attempt was made to limit inequalities of income to a moderate range of differential; from the middle of the 1930's on, however, with the inauguration of the era of purges, the last vestiges of equalitarianism were wiped out and an entirely new policy was brought into being. Wages based on performance rather than on fixed hourly rates became the policy, a policy that labor unions in free nations had opposed for two generations as a system of exploitation.

The old-fashioned capitalist appeal for higher production compensated by higher incomes was covered up with slogans like "socialist competition," and workers were driven on to greater production efforts by the policy of Stakhanovism, inspired by the alleged feats of a coal miner named Stakhanov. Whereas the original concern in communist theory had been with problems of just distribution, Soviet policy has in practice concentrated on maximum production. The *incentive of higher income* rather than service to the community has become the main appeal of Soviet social and economic policy, and equalitarianism has been derided as "petty-bourgeois prejudice," "hostile to socialism," and conducive to "wrong attitudes" toward work.

In line with Soviet anti-equalitarian policy, personal income taxes are among the lowest in the world. The Soviet government derives the bulk of its revenue from *sales taxes* and other indirect levies that proportionately hit the lowest income groups hardest. Only a small proportion of government revenue derives from income taxes. In the United States, the picture is the exact reverse: revenues are derived mainly from progressive income taxes, under which system the tax rate goes up as the income rises. In concentrating on sales and other indirect taxes, the Soviet tax system hits *consumption*, whereas income taxes in Western nations hit the *productive effort*.

The group with the highest income level is the same in the Soviet Union as in the United States: business managers and executives. Yet, whereas the income tax in the United States goes up to 70 percent (and is even higher in some other Western nations such as Britain and Sweden), the top tax rate for Soviet executives is only 13 percent. The top inheritance tax rate in the United States is 77 percent; in the Soviet Union, inheritance taxes were abolished in 1942—another bonus to the affluent elements in Soviet society.

According to official claims, the problem of social classes has been solved in Soviet society, because from the Marxist viewpoint there can be no class inequality except on the basis of the private ownership of the means of production.

Yet Soviet reality tells a different story. There are at least *three distinguishable classes*. In the first group—numbering a few hundred thousand families, perhaps as many as a million—are the top government officials, party leaders, military officers, industrial executives, scientists, artists, and writers. The second group is made up of the intermediary ranks of civilian and military officials, collective farm managers, and some of the more affluent skilled workers and technicians in industry; this group forms the middle class of Soviet society and numbers four to five million families. The third class is made up of the bulk of the population, the mass of workers and peasants, numbering more than fifty million families.

Upward social mobility in the Soviet Union largely depends, as in noncommunist countries, on access to higher education. Such access is unequally distributed in the Soviet Union, and the inequality reflects the reality of the Soviet class structure. Soviet researchers have found that only ten out of every hundred secondary-school graduates from families of collective farmers and state farm workers continue their education, whereas 82 out of every hundred second-ary-school graduates from families of urban nonmanual workers receive a higher education.

What is remarkable about social stratification in communist countries is that the *income spread between the different classes has remained very wide,* while it has been narrowed continuously in the democratic nations of the West through taxation and other measures. Moreover, within the bulk of the population, the working class, the *difference between wages of skilled and unskilled workers* has been kept at a high level in the Soviet Union, whereas in democratic nations this differential has been systematically reduced, largely by the pressure of free labor unions. The differential between skilled and unskilled worker is about three times greater in the Soviet Union than in the United States.

As Aristotle said over two thousand years ago, the main question is not *who* owns property, but *how* property is used.

In our own day, the experience of communist economic change teaches again that the principal issue is not whether the government owns the means of production, but *who owns the government.*

SOURCES OF STRENGTH
IN COMMUNISM

Among communism's sources of strength, the most important is probably the enormous *widening of the base from which the elite is recruited.* Before World War I, the Russian elite—in government, the army, business, science, and the arts—was drawn from a small social group of upper-class and upper-middle-class background. There was a tremendous gap between the small governing class of Russia, in intimate contact with western Europe, and the vast inchoate masses of peasants. The communist revolution, particularly in its first impetus, swept away distinctions of class, sex, or nationality and opened up a new world of opportunity for people who had hitherto been excluded from opportunity of any sort. Industrialization, perhaps the most dynamic key in creating new opportunities in science and government as well as in industry, formed a *new managerial class,* recruited on a very wide basis, for which there was no precedent.

A quick glance at the social background of the top leaders of the

Soviet Union today gives us a fair idea of the Soviet leadership as a whole:

Leader	Occupation of father
Aristov	fisherman
Brezhnev	steel worker
Gromyko	artisan
Kosygin	lathe worker
Mazurov	peasant
Podgorny	foundry worker
Polyansky	peasant
Shelepin	railroad worker
Shelest	peasant
Shvernik	poor worker
Suslov	peasant

These top leaders are typical representatives of the men who run Russia's industry, government, and armed forces. Those Westerners who have dealt with them agree that they are able and confident, full of drive and energy. In the United States, these men would be corporation executives, political and military leaders, and top government officials—the very same jobs they hold in the Soviet Union. Because their ideas and aims seem so different from Western ideas and objectives, many persons have been blinded to their high technical and executive ability.

The competition for leadership positions in the Soviet Union is stronger than in the democratic world, the premium for success greater, and the penalty for failure harsher. The successful manager who overfulfills his production quota is rapidly promoted and his rewards are—in relation to the rest of the population—more ample than in capitalist countries. The incentive system is more fully developed than in the United States and other Western nations, and generous bonuses are paid to successful executives.

The penalty for failure is also greater than in capitalist countries. Under Stalin, managerial failure could result in slave labor or even execution; in more recent years, the manager who fails in his production job is more likely to be fired and downgraded to a less responsible job. This harsh emphasis on performance may seem ruthless, but it works—if results are the only things that count.

The less a position in the elite is directly tied up with politics, the more recognition can be given to talent and merit. As long as a leading surgeon, chemist, mathematician, engineer, or industrial executive keeps his mouth shut (politically speaking), he will generally be left alone. The more a position in the ruling group is tinged with politics, the more criteria besides merit and talent become relevant and frequently decisive.

Rapid industrialization is the second main source of communist strength, in Russia as well as in other communized states. Before World War I, Russia was an overwhelmingly agricultural country; Russian industrial power was very low, ranking behind the United States, Britain, Germany, France, Japan, and Austria-Hungary. After World War II, Russia moved up to second place, preceded only by the United States. Industrialization in all communist states is concentrated on heavy industry, the base of military power.

In absolute figures, industry in Russia and the communist states still lags considerably behind the United States and other noncommunist nations. But what is impressive is the rapid rate of industrial growth in the communist states, which considerably exceeds that of many Western nations. Even if it be argued that the communist states have now the initial advantage of undeveloped countries undergoing rapid industrialization, and that their present rate of expansion cannot be indefinitely maintained, the Western nations will have to step up their own productivity and rate of industrial growth if the present balance of industrial power, still heavily in favor of the noncommunist states, is not to be lost.

Fast economic growth is not something which automatically comes out of either communism or capitalism but is the result of hard work and know-how. Within the communist group of nations, some have shown faster economic progress than others, and the same is true of the capitalist world. Specifically, the Soviet Union has no superior record of economic growth as compared with *all* capitalist nations. While it is true that the Soviet Union has, in the period of 1950–1967, grown faster economically than the United States, other capitalist nations have done better than the Soviet Union. As the table following shows, the growth record of the Soviet Union during 1950–1955 was more impressive than during 1956–1967, and the superior performance of Japan as compared with Russia in 1950–1967 is particularly striking. However, the eyes of the world are focused on

AVERAGE ANNUAL RATES OF ECONOMIC GROWTH
FOR SEVEN MAJOR ECONOMIES

Country	1950–1955	1956–1961	1962–1967
Japan	7.1	10.9	9.5
West Germany	9.0	6.2	3.2
Soviet Union	7.0	6.4	5.4
Italy	6.0	6.2	5.0
France	4.5	4.9	4.8
United States	4.3	2.1	5.1
Great Britain	2.6	2.9	3.1

Source: Joint Economic Committee, Congress of the United States, *Dimensions of Soviet Economic Power* (1963), and *Soviet Economic Performance: 1966–1967* (1968)

the comparative economic growth of the Soviet Union and the United States rather than of the Soviet Union and Japan. During 1950–1961, the Soviet rate of growth was more than double that of the United States; during 1962–1967, the Soviet growth rate was only slightly above that of the United States.

In gearing economic policy to the requirements of national power, the Soviet Union has made particularly strenuous efforts to close the gap with the United States in such key commodities as iron, steel, coal, and petroleum, but in electric power and natural gas the gap between Soviet and American production has widened in the period of 1950–1968.

The price for rapid Soviet economic growth has been steep. Millions of people were used for years in slave labor camps to provide cheap labor. The number of slave laborers in the two decades from the middle thirties to the middle fifties ranged from a conservatively low estimate of five million to the more likely figure of about ten million. Since 1957 slave labor camps have been closed, but, never having admitted their existence, the Soviet government does not divulge how many persons are still to be found in "correctional labor" camps.

Viewed in the long-term historical perspective, the Soviet economic achievement leads to several conclusions. First, there is no question that the Soviet Union is now the world's second industrial and military power. Second, Soviet levels of consumption still trail significantly those of many Western nations, and there is no likelihood of closing the gap in the near or intermediate future. Finally, the Soviet economic achievement, impressive as it is by any standard, does not validate the Soviet claim to having discovered or developed a method of rapid economic growth that cannot be achieved under any other social, economic, and political system. Japan's growth record between the late 1890's and late 1930's and again since 1950 is the outstanding refutation of the Soviet claim, but not the only one. During these periods, levels of personal consumption rose faster in Japan than in Russia between 1913 and the 1960's, and during the half-century of early American industrialization, from the 1870's to the 1920's, American consumption levels also rose at a faster rate than in Russia during its half-century of industrialization. The system of government within which an economy operates is an important factor, but it is only one factor among many. The potential of economic development in each country is related to many factors unique to it; a country that imitates Soviet, Japanese, or American political or economic institutions will not necessarily match Soviet, Japanese, or American economic achievements.

The third major area of Soviet strength is in *education and science*. The Soviet launching of the first satellite on October 4, 1957, came as a bombshell to those who still had the illusion that Russia was largely a country of illiterate peasants. This Soviet first was followed by many others: the Soviets sent the first man, the first woman, and the first team of astronauts into space; they sent the first satellite past the moon and around the moon, and theirs was the first to land on the moon; and they accomplished the first "space-walk" by an astronaut and the first link-up in space between two manned spacecraft. The successful landing of astronauts Armstrong and Aldrin on the moon in July 1969 boosted American morale at home and American prestige abroad, but this success does not minimize the importance and quality of the overall Soviet space effort.

The Soviet space effort is not the result of a crash program, but of sustained work and planning over many years. The increase in the years 1926–1952 of Soviet professional manpower was as follows: engineers, ten times; teachers, five times; and physicians, four times. Since 1958 the proportion of the age group 15–19 enrolled in second-

PRODUCTION OF SELECTED KEY COMMODITIES, 1950, 1965

	Year	Soviet Union	United States
Pig iron	1950	19	60
(million metric	1968	79	81
tons)			
Steel	1950	27	88
(million metric	1968	107	119
tons)			
Coal	1950	261	502
(million metric	1968	594	505
tons)			
Petroleum, crude	1950	38	266
(million metric	1968	309	463
tons)			
Natural gas	1950	6	193
(billion cubic	1968	171	547
meters)			
Electric power	1950	91	389
(billion kilowatt	1968	638	1,433
hours)			
Cement	1950	10	37
(million metric	1968	87	68
tons)			

Source: Bureau of the Census, and Soviet Central Statistical Administration

ary schools and of the age group 20–24 enrolled in institutions of higher learning has been higher in the Soviet Union than in the major Western countries, with the exception of the United States, which still leads in the absolute and proportionate sizes of secondary schools and college students. By the late 1960's, the median years of school completed by the Soviet population 16 or more years old was about 7 years, as compared with 12 years in the United States.

The intense demand for a higher education or advanced professional training in the Soviet Union is also expressed in the constantly rising proportion of fully employed students who receive their training through evening or correspondence courses. In the 1940's and 1950's regular day students outnumbered evening and correspondence students by a considerable, but steadily declining, margin. Since 1960, the number of regular full-time students has been consistently well below one-half the total number of students admitted to institutions of higher learning and professional training, whereas in the United States, as in other Western nations, the number of regular full-time students generally ranges around 90 percent of all students taking college and university courses.

Looking at Soviet and American higher education in the four decades of 1926–1965, we find the following results: the Soviet Union has trained 2.5 times more engineers than the United States and is continuing to train engineers at an annual rate that is about three times higher than in the United States. The total pool of engineers and physicists is now greater in the Soviet Union than in the United States, and the gap is growing year by year. By contrast, the United States has trained three times more graduates in the humanities and social sciences than the Soviet Union, and the American superiority in these areas largely accounts for the continuing overall lead of the total number of American college students over the total enrollments in Soviet institutions of higher learning and training.

In the field of medicine, the Soviet Union has trained 2.5 more physicians than the United States, and in the last several years the annual number of Soviet medical graduates has been three times higher than in the United States, although the Soviet population is only 15 percent higher than that of the United States. Currently, there are 22 physicians per 10,000 population in the Soviet Union but only 15 per 10,000 population in the United States. The shortage of medical training facilities in the United States is the most serious factor. At present about one in every six doctors first licensed to practice has received his medical training abroad, and of these graduates of foreign medical schools close to one-third are Americans. In American hospitals, about one out of four interns and resident physicians is a graduate of a foreign medical school. Many of the foreign physicians who immigrate to the United States come from developing countries in Asia and Latin America that suffer from an acute shortage of health personnel. The inferiority of health services in the United States can also be seen in the supply of hospital beds: in the Soviet Union, there are 100 hospital beds per 10,000 people as compared with only 85 beds in the United States. Most important of all, medical and health services in the Soviet Union are available to every Soviet citizen with little or no charge, whereas such services are paid for by the government in the United States only for persons over 65 years old under federal medicare and for low-income families regardless of age under various state medicaid programs.

The Soviet commitment to education as a major goal of national policy is expressed in many ways. With a national income that is less than half of that of the United States, the Soviets spend a greater proportion of their national income on education as is done in the United States. The Soviet professor receives five to eight times the wage of the average factory worker, whereas the American professor receives only one and one-half to two times the American worker's pay. Tuition, textbooks, and medical care are free of charge in Soviet universities and institutions of higher learning, and dormitory quarters—extremely crowded as they may be—cost only a few rubles per month (a ruble equals $1.11). In addition, 80 percent of Soviet students receive monthly stipends ranging from 30 to 60 rubles; the latter figure equals the minimum monthly wage of an urban worker. Students in fields such as mining, electronics, and chemical engineering receive the highest stipends, and an additional bonus of 25 percent is given to those students who maintain a consistently excellent record.

The Soviet system of higher education tries to utilize the maximum of available brainpower; the main method of recruiting talent is through written and oral examinations. By contrast, in the United States one-third of students graduating in the top quarter of their high school classes do not go to college—for economic reasons, in most cases.

Applying objective examination standards for admission to Soviet colleges and universities has created social problems of class. Workers' and peasants' sons and daughters are underrepresented in institutions of higher learning. In a study of Soviet education, the education editor of the *New York Times* found that "elite universities, such as Moscow and Leningrad, have a more select upper-middle-class urban enrollment than America's Ivy League" (*New York Times,* October 5, 1967). In recent years, therefore, Soviet educational authorities have set up special remedial and preparatory programs for children of peasants and factory workers—similar to such programs for blacks and Puerto Ricans in the United States—to improve their chances for obtaining a higher education.

Finally, the most direct source of communist strength lies in *military power*. Although the Soviet citizen consumes less than one-third of the American standard of consumption, and although the whole Soviet national product is less than one-half of the Americans, the Soviet government spends about the same amount on military preparedness as does the United States. The per capita income in China is less than one-fortieth that of the United States, but its armed

COMMUNIST EXPANSION SINCE 1939

	Year	Area (sq. mi.)	Population
U.S.S.R. annexed			
1. Part of Romania	1940	19,400	3,700,000
2. Estonia	1940	18,300	1,200,000
3. Latvia	1940	25,400	2,100,000
4. Lithuania	1940	23,000	3,000,000
5. Part of East Prussia	1945	5,400	1,200,000
6. Eastern Czechoslovakia	1945	4,900	730,000
7. Eastern Poland	1945	69,900	11,800,000
8. Part of Finland	1940	17,600	450,000
9. Tannu Tuva	1944	64,000	65,000
10. Japanese possessions	1945	17,800	433,000
Communist regimes established			
11. Albania	1946	10,700	1,300,000
12. Bulgaria	1946	42,800	7,300,000
13. Czechoslovakia	1948	49,300	14,000,000
14. East Germany	1949	41,500	18,500,000
(including Soviet sector of Berlin)			
15. Hungary	1947	36,000	10,000,000
16. Poland	1947	121,100	26,500,000
17. Romania	1948	91,600	17,000,000
18. Communist China	1949	3,281,000	582,000,000
(not including Tibet)			
19. Outer Mongolia	1945	626,000	1,000,000
20. North Korea	1948	48,500	9,000,000
21. North Vietnam	1951	72,000	12,000,000
22. Tibet (annexed by Communist China)	1951	469,000	1,200,000
23. Cuba	1958	44,218	6,000,000

forces are equal in size to those of the United States, and it has consistently devoted large resources to the development of nuclear weapons, even during the near-famine period of the early 1960's.

The vast expenditures on building up military strength have paid off in communist imperialist expansion. Since the outbreak of World War II in September 1939, the Soviet Union has acquired an area larger than all the New England and Middle Atlantic States, with a population of over 25 million. In addition to these outright annexations, the Soviet Union established, by armed force, communist governments in eastern Europe, with a combined population of over 100 million. Communist China conquered and annexed Tibet.

Never before in history has imperialistic expansion acquired so much in so short a time. By contrast, the Western powers have given freedom and independence to over 800 million people in former colonies since World War II.

SOURCES OF WEAKNESS
IN COMMUNISM

The first source of weakness is the stress on *conformity*. The most distinguishing quality of a leader is his courage to be different, to have new ideas, to be in a minority, even in solitude. Yet as time goes on, the leader in communist regimes is increasingly being replaced by the bureaucrat, the yes-man. The era of the purges in Russia in the middle 1930's was the conflict between the leaders who had made the revolution and the bureaucrats who administered it. Conformist as prerevolutionary Russia was, it allowed much more diversity than has been tolerated under the communist regime. In precommunist Russia, opposition parties of all types, including radical and socialist parties, functioned openly, and the press reflected all political viewpoints. *Pravda,* which became the official organ of the Communist party after the revolution, started publication in 1912; it suffered occasional harassments, but it was published.

Lenin, Trotsky, Stalin, and Khrushchev were all products of precommunist Russia. Malenkov, Stalin's immediate successor, was the first leader in Russia who was a product of communist rule. He proved not to possess the qualities of a leader; in 1955, he was removed as prime minister, and in 1957 he was purged by Khrushchev and exiled to central Asia. Both Brezhnev and Kosygin are products of communist rule. Brezhnev was trained in land surveying and metallurgical engineering, but his main profession became, early in his career, professional party work. Kosygin was trained as a textile engineer and spent most of his career in economic and administrative positions, avoiding involvement in ideological or political controversies and conflicts within the Communist party.

Both men lack the despotic ruthlessness of Stalin and the colorful flamboyance of Khrushchev. Brezhnev's and Kosygin's rise to power was marked by efficient bureaucratic performance rather than by impressive personal leadership. Instead of Stalin's limitless autocracy and Khrushchev's personal rule with its unpredictable periodic swings from more authoritarian to more lenient attitudes, the Soviet Union may be entering—if Brezhnev and Kosygin reflect a new long-term trend—an era of totalitarian organization men, of "totalitarians in grey flannel suits."

In some respects, this type of totalitarianism may be more liberal than under Khrushchev (not to speak of Stalin), as in the approach to the farm problem or in giving greater managerial authority to industrial executives. But in the more fundamental areas of political and intellectual unorthodoxy, the Brezhnev-Kosygin regime has persistently pursued a course of re-Stalinization. In 1956, Khrushchev delivered his famous secret speech on the crimes of Stalin at the Twentieth Communist Party Congress in Moscow, and during his rule he frequently attacked the "era of the cult of personality"—the official Soviet term for "Stalinism." By contrast, Brezhnev and Kosygin have sought to refurbish Stalin's reputation, and both have made it plain that they have no use for anti-Stalinist criticisms. As a result, a noted British specialist on Soviet affairs has observed from first-hand experience in Russia, "Stalinist terror may no longer be mentioned in books or articles" (Alec Nove, *Manchester Guardian Weekly,* July 10, 1969).

Khrushchev's ambivalence on repressing or allowing unorthodoxy was clearly shown in connection with the two greatest authors of the Soviet era, Boris Pasternak and Alexander Solzhenitsyn. When, in 1958, Pasternak received the Nobel prize in literature for his novel *Doctor Zhivago* (which was not allowed to be published in Russia), he was subjected to an organized campaign of vehement attacks and threats. Officially condemned as a traitor by the communist leaders, Pasternak was spared further humiliation by his lonely death in 1960. Even in his grave he is not left in peace. When playwright Arthur Miller visited Russia in 1969 and wanted to visit Pasternak's grave, he found that "a visit to this grave was forbidden or at least frowned upon from on high" (*Harper's Magazine*, September 1969, p. 53).

In the early 1960's, the Khrushchev regime relaxed repressive controls of literature, and the high point of this short era of "thaw" was marked by the publication of Solzhenitsyn's *One Day in the Life of Ivan Denisovich*. Although this story of life in a Soviet slave labor camp is cast in the form of a novel, the author wrote from personal experience, having spent the years 1945–1953 in such a camp. The novel was published in a Soviet literary magazine, *Novy Mir*, known for its more liberal leanings, but to this day *One Day* has not been published in book form in the Soviet Union. Unwilling to produce literature that is "cosmetics," as he put it, Solzhenitsyn has had the courage to plead in strong language for more intellectual freedom. As a result, his published works have been banned in the Soviet Union, and even the issues of *Novy Mir* that carried *One Day* have disappeared from the shelves of public libraries. Apart from an occasional defamatory reference to him in *Pravda*, his name must not be mentioned in print. His later novels, *The Cancer Ward* and *The First Circle*, were published in Western countries in 1968, but in Russia only a few people have read the originals in secretly circulating typed copies. Solzhenitsyn has not only been deprived of an income as a writer, but his personal safety has become so doubtful that he has been "compelled to conceal his movements and hide himself like a criminal" (*New York Times Book Review*, December 16, 1968).

Since 1966, the systematic repression of unorthodox writers and intellectuals has shown that the Brezhnev-Kosygin regime is committed to the revival of Stalinism, with the important difference that only harsh sentences of forced labor—but not executions—are inflicted on the victims. Some dissidents are put into insane asylums, but this policy has nothing to do with Marxism or Leninism; it goes back to a practice of tsarist government.

In 1966, two Russian writers, Andrei Sinyavsky and Yuli Daniel, were sentenced to seven years and five years of "strict regime labor camp" for having published "anti-Soviet" works in foreign countries under the pen names Abram Tertz and Nikolai Arzhak. Although the trial was closed to foreign reporters, its proceedings became known abroad. The conduct of the trial—and the official attacks on the two writers before the trial—as well as the stiff sentences shocked even communist leaders in some Western countries who publicly warned the Soviet rulers that the trial had done the Soviet Union more harm than the writings of Sinyavsky and Daniel.

The year 1966 also witnessed mass arrests in the Ukraine. More than two hundred Ukranian university professors, students, writers, scientists, and journalists were secretly tried for having distributed appeals in defense of intellectual freedom as well as Ukrainian cultural autonomy. A mass purge was also staged in Leningrad—Russia's "window to the West" and traditionally a hotbed of independent rebelliousness—in 1967. Large numbers—estimated between 150 and 300—of university professors, students, poets, and literary critics were arrested and secretly tried, and stiff sentences of hard labor, running up to 15 years, were handed down.

Of the many trials in 1968, two in particular attracted international attention. Early in 1968, four young dissidents—writers and their friends—were tried in Moscow for having put out underground literary magazines. The leader of the group, Alexander Ginzburg, was charged with having committed the additional crime of compiling a record of the Sinyavsky-Daniel trial and sending it abroad. The sentences for the three main accused ranged from two to seven years of "labor camp." The mildest sentence—one year—was given to a 21-year-old girl student who had typed manuscripts for the co-defendants.

In 1968, the trial of Pavel Litvinov and Mrs. Larissa Daniel attracted even more international attention than the Ginzburg trial had done. Pavel Litvinov, a 30-year-old physicist and grandson of Maxim Litvinov, Soviet foreign minister under Stalin for many years, had become actively involved in liberal circles. Because of his eminent social background, he was at first treated leniently, the punishment consisting solely in his being fired from his prestigious job. But on August 25, 1968, he and several of his friends, including Larissa Daniel, the wife of Yuli Daniel, unfurled a banner in the center of

Moscow protesting the Soviet invasion and occupation of Czechoslovakia. Litvinov was sentenced to five years of exile in a labor camp, Mrs. Daniel to four years, and several other sentences of three years were given to their co-defendants. Mrs. Daniel, a graduate in philosophy and in poor health, was sent to Siberia where she was assigned the job of hauling heavy pieces of lumber from the outdoors into a wood-processing factory.

The year 1969 saw numerous convictions of dissident writers and intellectuals, mostly under 30 years of age; these were supported by a more systematic cleansing of the editorial staffs of literary magazines suspected of liberal leanings. One of the prominent figures thus removed was Yevgeny Yevtushenko, one of the best known younger poets in the Soviet Union.

The literary sensation of the Soviet literary scene in 1969 was the defection of Anatoly V. Kuznetsov to Britain. Kuznetsov was at the peak of his literary fame at the time of his defection, and at his age (he was born in 1929) he had a great literary career ahead of him. Yet he chose to leave his mother, wife, and son in the Soviet Union, so that he could live in freedom and security in Britain. He received permission to go to Britain for two weeks only after he had informed on some of his fellow writers to the secret police and assured them that he would continue informing on writers at home and abroad. Once in Britain, he immediately asked for asylum, which was granted. Kuznetsov stated that the relations of Russian writers to the secret police fall into three categories: (1) writers who enthusiastically collaborate with the secret police "have every chance of prospering"; (2) writers who acknowledge their duty to work for the secret police but refuse to do so suffer numerous disadvantages, including loss of the chance to travel abroad; (3) writers who refuse all advances of the secret police and come into conflict with them—"In that case your works are not published and you may even find yourself in a concentration camp" (*New York Times,* August 10, 1969).

The Soviet concept of the writer as belonging to his government was also confirmed by Arthur Miller, one of the most popular American writers in the Soviet Union. After a journey to the Soviet Union, in which he met with leading "cultural officials" and top Soviet novelists and poets, Miller—a man of strong sympathies for the left—

concluded that "in the Soviet Union a writer is far more than an individual facing a piece of blank paper alone in a room; he is state property and accountable for his attitudes." Miller also noted that, despite periodic waves of witch-hunting in some Western countries (such as the United States in the 1950's, when he was a target of attacks), there is a vast difference between noncommunist and communist countries: in the former, publishing is carried on by many competing private companies, whereas "all Russian literature is published by the state and must meet the requirements of the Communist Party" (*Harper's Magazine,* September 1969, p. 42).

Adherence to the party line is demanded also in other fields, particularly the social studies and humanities. Even in scientific fields like psychology there is a party line. The fate of psychoanalysis is a case in point. Until 1930, psychoanalysis was tolerated in the Soviet Union, having attracted considerable attention in Russia long before the revolution. After 1930, psychoanalysis gradually fell into disfavor, and in 1936 the Communist party officially decided that psychoanalysis was incompatible with Marxism-Leninism-Stalinism. After having been branded by the Nazis as false because of its Jewish origin, psychoanalysis was condemned by communists as "the result of the extreme decadence of bourgeois culture" (*Soviet Psychology and Psychiatry,* Fall 1965, p. 45) and was finally assailed as an "ideological instrument of American imperialism."

In the field of pure and applied philosophy, Soviet educational authorities have done much housecleaning too. Their opposition to more conservative thinkers was to be expected, but eventually they took on progressive thinkers also. John Dewey, for example, has been roundly condemned for his pragmatic philosophy, which patient communist research has revealed to be yet another cleverly disguised instrument of American imperialism.

Another method of literary assassination is through enforced ignorance. Having talked to hundreds of Russians, a young American writer found that not one of them had ever heard of John Stuart Mill. After spending a year at Moscow University, the same writer summed up his impressions as follows:

You find fourth-year psychology students, for instance, who can quote Pavlov but have never read Freud; fifth-year economics students who have never examined a single criticism of the labor theory of value canonized by Marx; teachers of contemporary Western literature who know nothing about Nabokov, and an entire History of the Soviet Period Department which has not read, and has little hope of reading, Trotsky (George Feifer, *New York Times Magazine,* November 22, 1964, p. 50).

A few years later, another American at Moscow University reported what happened to a Soviet fellow student who tried to obtain a copy of Freud's *A General Introduction to Psychoanalysis* at the Lenin Library. The librarian told the student, "There are dozens of patriotic Soviet textbooks that explain everything you need to know about Freud." Then he added, "Why do you want such things in your record? It's not necessary for your development." The student took the hint. (Ivan Epstein, "Portraits from Moscow U.," *Harper's Magazine,* April 1968, pp. 55–56.)

Yet no totalitarian system is as efficient as it claims or as its critics fear. Despite all controls, some more enterprising and courageous students manage to get hold of forbidden Western books in the social sciences, literary criticism, philosophy, and psychology. An underground black market passes the books along, generally obtaining them from tourists and exchange students. Listening to foreign news is another source of serious information: the news service of the British Broadcasting Corporation holds first place in its reputation for objective reporting and lively scholarly discussions. Likeminded students meet in informal groups, and discuss not the dialectics of Marxism-Leninism, but Sartre and Camus. The students know that they are carefully watched by fellow students who report on them to the secret police, but this is considered a fact of life one must accept. More rebellious students and young writers and poets even put out underground magazines, mostly devoted to poetry, literary essays, and social criticism. Since there are no private printers in a collective communist economy, such underground magazines are put out in mimeographed form, circulating in a few dozen or a few hundred copies, often only in a few issues, until the secret police discovers the identity of the editors and puts them into prison. Even typing such literature is, as we saw earlier, a serious political crime.

As to foreign newspapers, the general policy is to permit only the sale of official organs of foreign communist governments and parties. However, even such papers are banned whenever they carry criticisms of Soviet actions or conditions. Yugoslav, Romanian, French, British, and Italian communist papers are thus frequently forbidden, as were Czech papers before the invasion in 1968. Major Soviet libraries subscribe to noncommunist newspapers, but do not display them. A special permit is needed to use them in the library, and such permit is granted only if it is in the interest of the party and government. Chinese communist publications—easily available in American libraries and publicly sold in major American cities—are subject to the most severe Soviet ban. An American tourist can bring into the Soviet Union copies of the *New York Times* or the *Wall Street Journal,* but not of the *Peking Review.*

Censorship of news is also practiced on Western correspondents in Moscow. First, there is physical isolation. Correspondents have to live in apartment houses reserved exclusively for them; police are stationed in front of the buildings to prevent unauthorized Soviet citizens from entering. Next, Western correspondents are not allowed to dig for news on their own. All contacts for news-gathering purposes must first be cleared and approved by the press department of the Soviet foreign ministry. Finally—and most importantly—there is the fact of self-censorship of many Western correspondents. After two years in Moscow as the bureau chief of the *New York Times,* an American journalist wrote: "The threat of being expelled hangs over Western newsmen, and those who think twice almost always conclude that expulsion is a greater evil than silence. The Western news agencies have minimized their coverage of Soviet dissidents, for example, because their bureaus might be closed" (Henry Kamm, "Brezhnev Sets the Clock Back," *New York Times Magazine,* August 10, 1969, p. 30).

With respect to music and the fine arts, Lenin allowed a lively and varied experimentation in all fields. Under Stalin, the tradition of a party line in the arts was firmly established; in music, for example, the "formalism" of composers such as Prokofiev and Shostakovich was condemned, and composers were urged to make music that is simple, popular, and tuneful. Khrushchev interfered less with music, but asserted his authority more in painting and sculpture. After visiting the first Soviet exhibition of abstract paintings in Moscow in 1962, Khrushchev summarized his artistic judgment by saying they could have been painted by a "donkey's tail." In 1967, when avant-garde Soviet painters attempted to display their forbidden abstract and surrealist paintings in Moscow, the show was closed after one hour.

Under the Brezhnev regime, the systematic attack on abstract art has been intensified. In 1966, for example, Oskar Rabin, perhaps the best known of contemporary young Russian painters, was attacked for having permitted an exhibition of his expressionist and symbolist paintings in London. For years, Rabin earned his living as a railroad laborer but devoted his spare time to painting. His "underground" paintings appealed to foreign residents in Moscow who recognized his talent and bought his pictures. This support enabled him to devote all his time to painting. Because of his unorthodox style, he was denied membership in the Artists Union, thus being barred from officially permitted showings of his works in the Soviet Union. After committing the crime of allowing the exhibit of some of his paintings in London, Rabin was attacked by Soviet spokesmen as a painter of "paranoiac visions," as a "miserable wretch who has gone astray in his ideas and in his art." The official cultural journal in the Soviet Union, *Soviet Culture*, urged Rabin and other "underground artists" to discontinue any connection with Western art dealers: "Do you think that these profiteers value you as artists? They spit on you. You are useful to them only as political commodities to help bourgeois propaganda. This is your only value to the West." By contrast with the official Soviet damnation of Rabin as a "paranoiac" and "miserable wretch," Western students of Russian life and civilization find Rabin in the great artistic tradition of his country: "He evokes the same profound melancholy and human nostalgia that we find in the great Russian writers" (Jacques Catteau, "Oskar Rabin, Painter," *Survey*, October 1965, p. 84, with reproductions of some of Rabin's paintings).

Why this persistent Soviet hostility to modern trends in art, music, and literature?

Fifty years ago, abstract music and painting and expressionism in literature started out as small movements; while the following has grown, it is still a minority everywhere. Simple folk tunes in music, smiling factory workers and collective farmers in paintings—

these types of art are not only more suitable for communist propaganda, but they also express the level of taste of a Stalin, Khrushchev, or Brezhnev. It does not matter too much whether a British prime minister or an American president likes modern art or not, but it matters a great deal how the first secretary of the Soviet Communist party feels about it.

Second, there is the element of individual revolt in modern art and music, including jazz. Modern art is a rebellion against centuries-old conventions and forms and is therefore suspect. Moreover, modern art expresses free-flowing individuality and imagination, thus lessening the importance of the group, the people. The Soviet leadership thus looks with suspicion at this individualistic streak in modern art and literature, just as Dostoevsky was long consigned to relative obscurity, for he stresses individual tragedy, guilt, and responsibility rather than class war as the ultimate source of the human condition.

Finally, there is in modern art a deliberate split between the minority of the artistic vanguard and the mass of the people. While this is true everywhere, it is more serious in communist countries that uphold the official dogma of the identity of party leaders and the people. According to this dogma, there is always perfect identity of outlook and feeling between the intellectual leadership and the masses of the people. Modern art, on the other hand, provides an illustration of an intellectual and artistic minority being ahead of —or at least separate from—the people. This separation of artistic minority and people runs counter to the Soviet-communist dogma of identity between the "toilers of the mind" and the mass of peasants and workers. This disparity could be resolved either by foisting modern art on the people or by silencing the artists. The second solution is politically much easier, and it also has the advantage of reflecting the aesthetic reactions of the Soviet political rulers.

One of the basic freedoms most systematically denied by the Soviet government to its subjects is the freedom of movement. The political dissident may be banished to a correctional labor camp in Siberia or the far north. The ordinary citizen may be denied permission to take up residence in a city which, in the judgment of the police, is overcrowded. Going abroad—a privilege granted by many other authoritarian and even totalitarian governments—is for the average Soviet citizen a dream never to be realized, particularly if travel to a noncommunist country is involved. In recent years, a few hundred Soviet citizens have annually traveled as tourists to the United States. Generally, they travel in groups, always accompanied by secret police representatives, and the tourists always have to leave hostages behind—wives, children, parents, or brothers and sisters. Under constant surveillance of the Soviet secret police, the Soviet tourist in New Delhi or London has to plan carefully how to defect—as the cases of Svetlana Alliluyeva (Stalin's daughter) in 1967 and Anatoly Kuznetsov in 1969 dramatically demonstrated. By contrast, Western tourists freely visit the Soviet Union without any restrictions from their own governments, and the annual number of American tourists to the Soviet Union, for example, runs into several tens of thousands.

When it comes to permanent emigration, Soviet citizens generally do not even bother to apply, as the desire to emigrate is considered evidence of hostility to the government. In 1969, a radio engineer who vigorously petitioned the Soviet authorities to grant him and his family permission to emigrate to Israel was fired from his job (his wife, too, was dismissed) and then sentenced to three years of prison camp on charges of slander against the Soviet state (*New York Times,* June 5, 1969). Adventurous souls try to leave the country illegally—a very dangerous undertaking. According to Soviet law, high treason—punishable by death—includes "fleeing abroad or refusing to return from abroad." Under Stalin, the death penalty was often used. Under Khrushchev and Brezhnev the milder punishment of stiff sentences to forced labor has been meted out.

There is no way of knowing how many Soviet citizens would leave their country if they had the legal right to do so. The case of East Germany, however, throws some light on the extent to which a communist regime makes involuntary prisoners out of its subjects. Between 1950 and 1961, when movement between communist East Germany and noncommunist West Germany was comparatively easy, about four million East Germans—almost a quarter of East Germany's population—fled to West Germany. In 1961, the East German government put up the Berlin Wall and installed barbed wire and mine fields along the intra-German border to prevent the mass exodus of East Germans to West Germany. Despite such barriers, however, 125,000 East Germans managed to get across in the years 1961–1969, but more than a hundred lost their lives in the attempt to escape from East Germany. The Wall—dividing communist East Berlin from noncommunist West Berlin—is the most impressive symbol and monument of communism as a movement of "human liberation."

Finally, the problem of nationalism has increasingly bedeviled communism—contrary to all theories of Marxism-Leninism. According to basic communist doctrine, nationalism is a bourgeois prejudice which the proletariat rejects, and among communist societies the peaceful internationalism of "fraternal" socialist communities based on equality would replace bourgeois nationalism and imperialism based on inequality. The political reality is different. In the Soviet Union itself, a cult of the Great Russians as the "leading" nationality has been fostered in recent years. In the east European communist states—particularly in Yugoslavia, Romania, and Czechoslovakia—nationalism is stronger than ever, and it derives its strength from resistance to the actuality or threat of Soviet domination. The supreme failure of communist internationalism lies in the fact that, at present, the most serious danger of war between two major powers is between communist Russia and communist China.

REVOLTS AGAINST
SOVIET COMMUNISM

In 1948, Yugoslavia was more communized than any of the communist states in eastern Europe. Tito's crime in 1948 was not abandoning communism in favor of capitalism, but the much worse offense of trying to regain national independence for the peoples of Yugoslavia from Moscow. The Soviet Union mobilized all its resources of propaganda and subversion to overthrow Tito and his brand of national communism. At the time, few people thought Tito could defy Moscow successfully. Yet the unlikely happened, and Yugoslavia is still independent. The Soviet Union has come to realize that an independent Yugoslavia is here to stay and has been compelled by the force of circumstances to come to a *modus vivendi* with the Tito regime. Yet Yugoslavia has no illusions about the precariousness of that *modus vivendi*, and relies on its determination to defend its independence against the Soviet danger. The Yugoslav Constitution of 1963 forbids its citizens and officials to sign any document recognizing capitulation to, or occupation by, another power. On August 21, 1968, President Tito immediately condemned the Soviet invasion of Czechoslovakia as "a grave blow to the socialist and progressive forces in the world." After the Soviet occupation of Czechoslovakia, Yugoslavia was in imminent threat of Soviet invasion, and it made clear that it would resist with all its strength. In addition to regular armed forces of considerable size and quality, Yugoslavia has organized a Territorial Army of three million volunteers—out of a population of twenty million. Ranging in age from 18 to 60, all members are volunteers, and every organization and local community has its units, ready to spring into action. Nazi Germany was never able to defeat the Yugoslav guerrillas behind the lines in World War II, and Yugoslavia is confident that its people will be equally successful in fighting Soviet invaders in the same manner.

The break with Moscow in 1948, combined with Yugoslavia's determination to defend its independence against all Soviet threats, has led to considerable liberalization in political and economic affairs. The peasants were given the choice of returning to individual farming, and the overwhelming majority chose without much hesitation to abandon the collective farms. Workers in industry enjoy a substantial amount of "self-management," and privately owned enterprises employing fewer than five people are permitted and do a flourishing business, particularly in the repair, service, and handicraft industries. Also, American economic and military aid—in excess of three billion dollars by the late 1960's—has greatly helped Yugoslavia to maintain its independence and improve its economy. Four-fifths of the Yugoslav combat aircraft, for example, are American jets.

Foreign books and newspapers are more easily available in Yugoslavia than in any other communist country, and there is considerable exchange of students and teachers with western Europe and the United States. Foreign movies are freely shown, and Western plays are performed on the stage. Yugoslavia is also the only communist country which allows its citizens to visit and work abroad and to emigrate. Unlike other communist states, Yugoslavia admits a serious unemployment problem, and hundred of thousands of its workers have been encouraged to seek employment abroad. The main labor-importing countries—West Germany, France, and Sweden—have set up recruiting offices in Yugoslavia, and the government even pays the workers' travel cost to their place of work. Aside from ideological liberalization, the Yugoslav government favors these moves for two practical reasons: Yugoslavs employed abroad send their families funds in hard currency, and during their employment abroad workers acquire advanced industrial skills that are common in West Germany or France or Sweden but still scarce in developing Yugoslavia.

Yet the communist leadership in Yugoslavia reminds the people from time to time that there are limits to freedom in a communist state. The fate of Milovan Djilas is a case in point. Djilas was a lifelong friend and one of Tito's closest aides both during and after World War II. But in the early 1950's, Djilas began to express democratic ideas. He urged a free press and free public discussion, and he even dared to suggest that Yugoslavia be permitted to have more than one party. This was too much for the communist rulers. Djilas was tried in 1955 and sentenced to three years in prison. In 1957, a book by Djilas entitled *The New Class* was smuggled out of Yugoslavia and published in New York. In his book, Djilas exposed communism as an instrument of the communist ruling class (the "new class") for the exploitation and domination of the Yugoslav people. A new trial followed in which he received another seven years of imprisonment. Released from prison in 1961 for reasons of health, Djilas went to work on another book, *Conversations with Stalin*, describing the talks he had had with Stalin in 1944–1948. The book was published in 1962 in New York; Djilas was tried again, and this time he received nine years of prison. He was released, for reasons of ill health, on December 31, 1966, but placed under the restriction of making no public statements for five years. Yet he defied the ban by publishing *The Unperfect Society: Beyond the New Class* in Western countries in 1969. A communist from early boyhood, Djilas spent three years in prison under the anticommunist regime in Yugoslavia before World War II. Under communism, he found out how much more repressive is communism than the system he had helped to destroy.

After Tito's rebellious break with Moscow in 1948, the next major explosion took place on June 16 and 17, 1953, in East Germany. Food conditions had steadily deteriorated under Soviet exploitation and East German communist mismanagement, and there was less food than during World War II. Even bread and potatoes, the staple diet of communist economic planning, were scarce.

The spark which fired the smoldering resentment of the people was a government announcement on May 28, 1953, that workers' wages would be cut further unless they produced at least ten percent more than in the past. On June 16, building workers on Stalin Avenue in East Berlin started a spontaneous strike and marched toward government headquarters. The strike spread quickly throughout East Germany on that day and the next, and in many communities the workers were in command of the situation, occupying police offices, liberating political prisoners, and setting government and Communist party buildings on fire. Many members of the police either took a wait-and-see attitude or even went over to the rebels. Before long, the rebels demanded, in addition to more tolerable living conditions, free elections, free labor unions, and the end of Soviet domination.

Hesitating at first to intervene directly, the Soviet forces quickly realized that the communist regime would soon be overthrown completely, and thousands of Soviet tanks moved into the major strongholds of rebellion, suppressing it in a few days. Several hundred Germans died in the uprising, hundreds were wounded, and about 50,000 were imprisoned.

Exactly three years after the uprising in East Germany the Poles revolted. On June 28, 1956, thousands of workers of the Stalin Steel Works in Poznan went on strike early in the morning and moved toward the center of the city, chanting "bread, bread, bread," singing Polish national songs, carrying the old Polish national flags, and refusing to disperse despite the tank formations quickly brought into the city by the communist authorities. Before long, the striking workers occupied the Communist party headquarters and the radio station and set the city prison on fire after freeing the prisoners. In the ensuing battle with army and police, a battle that lasted for several days, about 200 Poles lost their lives, thousands were wounded, and many more thousands were arrested.

Militarily, the rebellion was successfully repressed, but politically it unleashed a chain of events which is still in the making. In October, 1956, Wladyslaw Gomulka was elected first secretary of the Polish Communist party. This announcement came as a bombshell, because Gomulka was known as the leader of Titoism or "national communism" in Poland and had spent several years in prison for that crime.

For a while, the Russians considered full-scale occupation of the country and the reestablishment of Stalinism by force. But the Poles stood their ground, and Poland had won, for the time being, its struggle for some degree of national independence, although its government continued to be communist dominated.

One of the most popular moves of the new government under Gomulka was to permit the peasants to dissolve collective farms and go back to private farming. As a result, food production rose, leading to improved living conditions of the urban population as well. In industry too, the harsh controls over workers were relaxed, and industrial production moved steadily forward from its previous low. Private enterprise in business and trade has been permitted on a moderate scale, such as in the case of bakers, tailors, plumbers, repairmen, and skilled craftsmen in the building and tourist trades. In addition to these internal measures aiming at the improvement of its economy, Poland has also benefited from American economic aid, amounting to more than a billion dollars by the late 1960's.

In 1957, the Polish government released Cardinal Wyszynski, the symbol of Catholic resistance, from prison and also permitted religious instruction in public schools. This new attitude of greater tolerance was also extended, for a few years, to literature and the arts, and Western books and papers became available. Arriving in Warsaw from Moscow, one is amazed to see large quantities of French, English, and German books in display windows of Polish bookstores—a sight one cannot yet even dream of in the Soviet Union.

From the early 1960's on, the Polish government under Gomulka has gradually nibbled away at these liberties, without attempting to abolish them in a single stroke. Censorship of newspapers has been tightened, more liberal magazines have been banned, plays have been forbidden, and theater directors have been dismissed. In 1968 and 1969, the government purged the universities and student bodies of "revisionist" (that is, liberal) elements, and the pattern of re-Stalinization followed closely that of the Brezhnev regime in Russia. After the Israeli-Arab war in 1967, Poland also engaged in an intense antisemitic campaign under the guise of "anti-Zionism." Before World War II, the Jewish population in Poland was three million. At the end of the war, largely as the result of German mass murder of the Jews, only about 30,000 were left. The Gomulka government in 1968 and 1969 allowed Jews to emigrate—empty-handed in most cases—and by the end of 1969 only about 10,000 Jews were still in Poland.

The hardening of government policy has also been seen in the growing harassment of the Catholic church. In 1961, the government prohibited religious instruction in public schools, closed most Catholic schools and some seminaries and harassed others through discriminatory and harsh tax measures. The Catholic church has carefully avoided taking a public stand on specific political issues that deeply concern it. Thus, the church did not comment on the Soviet-led invasion of Czechoslovakia, in which Polish troops were the second-largest in number. Yet, from time to time church leaders do speak out on more general issues of religion and morality. Thus, Cardinal Wyszynski in his Palm Sunday sermon of April 11, 1965, said: "It is monstrous that we Catholics must reject God because there is a group of people, with power and public funds, wishing it. Where is reason? Where is democracy." On March 21, 1968, the Polish bishops in a letter read in all churches made this statement: "Brutal use of force disgraces human dignity and does not lead to the true solution of tensions between people and between social groups."

The events in Poland in 1956 immediately raised hope and passion in Hungary. On October 23, 1956, university students, quickly joined by thousands of industrial workers, held a mass meeting in Parliament Square. Expressing their sympathy for the Polish fight for freedom and independence, they put forward a series of demands, including among others: the evacuation of Russian troops from Hungary; free elections; free labor unions and the right to strike; revision of workers' wages and a complete reorganization of the economy; the immediate release of political prisoners and the return of Hungarians deported to the Soviet Union; removal of the statues of Stalin; and, finally, reorganization of the compulsory system of farm collectives.

The political police turned a peaceful meeting into bloody rebellion by firing on the students and workers. The fighting quickly spread throughout the whole country. The workers declared a general strike, and the freedom fighters were soon joined by the regular Hungarian army and police. On the communist side, the Hungarian political police were joined by powerful Russian tank forces. Yet the incredible happened. The freedom fighters won their struggle, and on October 29, 1956, Hungary was free. Political authority was exercised by the representatives of popular organizations, and almost at once dozens of democratic newspapers began to be published. Communists were nowhere to be seen, and statues of Stalin were publicly burned. Also, political prisoners were set free. The best known among them was Cardinal Mindszenty, who had been imprisoned since 1948.

However, this period of Hungarian freedom and independence lasted for only five days. On November 3 close to 200,000 Soviet troops and 5,000 tanks moved into Hungary to suppress Hungarian freedom. After a week of heavy fighting, the revolution was put down. Prime Minister Nagy was kidnaped by the Russians and later executed. Over 35,000 Hungarians were killed in the fighting, and many more wounded. Many thousands were deported to Siberia, and over 200,000 managed to escape to Austria. The physical destruction of the towns was worse than that suffered by Hungary in World War II, when she was a major battleground for many months.

Despite their military defeat by Soviet tanks, the Hungarians learned several lessons. First, the spectacle of rebelling workers trampling and burning the red flag as the symbol of oppression destroyed the myth, once and for all, that Soviet communism represents the cause of the workers. Throughout the whole Hungarian Revolution, the Hungarian Workers' Council, and local workers' councils across the nation, were the center of anti-Soviet and anti-communist activity.

Second, the Hungarian Revolution revealed the inefficacy of communist indoctrination. The revolution was touched off by university students—the products of communist education and indoctrination.

Finally, the Hungarian Revolution gave the death blow to the theory, obsessively clung to by many noncommunists, that revolution in a totalitarian state is impossible. According to this theory, revolution was possible in the eighteenth or nineteenth century because the government did not then possess the powerful weapons of suppression available to it in this century. The Hungarian Revolution has proved that the mind of man is still king, as it has always been, and that totalitarian governments of the twentieth century cannot rely exclusively on terror any more than could despotism in the past.

During the first years after the crushing of the Hungarian Revolution, many people inside and outside Hungary thought that the heroic effort of the nation had been in vain. Communist dictatorship was harsher than before the Revolution, and for a while it seemed more Stalinist than the Soviet Union itself. In the end this reasoning—an implied defense of inert submission to communist totalitarianism—proved wrong. The very fact of the revolution encouraged tendencies toward more national independence in other communist states. Even little Albania has been able, from the late 1950's on, to defy the Soviet Union by enthusiastically siding with communist China in its conflict with Russia.

In Hungary herself, the harsh government installed by the Soviet army after the repression of the revolution in 1956 gradually realized that Soviet tanks were not enough if the country was to regain some measure of political stability. By 1963, this movement of relaxing the most oppressive controls gathered considerable momentum; thousands of political prisoners were released under a general amnesty, and the government eased its stringent controls in industry and farming. Writers and artists were given greater freedom of expression, and noncommunists were appointed to important positions. Whereas the previous slogan had been "He who is not for us is against us," the new official slogan became "He who is not against us is with us." In 1965, Janos Kadar, the head of the Hungarian Communist party, publicly expressed his concern about the continuing lack of popular acceptance of communism, in spite of the more lenient methods used in the preceding few years. In urging intensified party efforts, he asked, "What would be the good of having a few hundred thousand very radical communists if the rest of the people turned against the ideas of communism?" (*The Economist*, August 28, 1965).

In 1968, Hungary embarked on a major reform of her economy, with the objective of creating market competition and incentives for managers and workers. The program had to be limited in its scope by one basic consideration: keeping the Hungarian economy tied to Russia's plan for the economic integration of eastern Europe through COMECON. One-third of Hungary's trade is with Russia and over one-third is with other communist states, although the new generation of Hungary's planners and economists would like to expand economic ties with Western countries. In her foreign policy, too, Hungary has followed the Soviet line, but with much less enthusiasm than has been displayed by Poland, East Germany, and Bulgaria. The low point of doubt and despondency was reached in 1968, when Hungary, still remembering 1956, had to contribute troops to the Soviet-led invasion of Czechoslovakia.

Romania, held up until the early 1960's as a model and docile satellite of the Soviet Union, has in recent years increasingly asserted its national independence. A Latin island in a Slavic sea, Romania has returned to its historic cultural ties with the West. In 1963, the government abolished the compulsory teaching of Russian in grade and high schools and closed the official Soviet Russian Language Institute and Russian bookstore in Bucharest. In 1969, according to official statistics, 55 percent of university students taking a foreign language chose French, 33 percent chose English, and only 10 percent took Russian. Foreign authors are published and widely discussed, and Franz Kafka's works—considered by many to be the most penetrating critique of totalitarianism—are the most popular among the younger and avant-garde intellectuals.

In the economic field, Romania has led the opposition inside COMECON (made up of the Soviet Union, East Germany, Poland,

Czechoslovakia, Hungary, Bulgaria, and Romania) against the Soviet concept of "integrating" eastern Europe for the benefit of the
Soviet economy. In particular, Romania is intent on developing its
industry and refuses the Soviet-assigned role of being a perpetual
supplier of raw materials for the other communist states. Also,
Romania is eager to break out of the confining limits of COMECON
and to expand its trade with noncommunist states. In 1956, only
29 percent of Romania's trade was with noncommunist nations; in
1968, the percentage jumped to 49 and is constantly rising. More
significantly, in 1956 Russia's share in Romania's foreign trade was
54 percent; in 1968, the percentage dropped to 28. Under its re-
vamped economic policies Romania's gross national product has
grown at a faster annual rate than that of the other eastern European
communist states, and its government therefore insists that the
economic reforms are guided by pragmatic considerations rather
than by any ideological criteria.

In its foreign policy Romania has shown the highest degree of
independence of all members of the Warsaw Pact (Soviet Union,
Poland, East Germany, Hungary, Bulgaria, Czechoslovakia, and
Romania) with respect to Soviet policy. Although Romania continues its membership in the Warsaw Pact alliance, its policy has,
in fact, been one of strict neutrality. Romania maintains active ties
with both China and Albania and has refused to be a party to Soviet-
led efforts at condemning China in its conflict with Russia. When
Russo-Chinese border clashes are reported, the Romanian press—in
the time-honored style of neutrality in wartime—publishes the official Soviet and Chinese communiqués, giving equal space to each
side. In its relations with the West, Romania is the only member
of the Warsaw Pact—other than the Soviet Union itself—that maintains full diplomatic relations with both West Germany and East
Germany. At the outbreak of the Israeli-Arab war in 1967, all Warsaw Pact countries except Romania broke off diplomatic relations
with Israel; Romania has not only refused to join the other Warsaw
Pact countries in their anti-Israel campaign but has maintained
friendly relations with both Israel and the Arab states and has
quietly allowed Jewish emigration to Israel.

In connection with the Soviet-led invasion of Czechoslovakia in
1968, Romania was the only Warsaw Pact country that refused to

contribute troops or condone the act. Only a week before the invasion, President Ceausescu of Romania had demonstratively visited Prague and signed a treaty of mutual help and assistance with the liberal Dubcek government in Prague. After the invasion of Czechoslovakia, Ceausescu warned the Soviet Union that no foreign troops would be allowed to enter Romania and ordered the immediate creation of a "people's militia" of workers, peasants, and intellectuals for "the defense of freedom and independence" of his nation. Ceausescu bluntly condemned the Russian aggression as "a grave mistake and a serious danger not only to peace in Europe but to socialism throughout the world, too."

When Romania invited President Nixon to visit Romania on August 2, 1969, it took a calculated risk in its relations with the Soviet Union. Although the Romanian government tried to keep popular manifestation at a low key, the enthusiasm of the people went beyond the boundaries of the planned low key. A few days later, the Soviet representative at the Romanian Communist Party Congress in Bucharest attacked "bridge-building" (as exemplified in the Nixon visit) as a "perfidious tactic" that was undermining the cohesion of the communist countries in eastern Europe. Yet the Romanians stood their ground, and President Ceausescu announced that the "people's militia" would continue to defend Romanian independence against "imperialism." "He did not say what 'imperialism,'" an American observer of the party congress reported, "but the delegates' wild applause at his announcement made it obvious that it was not the imperialism of the United States he had in mind" (Tad Szulc, "Letter from Bucharest," *The New Yorker*, September 6, 1969, p. 118).

SOCIALISM WITH A HUMAN FACE

Communist rule in Czechoslovakia was established in 1948 through a coup of the Communist party, combined with threats of Soviet military intervention in case of resistance to the takeover. Czechoslovakia was the only country in central Europe, apart from Switzerland, that had a genuine democratic and libertarian tradition in politics, economics, and religion, and its standards of education and industrial skill compared favorably with those of its neighbors.

The communization of Czechoslovakia in 1948 shocked the Western nations into a renewed awareness of Soviet imperialism, and the creation of NATO was the most significant response to that shock. From 1948 to the early 1960's the communist regime was rigidly Stalinist in its internal policy and docile in its relations with the Soviet Union.

From the middle 1960's on, a new generation of communist leaders began to reappraise the effects of communist rule on Czechoslovakia. In the economic field, the country had fallen behind as a result of both domestic and foreign policy. Domestically, rigid central planning and bureaucratic routine had stifled the traditional initiative and enterprise of the highly skilled Czechs. In its foreign economic policy, the Czech economy had to adapt to the role assigned to it by the Soviet-led COMECON. The Czech economy had to neglect the industries in which it had developed world-renowned skills and profitable markets in the West, such as textiles, glass, china, leather goods, and jewelry, and had to concentrate on basic industries for which it was not suited. As a result, the growth record of the Czech economy was very unimpressive—even as compared with the other communist states in eastern Europe. In politics, the democratic habits of the people increasingly reasserted themselves among workers, students, and intellectuals, as well as among growing numbers of Communist party leaders. In January 1968, Antonin Novotny—the leader and popular symbol of Stalinist communism—was replaced by Alexander Dubcek, a liberal communist, as first secretary of the Communist party. Under Dubcek's leadership, communism in Czechoslovakia embarked on a unique experiment in the history of communism: the transformation of totalitarian communism into *socialism with a human face* by peaceful means, that is, the combination of public ownership in the economy with political democracy in government.

One of the first things done by the Dubcek leadership was to release more than 30,000 victims of the Novotny regime from prison and to abolish the secret police. Prominent victims of Czech Stalinism executed in the 1950's were rehabilitated posthumously. Old-line Stalinist communists were dismissed from their positions, but the new government was careful not to use any force against the discredited Stalinists. This treatment was in line with the new emphasis on the rule of law and also grew out of the conviction that the popular condemnation of Stalinist communists was so profound that no other penalties were needed. All travel restrictions on Czechoslovaks wishing to leave the country or foreigners wishing to visit it were lifted. This freedom to travel was an indirect blow at the Berlin Wall, since East Germans could visit Czechoslovakia and from there make their way to West Germany.

Freedom of speech, the press, and assembly spread spontaneously as the government did nothing to discourage it. In fact, the government finally abolished all censorship of the press—probably the most sensational step of all. Noncommunist papers were freely published, and criticism of communism itself was expressed. In the most famous document of the period—"2,000 Words," a manifesto of intellectuals and workers—the following passage appeared: "The Communist party, which after the war possessed the great trust of the people, gradually exchanged this trust for offices, until it had all the offices and nothing else." The signers of the manifesto declared their commitment to socialism, but it had to be a socialism regenerated by democracy: "The regenerative process introduces nothing particularly new into our life. It revives ideas and topics, many of which are older than the errors of socialism." What many Czechoslovak communists wanted for their country was Marxism without Leninism. Some publicly stated that Leninism might be suitable for a country like Russia, but not for Czechoslovakia in its advanced stage of political and economic development.

Finally, the Dubcek leadership even allowed the formation of noncommunist clubs and associations, and Wenceslas Square in the center of Prague became the Hyde Park of Czechoslovakia in which any group and individual could freely express their views. The extent of the freedom enjoyed in the spring and summer of 1968 can be seen in the fact that a public opinion poll was taken on the question of allowing opposition parties. On June 27, 1968, the official daily of the Communist party reported the results of the poll: *90 percent of noncommunists favored the creation of opposition parties, and even more than half of the communists polled did so.*

During the spring and summer of 1968 the Dubcek leadership was warned by Brezhnev and Kosygin to give up the experiment in "socialism with a human face." The main fear of the Russians—

supported principally by East German and Polish leaders—was that the process of liberalization would undermine the monopoly of the Communist party in Czechoslovakia and that an opposition, once given freedom of organization and expression, might provide an alternative government some day. The Czechoslovak leaders defended themselves by arguing that they were fully confident that liberalization under communist leadership would strengthen the cause of communism, and that no political groups would be allowed that challenged the economic principles of public ownership of the means of production. In the area of foreign policy, the Dubcek leadership repeatedly reassured the Soviet leaders that Czechoslovakia would continue its membership in the Warsaw Pact. If the Soviet leaders had permitted the people of Czechoslovakia to continue the experiment of combining public ownership with a high degree of political democracy under the leadership of the Communist party, we should have been provided with an answer to the question whether a communist society can maintain itself by processes of consent or whether it must rely on prisons and the secret police.

The Soviet leaders were unwilling to accept either possible outcome of the experiment: if the experiment led to the gradual removal of communist influence in Czechoslovakia in politics and economics, it might give an example to other communist countries that communist rule is not a dead end and that a return journey to a noncommunist society is possible—even under liberal communist leadership. Conversely, from the Soviet viewpoint, should the experiment in Czechoslovakia succeed and the party maintain itself in a place of leadership by moral authority rather than by force, the repercussions of such a success in Czechoslovakia might be disastrous for the communist regimes in the Soviet Union and other communist states that relied on prisons and labor camps for the maintenance of communist rule.

The Soviet leadership decided that the experiment in Czechoslovakia had to be ended by armed force, since a voluntary return to Stalinism in Czechoslovakia was out of the question. On August 21, 1968, 200,000 troops, mostly Soviet but including East German, Polish, Bulgarian, and Hungarian contingents, invaded and occupied Czechoslovakia. There was sporadic individual fighting, a few dozen people were killed, but the Czechs had decided not to resist the invasion with their armed forces. Swastikas were painted on Soviet tanks, and numerous inscriptions on buildings explained to the Soviet "liberators" that to the people of Czechoslovakia, German Nazism and Soviet communism were the same.

Entering Prague during the night, the Soviet invaders did not waste any time. Dozens of unmarked cars of the secret police raced through Prague and arrested known liberals. At 4 A.M., Soviet airborne units surrounded the building of the Communist party. Dubcek and three other top government leaders were removed by Soviet soldiers and civilians. Then "the four men were led to a Soviet transport plane, pushed with rifle butts. . . . They were treated harshly and insulted. As Premier Cernik was to tell the Cabinet later: 'I feared for my life and that of my comrades' " (*New York Times,* September 2, 1968). The four top leaders were flown to the Soviet Union and kept prisoner. President Svoboda of Czechoslovakia flew to Moscow on August 23, 1968, and he made it clear to the Soviet government that he would not participate in any negotiations until the imprisoned leaders had been freed. He reportedly even threatened to commit suicide in the Kremilin if the imprisoned leaders were killed—as had happened to Imre Nagy in Hungary. The Soviets freed Dubcek and his colleagues, and the Czechoslovak leaders surrendered the independence of their country to the Soviets on August 26, 1968. As Josef Smrkovsky, president of the National Assembly of Czechoslovakia and a member of the delegation, later explained, the Czechoslovaks had negotiated "in the shadow of tanks and planes." Soviet troops were to stay indefinitely on Czechoslovak soil—to make sure that totalitarian communism of the Soviet type would prevent any recurrence of the virus of "socialism with a human face."

Whereas the communist coup in Czechoslovakia in 1948 was hailed by other communist states and parties as a victory of the cause of Marxism-Leninism, the Soviet occupation of Czechoslovakia in 1968 fragmented the communist world more profoundly, and probably more permanently, than ever before. Three communist states—Yugoslavia, Romania, and China—sharply denounced the Soviet action, and only the governments of Poland, East Germany, Bulgaria, and Hungary—who had themselves participated in the aggression—defended the Soviet Union. Not a single Communist party leader in Western Europe defended the Soviet move, and the large Communist parties of Italy and France were particularly outspoken in their condemnation.

Seeing the disintegration of communist unity even in its own backyard, eastern Europe, the Soviet leadership determined that its policy of coercion in relation to other communist states had to be raised from the level of practice to that of principle. Speaking on November 12, 1968, at the congress of the Polish Communist party in Warsaw, Brezhnev made it plain that the action in Czechoslovakia was not an isolated incident, but the application of a broader principle, since then known as the "Brezhnev Doctrine." Under this policy principle, the Soviet government reserves to itself the right to use military force in *any* communist country where, in its judgment, a threat emerges to the cause of communism, "a threat to the security of the Socialist Commonwealth as a whole." Significantly, Brezhnev did not confine the applicability of his new doctrine to Warsaw Pact countries, but spoke of "any socialist country"—including, apparently, such states as Yugoslavia and China.

The dilemma posed by the Brezhnev Doctrine to the noncommunist world and to the concept of coexistence between East and West was aptly formulated by the London *Economist*:

Mr. Brezhnev was saying that once a country has got a communist form of government it will never be allowed to get rid of it; and this, presumably, even if the majority of its people say they want to try something else. The Russians are inviting the Western world to take part in a competition in which, on the principle of democratic choice, noncommunist countries are allowed to go communist but, on the principle of the socialist commonwealth, communist ones are forbidden to make the return journey. Heads we win, tails you lose. It is an odd way to invite people to play ball (December 7, 1968, p. 18).

THE SINO-SOVIET CONFLICT

The most explosive conflict within world communism is yet to come: communist China against the Soviet Union. Basically, it is a struggle over power, but like every power struggle it has other elements as well.

First, there is the issue of nationalism, Chinese against Russians. For more than three hundred years, Russia has expanded her empire in Asia, frequently at the expense of China. Russia has, therefore, traditionally feared the prospect of a strong and united China ruled by an effective central government, the kind of government that communist rule has established in China since 1949. From the traditional Chinese viewpoint, the Russians are meddlesome troublemakers, imperialist expansionists, and—by the standards of ancient Chinese civilization—a horde of crude barbarians. In the eyes of the Chinese, Russians are not (as they appear to some Westerners) semi-Asiatic or semi-Oriental, but full-fledged Europeans and, as such, barbarians by definition.

Even under Stalin, Titoism showed that the force of nationalism was stronger than the myth of "international proletarian solidarity and fraternity." If the nationalism of little Yugoslavia could prevail against Stalin, the nationalism of a great power like China, the Chinese feel, is even more destined to prevail against a mere Khrushchev or Brezhnev. Marx or no Marx, more than 800 million Chinese will not forever accept the idea that the 235 million people of the Soviet Union are the leaders of the communist world. The Chinese are quite familiar with the Confucian saying, "When two men ride on a horse, only one can sit in front." The Chinese are determined that they, not the Russians, will sit in front.

Closely connected with the traditional force of nationalism is the issue of population and resources. More than 800 million Chinese inhabit a densely populated area, with an annual increase of population running to about 12 million people. By contrast, the 235 million inhabitants of the Soviet Union live in a much vaster territory, and the annual increase of population is only about three million. On the Russian side of the common border, the land is empty and the population very sparse. On the Chinese side, the land is overcrowded. This growing gap between the Soviet ratio of people and resources on the one hand and the Chinese ratio on the other may someday lead to Chinese expansion at the expense of Soviet territory.

In particular, the Chinese have publicly proclaimed in recent years that they do not recognize the imperialist treaties and conquests at the expense of China in the past. This is of particular

SOVIET TERRITORIES CLAIMED BY CHINA (1970)

LINE CLAIMED
BY CHINA

SAKHALIN.
Khabarovsk
Domansky
Ussuri R.
Vladivostok
JAPAN
Sea of Japan

N.KOREA
Seoul
S.KOREA
Tsingtao

Blagoveshchensk
Amur R.
Harbin

TRANS-SIBERIAN RAILWAY

Shenyang
Tientsin
Peking

U. S. S. R.

Lake Baikal
Chita
Ulan Bator
MONGOLIA

Taiyuan
CHINA

1000 miles
800
600
400
200
0

Krasnoyarsk

Novosibirsk
Barnaul

NUCLEAR
PROVINCE TEST SITE
SINKIANG

Omsk
Kuldja

Magnitogorsk
L. Balkhash
Alma Ata
Kashgar
Yarkand

LINE CLAIMED
BY CHINA

Tashkent

KASHMIR
TIBET

AFGHAN-
ISTAN
PAKISTAN

concern to Russia, since she took more territory from China than any other imperialist power. The major areas in dispute include vast Far Eastern stretches of land, from the mouth of the Amur River down the Pacific coast of Siberia and reaching west as far as Lake Baikal. Today, this area of untold natural riches is inhabited by nine million Soviet citizens. The Chinese feel that, with more intensive cultivation of the soil, at least 100 million Chinese could live there—albeit on a lower Chinese standard of living. Next, China has also shown desires for the "liberation" of formerly Chinese territories in Soviet central Asia, covering an area of about half a million square miles and ten million people. This is rich land with a great potential in food and fibers. Finally, there is Mongolia, with over half a million square miles and only one million population. A Chinese province from 1686 to 1911, it became a Russian protectorate in 1912–1919 and again a Chinese province in 1919–1921. In 1921, Mongolia became an independent state in form, but in fact it was closely linked with Moscow. China has tried to gain a foothold in Mongolia, playing on racial affinity and historical ties, but Russian influence has so far remained uppermost. One of the main reasons for Russia's success is the fact that she has been giving considerable economic aid to Mongolia—about $200 million and more annually, one of the highest per capita aid expenditures of any country anywhere. In 1966, the Soviet Union and Mongolia concluded a military security treaty, giving the Soviet Union the right to station troops in her ally's territory, thus bringing Soviet armed forces right up to the Chinese border. In 1968 and 1969, the Soviets also introduced rocket and missile forces into Mongolia, only a few hundred miles from China's major nuclear installations. Should Russia decide on a preemptive strike against China, knocking out these nuclear plants would be one of the first objectives.

While the Soviet leaders have repudiated many of the internal policies of the tsars, they are not willing to give up the fruits of tsarist conquest, be it in favor of the Chinese or of anybody else. So far, the Chinese have publicly stated that they wish to settle the issue of these disputed areas not by force but by peaceful negotiation at "the appropriate time," that is, when China is strong enough to bargain effectively with the Soviet Union. Chinese maps now indicate the area of the country before and after the foreign imperialist grabs of Chinese territory. By coincidence, Russia always appears in these maps as the foremost imperialist, helping herself to more Chinese territory than any other imperialist state of the past. Since such maps are published in the officially prescribed school books in China, a whole generation is growing up eager to regain the lost territories. On June 13, 1969, the Soviet government delivered a major policy statement to the Chinese government in which it protested against the Chinese publication "of textbooks and maps in which a number of lands of other states were presented as belonging to China." The Soviet government also warned China in the same message that "any attempt to encroach upon the Soviet frontier will meet with a crushing rebuff."

Far from dismissing these territorial ambitions of the Chinese as idle speculation, the Soviet government has taken them seriously. In 1963, the Soviet government began a drive to double the population of the disputed areas in the east within a decade and supplemented this campaign with detailed economic plans designed to attract, and provide for, a rapidly growing population. Even if this project of doubling the population of the Soviet Far East were to succeed, the Chinese population is multiplying so much faster than the Soviet that it is doubtful whether the Soviets can ever match the Chinese population pressure by transferring its own people in sufficiently large numbers even to approximate the Chinese density of population. In the meantime, the Chinese have embarked on an intensified settlement program at two crucial frontiers with the Soviet Union: northern Manchuria and Sinkiang. The Soviet authorities are aware of this Chinese pressure on their borders, and Soviet border guards in the Far East and central Asia are on constant alert against "enemy violators." Border clashes have occurred on numerous occasions, and each side blames the other for the intense military activities on the 4,500-mile border. Since early 1969, border "incidents" have escalated sharply in intensity and duration, and major battles between border troops have resulted in hundreds of casualties. The combined armed strength of the Soviet Union and China along their borders exceeded 1.5 million men in 1969, and the leaders of both countries publicly stated that they were ready for both conventional and nuclear war. The airport at Omsk in western Siberia has been made into one of the largest airports of the world, and Russia has developed an extensive delivery system of nuclear weapons close to China's borders. The Chinese possess massive manpower, but are no match for Russia's airpower and nuclear capability. The prospect of a major Sino-Soviet war has become of such concern to Soviet leaders that they have tried to transform the issue from an intracommunist dispute into one that is, or should be, of concern to all nations. War between Russia and China, *Pravda* editorialized on August 28, 1969, "what with the existing weapons and lethal armaments and modern means of delivery, would not spare a single continent."

Soviet fears of a resurgent China have also been seen in the economic field. During the first years of the communist regime in China, from about 1950 to 1957, Soviet aid and advice were significant in the total economic planning of China. After 1957, tensions gradually developed, and the Soviets took measures against China where they could be most painful: in the economic sphere. In 1959, the first repatriations of Soviet advisers, experts, and other technicians took place; by the middle of 1960, these repatriations were about finished. Interestingly, in some instances the departing Soviet technicians even took with them the plans of the projects they were engaged on, as was the case in the huge Sammen Narrows Dam on the Yellow River. Trade between Russia and China has also slumped. Soviet trade with China dropped from more than $400 million in 1964 to less than $100 million in 1967, and is less than Soviet trade with any other communist country, even less than with Mongolia, a nation of one million people. To make up the loss of trade with Russia and the eastern European communist states, China has greatly intensified its commercial relations with Japan and western Europe.

Diplomatically, too, the Soviet Union and China have different interests, for reasons of geography if for no other. For the Soviet Union, the problem of Germany and the more specific issue of Berlin are the key problems in Europe—in both of which China has shown very little interest. By contrast, China's number one issue in Asia is the conquest of Taiwan—a matter which is of little concern to Russia. In the struggle between India and China, the Soviet Union has not even pretended to be a neutral. From the beginning of the

Chinese aggressions against India in 1959, the Soviet Union at first refused to side with the aggressor and later openly aided India with jet fighters, transport planes, helicopters, and other equipment. It also helped India to build her own factory producing Soviet-type jet fighters. Elsewhere in southeast Asia, China apprehensively watches growing Soviet influence in Indonesia, Vietnam, Thailand, Malaysia, and Singapore. China is particularly worried over the prospect of seeing the waning American presence in southeast Asia being replaced by expanding Soviet influence in areas that it has traditionally considered its own sphere of influence. From the Chinese viewpoint, Soviet meddling in southeast Asia is as offensive and intolerable as that of the United States.

The case of India illustrates the divergent approaches of Russia and China to the goal of spreading communism, particularly in the developing countries. In its first phase, the Soviet approach is essentially a "strategy of denial." The objective is to get a foothold in a developing country through economic aid and propaganda, thus minimizing and neutralizing Western influence, and then to create a power vacuum in which Soviet power can firmly entrench itself, as it has done, for example, in the Arab states in the Middle East. If events develop along hoped-for lines, the Soviet approach fully envisages support for local civil wars and minor international wars fought with weapons.

The Chinese approach to the problem of communizing the developing countries is different. In the first place, the Chinese argue that Soviet economic aid should go only to communist states (like China herself), or those well on the road to becoming communized, but not to "capitalist regimes" like India. As to the spreading of communism in developing countries, the Chinese urge more direct—that is, armed—action. Chinese communist leaders often quote Mao's famous statement that "political power grows out of the barrel of a gun." In looking at the world at large, the Chinese communist leadership seeks to apply the lessons of its own conquest of power. In China, the communist revolutionaries established strongholds in the countryside and then proceeded to encircle and conquer the beleaguered cities. In Chinese communist thinking, North America and western Europe are "the cities of the world," and the "contemporary world revolution also presents a picture of the encirclement of cities by the rural areas" (*Peking Review*, September 3, 1965, p. 24). This means that "the cities of the world" (North America and western Europe) must be conquered by the "rural areas of the world," or Asia, Africa, and Latin America, in the same way in which the cities of China were conquered by the rural areas during the communist civil war in China. The Chinese leaders frankly admit that China must be the "base area for the world revolution."

The Soviet Union hopes to spread communism through leadership in economics and science, propaganda, subversion, and minor wars short of all-out nuclear war. The Chinese position is that such a nuclear world war is not inevitable, because the West is unlikely to strike back with nuclear weapons if pushed harder than the Soviets are willing to do. However, the Chinese reason, should the risk of nuclear war materialize, such risk must be accepted, because nuclear war would see the end not of mankind but of capitalism, on the ruins of which communism would triumph everywhere. For the Chinese, a loss of 200 million people in a nuclear conflict would still leave enough Chinese to carry on. For the Soviet Union, a similar loss of 200 million people would mean the destruction of the whole country, and Soviet leaders are therefore less comfortable about the prospect of nuclear warfare.

Thus, Sino-Soviet differences are not primarily based on different interpretations of communist dogma. In a general way, the Soviet approach to the spread of communism expresses the attitude of a country that has acquired much self-confidence and that feels that time is on its side. By contrast, China has accomplished relatively little, as measured by the standards of other great powers (like the United States or the Soviet Union), either in economic development or in scientific leadership. She is therefore in a hurry and willing to take greater risks in direct action. Moreover, in the case of India, for example, the national interests of China and Russia would be different and very likely opposed, even if Lenin or Mao had never laid down any guidelines for action. Both Russia and China have one major interest with respect to India: to see to it that India does not become subservient to China (as viewed by Russia) or to Russia (as viewed by China).

The competition between China and Russia is taking place on

Oliphant in the Denver Post; *reprinted by permission*

"RATIONALIZE IT! IF WE DON'T FIGHT THEM HERE, WE'LL BE FIGHTING THEM IN DOWNTOWN MOSCOW—WE HAVE TO CONTAIN CHINESE COMMUNISM IN ASIA."

all continents, within communist states as well as within communist parties in noncommunist states. In Europe, Albania, the poorest of the communist states, has come under the influence of China. In Asia, Africa, and Latin America, China portrays herself as the true leader of the poor, have-not nations, whereas Russia is pictured as being too busy with keeping what she has, and no longer dedicated to world revolution. The Chinese also charge that the "Soviet revisionist renegade clique" (as the Soviet government is persistently called in the Chinese press) is working for the restoration of capitalism, and that "stinking egoism" has replaced the communist morals of Lenin and Stalin in the Soviet Union. In Asia, Chinese influence is strong in North Korea and Vietnam, whereas Soviet influence is paramount in the communist regime of Mongolia. Among the Asian communist movements, Soviet influence is dominant in Ceylon, Japan, and India, although in all three cases there are strong pro-Peking factions.

Many Asian Communist parties deliberately adopt an attitude of nonalignment in the Sino-Soviet conflict in order to obtain greater freedom of action by playing one side against the other. Some of the Asian, African, and Latin American parties are truly neutral between Moscow and Peking; others are nonaligned but favoring

Drawing by J. Mirachi; © 1963 The New Yorker Magazine, Inc.

"JUST FOR KICKS, I'D LIKE TO PROPOSE THE ADMISSION OF RED CHINA AND WATCH HIS REACTION."

to some degree one side or the other. In some cases, the local Communist parties have been rent by internal dissension over the Sino-Soviet issue to such an extent that factions and splinter groups have developed, threatening the unity of the movement as a whole.

From the beginning of 1963 on, the Chinese communists have persistently played on one major theme in their conflict with Russia, a theme that has particular relevance in the underdeveloped countries: color. A mockery of anything even remotely related to Marx or Lenin, the theme of race and color may well become the most powerful weapon in the hands of the Chinese against the Russians. Fully aware that the majority of the world's people are nonwhite and that in most developing countries the colored vastly outnumber the whites, China is trying to create the image of Russia as but another white imperialist power, seeking to impose its will on the poor, nonwhite masses in Asia, Africa, and Latin America. Thus, when the Soviet Union signed the partial nuclear test-ban agreement with the United States and Great Britain in 1963, China refused to join, because she was eager to get ahead with her own atomic weapons program. Yet very soon she publicly attacked the agreement as another example of the Russians joining with the white imperialist "haves" against the "toiling masses" of the non-whites throughout the world. In the last few years, a favorite propaganda theme of China against the Soviet government has been the charge that Russia "is pursuing a policy of Soviet-U.S. collaboration for world domination" (*Peking Review,* September 2, 1966). In its campaign against the "filthy Soviet revisionist swine" (*Peking Review,* February 3, 1967), the Chinese have charged that the "Kremlin's new tsars" (another standard Chinese name for the Soviet government) "indoctrinate and drug Soviet youth with fascism and militarism," and that they behave "exactly like Hitler, Mussolini, and Tojo in their time" (*Peking Review,* August 6, 1969).

The struggle between the Soviet Union and communist China has shown that in their practical conduct communist states follow Lenin's emphasis on political power rather than Marx's "laws" of economic development. However, the doctrine and practice of political power are not novel contributions by Lenin and communism, but have existed throughout history. Similarly, communist states and parties have been guided in their attitudes toward Russia and China by considerations of national interest. This emphasis on national interest is an important stage in the process of denuding Marxism and Leninism of one of their fundamental doctrinal elements: faith in internationalism and the universal brotherhood of mankind. At first, the Sino-Soviet conflict was minimized by official communist rhetoric as a mere ideological controversy between two "fraternal" proletarian parties. Later, the dispute was recognized as a quarrel between two states, two systems of power. Today, the Sino-Soviet conflict is viewed everywhere as the most important potential danger of nuclear war between any two major powers in the world, possibly engulfing all continents.

FOR FURTHER READING

Alliluyeva, Svetlana. *Only One Year.* New York: Harper & Row, 1969.

Aron, Raymond. *Marxism and the Existentialists.* New York: Harper & Row, 1969.

Avineri, Shlomo. *The Social and Political Thought of Karl Marx.* New York: Cambridge University Press, 1968.

Berlin, Isaiah. *Karl Marx.* 3rd ed. New York: Oxford University Press, 1963.

Conquest, Robert. *The Great Terror.* New York: Macmillan, 1968.

Debray, Régis. *Revolution in the Revolution?* New York: Grove Press, 1967.

Djilas, Milovan. *The Unperfect Society: Beyond the New Class.* New York: Harcourt, Brace & World, 1969.

Drachkovitch, Milorad M. (ed.). *Marxism in the Modern World.* Stanford, Calif.: Stanford University Press, 1965.

Easton, Lloyd D., and Kurt H. Guddat (trans. and eds.). *Writings of the Young Marx on Philosophy and Society.* "Anchor Books." Garden City, N.Y.: Doubleday, 1967.

Ebenstein, William. *Great Political Thinkers.* 4th ed. New York: Holt, Rinehart & Winston, 1969. Chap. 23.

Fischer, George. *The Soviet System and Modern Society.* New York: Atherton, 1968.

Fischer, Louis. *The Life of Lenin.* "Harper Colophon Books." New York: Harper & Row, 1966.

Fromm, Erich. *Marx's Concept of Man.* New York: Ungar, 1961.

Goldhagen, Erich (ed.). *Ethnic Minorities in the Soviet Union.* New York: Praeger, 1968.

Goldman, Marshall I. *The Soviet Economy: Myth and Reality.* Englewood Cliffs, N.J.: Prentice-Hall, 1968.

Hanson, Philip. *The Consumer in the Soviet Economy.* Evanston, Ill.: Northwestern University Press, 1968.

Horowitz, Irving Louis. *Three Worlds of Development: The Theory and Practice of International Stratification.* New York: Oxford University Press, 1966.

Inkeles, Alex. *Social Change in Soviet Russia.* Cambridge, Mass.: Harvard University Press, 1968.

Joint Economic Committee, Congress of the United States. *Soviet Economic Performance, 1966–1967.* Washington, D.C.: U.S. Government Printing Office, 1968.

Kassof, Allen (ed.). *Prospects for Soviet Society.* New York: Praeger, 1968.

Kautsky, John H. *Communism and the Politics of Development: Persistent Myths and Changing Behavior.* New York: John Wiley, 1968.

Korol, Alexander G. *Soviet Research and Development: Its Organization, Personnel, and Funds.* Cambridge, Mass.: M.I.T. Press, 1965.

Littell, Robert (ed.). *The Czech Black Book: A Report on the Soviet Invasion.* New York: Praeger, 1969.

Little, D. Richard (ed.). *Liberalization in the USSR: Facade or Reality?* Lexington, Mass.: Heath, 1968.

Lobkowicz, Nicholas (ed.). *Marx and the Western World.* Notre Dame, Ind.: University of Notre Dame Press, 1967.

Lowenthal, Richard. *World Communism: The Distintegration of a Secular Faith.* "Galaxy Books." New York: Oxford University Press, 1966.

Nove, Alec. *The Soviet Economy.* 2nd rev. ed. New York: Praeger, 1969.

Pasternak, Boris. *Doctor Zhivago.* New York: Mentor Books, 1959.

Petrović, Gajo. *Marx in the Mid-Twentieth Century: A Yugoslav Philosopher Considers Karl Marx's Writings.* "Anchor Books." Garden City, N.Y.: Doubleday, 1967.

Rubinstein, Alvin Z. *Communist Political Systems.* Englewood Cliffs, N.J.: Prentice-Hall, 1966.

Scalapino, Robert A. (ed.). *The Communist Revolution in Asia: Tactics, Goals, and Achievements.* 2nd ed. Englewood Cliffs, N.J.: Prentice-Hall, 1969.

Schram, Stuart R. *The Political Thought of Mao Tse-tung.* Rev. ed. New York: Praeger, 1969.

Schurmann, Franz, and Orville Schell (eds.). *Communist China: Revolutionary Reconstruction and International Confrontation, 1949 to the Present.* "Vintage Books." New York: Random House, 1967.

Schwartz, Benjamin I. *Communism and China: Ideology in Flux.* Cambridge, Mass.: Harvard University Press, 1968.

Schwartz, Harry. *Prague's 200 Days: The Struggle for Democracy in Czechoslovakia.* New York: Praeger, 1969.

Solzhenitsyn, Alexander. *One Day in the Life of Ivan Denisovich.* New York: Bantam Books, 1963.

Strauss, Erich. *Soviet Agriculture in Perspective: A Study of Its Successes and Failures.* New York: Praeger, 1969.

Wesson, Robert G. *Soviet Foreign Policy in Perspective.* Homewood, Ill.: Dorsey, 1969.

Zawodny, J. K. *Death in the Forest: The Story of the Katyn Forest Massacre.* Notre Dame, Ind.: Notre Dame University Press, 1962.

Zeman, Z. A. B. *Prague Spring.* New York: Hill & Wang, 1969.

totalitarian
fascism

chapter two

SOCIAL BACKGROUND OF FASCISM

Communism was the first major twentieth-century revolutionary, totalitarian revolt against the liberal way of life; *fascism* was the second. Stripped to its essentials, fascism is the totalitarian organization of government and society by a single-party dictatorship, intensely nationalist, racist, militarist, and imperialist. In Europe, Italy was the first to go fascist in 1922, and Germany followed in 1933. In Asia, Japan became fascist in the 1930's, gradually evolving totalitarian institutions out of its own native heritage. In the western hemisphere, a semiconstitutional government of a landed oligarchy was destroyed in Argentina in 1943 in a revolt of dissatisfied officers, and a fascist dictatorship was subsequently built up under the leadership of Colonel (later General) Perón, lasting until its overthrow in 1955.

Clearly, then, whereas communism is typically linked with poor and underdeveloped nations (Russia in Europe, China in Asia), fascism is the form of totalitarianism that typically grows in wealthier and technologically more advanced nations (Germany in Europe, Japan in Asia). In the Americas, Guatemala, one of the poorest and most backward nations, for years encouraged the growth of communism until the procommunist regime of President Arbenz was overthrown in June 1954 with American aid. Cuba, less poor than Guatemala, is a more recent example of communism in the Americas. Significantly, Castro fought his rebellion under the banner of democracy, not of communism, and turned to Marxism-Leninism only after his victory. Fascism, on the other hand, saw its most intense development in Argentina, the wealthiest of the 20 Latin American republics.

Whereas communism is very largely the product of predemocratic and preindustrial societies, fascism is *postdemocratic* and *postindustrial:* fascism is unlikely to seize power in countries with no democratic experience at all. In such societies, dictatorship may be based on the army, the bureaucracy, or the personal prestige of the dictator, but it will lack the element of mass enthusiasm and *mass support* (not necessarily majority support) characteristic of fascism. Moreover, although no fascist system is apt to arise in a country without some democratic experience (as in Germany or Japan), there is not much likelihood of fascist success in countries that have experienced democracy over a long period.

Paradoxically, experience has proved that, in general, the more violent and terroristic fascist movements are, the more popular support they tend to have. Thus fascism in Germany was both the most brutal and the most popular political movement; in Italy fascism was less popular and less brutal. Such fascist dictatorships based on mass support are not to be confused with traditional dictatorships such as existed in Europe in several countries during the 1930's, particularly in the Balkans and eastern Europe. The present authoritarian dictatorships in Spain and Portugal, too, are essentially traditional, and rest on the established forces of the bureaucracy and army.

In Latin America, there also are numerous dictatorships, but they are not fascist (with the exception of Argentina from 1943 to 1955) because they typically rest on the personal magic or force of one man, usually a general. Relying as he must on the good will of his army, the Latin American dictator has no need for, and rarely has, the mass support that characterizes fascism. Popular political movements hardly enter the picture.

The second condition essential to the growth of fascism is some degree of industrial development. There are at least two principal points of contact between fascism and relatively advanced industrialization. First, fascist terror and propaganda require a good deal of technological organization and know-how. Second, as a system of *permanent mobilization for war,* fascism cannot hope to succeed without considerable industrial skills and resources.

It may be argued that the connection between fascism and modern industry goes even deeper. Every industrial society brings about social and economic tensions. Such tensions can be dealt with in one of two ways: the liberal way or the totalitarian way. The liberal society recognizes the variety of economic interests and their necessary conflict (such as between labor and management, agriculture and industry, skilled and unskilled workers) and seeks to reconcile such conflicts by the experimental method of peaceful, gradual adjustment. The fascist state either denies that there are divergent social interests (abhorring as it does the notion of variety, especially in the form of departures from state-imposed uniformity) or, if it half-heartedly concedes the existence of divergent social interests, it resolves such differences by force.

The difference between communism and fascism on this point may be briefly (and with some oversimplification) formulated in this way: communism is the totalitarian way of *industrializing an underdeveloped society;* fascism is the totalitarian method of *solving conflicts within an industrially more advanced society.*

In its social background, fascism has particularly appealed to two groups: first, a numerically small group of *industrialists* and *landowners* who are willing to finance fascist movements in the hope of getting rid of free labor unions. Industrialists are not, as a class, any more fascist-minded than other social groups; in countries with strong liberal and democratic traditions, for example, industrialists are no better and no worse than other people as far as their faith in the democratic process is concerned. But where democracy is weak, as in Germany, Italy, or Japan, it took only a few wealthy industrialists and landowners to supply fascist movements with ample funds.

Where the pressure of public opinion is strongly democratic and liberal, individual industrialists who are inclined toward fascism will find that supporting fascist groups is bad business; but where democratic traditions are weak, leaders of big business like Thyssen and Krupp in Germany, or the Mitsui trust in Japan, found it possible to side openly with the cause of fascism.

The second main source of fascist support—and numerically by far the most important—comes from the lower middle classes, mostly in the salaried group. Many persons in this class dread the prospect of joining (or rejoining) the proletariat and look to fascism for a salvation of their status and prestige. The salaried employee feels jealous of big business, into whose higher echelons he would like to rise, and fearful of labor, into whose proletarian world he would hate to descend. Fascism very cleverly utilizes these jealousies and fears of the salariat by propagandizing simultaneously against big business and big labor. Although such propaganda is neither logically nor politically consistent, its very inconsistency both reflects and appeals to the confusion of the salaried class, uncertain as that class is where to turn politically.

In the United States, anxiety over preserving one's threatened status has been one of the main psychological forces exploited by the Radical Right (John Birch Society, Minute Men) and by fascist groups. This status anxiety has been centered, above all, on the rising power of organized labor, which is perceived as a threat to the existing status quo. In addition, American fascist and semifascist propaganda has focused on white fears of the rising status of blacks. As in other countries, racial hostility is stronger in psychologically more insecure lower-middle-class groups than in the better educated and more affluent middle and upper classes.

Paradoxically, organized labor frequently contributes to this uncertainty and demoralization of the salariat without meaning to do so. For psychological reasons, white-collar workers are generally unwilling to organize into unions. As a result, the *incomes of workers,* particularly those organized in unions, *have tended to improve much faster than the incomes of salaried employees.* As the gap between the economic status of workers and that of salaried persons widens, the latter become more and more resentful of losing what they consider their rightful place in society and may turn to fascism, which promises to keep unions under control. The leaders of organized labor may point out that the weak economic position of salaried persons is their own fault and that such persons are in error in refusing to organize and bring pressure upon their employers; such arguing points, however, though they may be logically valid, are psychologically ineffective. In times of prosperity the divergence between labor and the salaried class may not be too upsetting politically, but in times of crisis and depression the smallest class antagonisms may turn into political dynamite.

Another important social group that has shown itself particularly vulnerable to fascist propaganda is the military. Even in a strong and well-established democracy, professional military people tend to overestimate the virtues of discipline and unity; where democracy is weak, this professional bias of the military becomes a political menace. Thus, in the early stages of Nazism in Germany, the military class of the nation either openly supported Hitler or at best maintained an attitude of benevolent neutrality. The top military leaders of Germany knew that a high proportion of Nazi bosses were criminals and unscrupulous psychopaths, yet they supported the Nazi movement as a step toward the militarization of the German people. In Italy too, fascism in its early stages received considerable support from army circles, and in Japan fascism developed with the active and enthusiastic support of the army, which had every reason to be the main pillar of a regime committed to imperialist expansion. In Argentina, semiconstitutional government was overthrown in 1943 in a revolt of the "younger officers," under Perón, who set up his own brand of fascism, named *peronismo* after him.

Yet it should be pointed out that the military often play a leading part in getting rid of fascist and other kinds of dictatorial government. Perón himself learned this lesson in 1955, and the same thing has happened to several other Latin American dictators since the end of World War II. Once fascism is established, people often look to the army as one of the last remaining bulwarks of decency and legality. Therefore, fascism (like communism) indulges in periodic purges of the armed forces, because fascist leaders realize that the army is one of the few institutions left that enjoy genuine popular respect.

Although fascism is not a direct or necessary result of economic depression, as Marxist-communist theory suggests, there is a relation between the two. In times of depression, fear and frustration undermine faith in the democratic process, and where the faith in rational methods weakens, fascism is the potential gainer. The small businessman blames big business for his troubles; big business puts the blame on the unreasonableness of the labor unions; labor feels that the only way out is to soak the rich; the farmers feel that they are not getting enough for farm products and that they are made to pay too high prices for manufactured goods; and—worst of all—there is the large mass of unemployed people.

What democratic nations have failed to understand sufficiently is that the worst feature of unemployment is not economic suffering (which can be mitigated by adequate relief), but the feeling of being useless, unwanted, outside the respectable ranks of society. It is among these spiritually homeless that fascism makes serious inroads during a depression: by putting an unemployed person into a uniform, a fascist movement makes him feel that he "belongs," and by telling him that he is a member of a superior race or nation, such a movement restores some of his self-respect.

The Black Muslims have sought to exploit the feeling of "not belonging" among American blacks. The rate of unemployment is, in prosperity and depression, twice as high among nonwhites as it is among whites, and many nonwhites therefore feel excluded from existing society both racially and economically. In their propaganda the Black Muslims have tried to make the Negro feel that he belongs to a superior race and that he must dissociate himself from the corrupt and unjust white world, by force if necessary. In their appeal to racialism and change by force, in their pride in African culture, and in their promise of building independent black political communities on American soil, the Black Muslims thus aim at restoring Negro self-respect.

The sense of not belonging is, in a way, characteristic of life in modern industrial society in general. Industrialization and urbanization have debunked and frequently destroyed traditional values, without always providing adequate substitute values in their place. The disorientation and confusion resulting from these effects of industrialization provide the social and psychological background of fascism and its attempt to restore the old, preindustrial way of life in a modern nation.

It can thus be seen that the Marxist interpretation of fascism in terms of class (identifying fascism with capitalism in decay) is not borne out by the facts. *Fascism cuts across all social groups;* wealthy industrialists and landowners support it for one reason, the lower middle classes for another, and some blue-collar workers for another still. Finally, there are the many nationalists and chauvinists in every country who prove themselves vulnerable to promises of conquest and empire. In terms of explicit programs, fascist movements must make the most contradictory promises to satisfy all their adherents; such contradictions are one main weakness of fascism. Yet in terms of implicit psychological background, fascism looks within all social groups for the great common denominators, *frustration, resentment,* and *insecurity.* These psychological attitudes can easily be turned into hatred and aggression, against both internal and external "enemies."

Because these social and psychological attitudes are not the monopoly of any one social class, fascism manages to appeal to large masses of people in some countries. When Adolf Hitler joined the Nazi party in 1919, he was Member No. 7. Yet within fourteen years Nazism became the greatest mass movement in German history, including in its ranks members of all groups of German society, from hobos to members of the imperial family and the royal houses of the German states. By 1932, the Nazi vote had mounted to 14 million, and in March 1933, 17 million Germans (almost half the total vote) voted for Nazism; several more millions voted for nationalist and militarist parties that were Nazi in all but name. It is obvious that 17 million voters cannot consist exclusively of wealthy bankers and industrialists and that only a party with national, rather than class, appeal can obtain such large votes. In no other country has fascism ever been as widely popular as in Germany, but there has been no fascist regime anywhere without some popular support.

PSYCHOLOGICAL ROOTS OF
TOTALITARIANISM

In countries like Germany and Japan, the clue to the understanding of fascist tendencies lies in broad social forces and traditions. In those countries, the authoritarian tradition has been predominant and democracy is still a very frail plant. As a result, a German or Japanese with fascist tendencies is no outcast and may be considered perfectly well adjusted to his society. Even when his society explicitly condemns fascism, much in the implicit habits and customs of German and Japanese life tends toward the authoritarian way of life, and from authoritarianism to fascism is only a step. In democratic societies, on the other hand, the appeal of fascism can be more fruitfully judged from the angle of individual psychology. Empirical studies in the United States have shown that ten percent of Americans are strongly authoritarian and about 20 percent partly authoritarian (T. W. Adorno and others, *The Authoritarian Personality*, 1950).

Traditional analysis of political dictatorship has been centered on the motivations of dictatorial leaders, driven by lust for power and sadistic cravings for domination. The followers and subjects of a dictatorship are viewed exclusively as "victims" who just happen to fall into the misfortune of oppressive rule. Every insurance company knows that some persons are more accident-prone than others, and every policeman knows that some persons are more likely to attract criminals than others.

Similarly, it is not too farfetched to suggest that some people and some nations are more "dictatorship-prone" than others. Plato's psychological insight led him to suggest in his *Republic* that constitutions grow not "from stone to stone," but "from those characters of the men in the cities which preponderate and draw the rest of the city after them." The very existence of an authoritarian mass movement like fascism depends on the *desire* of many persons *to submit and obey.*

Rational democrats may not understand why anyone should prefer to obey rather than take the responsibility of making decisions for himself; they take it for granted that men *should* make their own decisions rather than have their actions dictated by others. But this democratic stereotype overlooks the *comforts of irresponsibility* to many persons. Children love the feeling of being sheltered and secure behind the benevolent power and authority of their parents. The mark of the mature adult is his willingness and capacity to stand on his own feet, to take responsibility and be independent of others. Yet relatively few persons ever attain this sort of maturity; the process of growing up, as every adolescent knows, is painful, and many rebel against a cold world where they must struggle for themselves without the omnipotence and omniscience of parental love and security. In all human beings there is a *latent tendency toward dependence* based on the parent-child relationship, although some people manage to achieve a more self-reliant adulthood than others. The totalitarian system, whether communist or fascist, appeals to people who, for whatever personal reasons, look for the father-child relationship, for security through dependence.

What are some of the empirically ascertainable traits that characterize the authoritarian personality, particularly the personality attracted to the fascist type of authoritarianism? First, a tendency to conform compulsively to orthodox ideals and practices; emotional rigidity and limited imagination; excessive concern with problems of status and strength; strong loyalty to one's own group coupled with vehement dislike of outsiders; and stress on discipline and obedience rather than freedom and spontaneity in human re-lations (education, sex, family, religion, industry, government). The "herd-minded" (or ethnocentric) element in the fascist personality is perhaps the single most important one, although no one element in itself conclusively defines a personality as authoritarian.

The key role of the *family* in the formation of basic attitudes seems to be brought out by all clinical and theoretical studies; but the family is not, after all, an isolated and independent agent. Rather, it reflects the predominant social goals and values and con-stitutes to the child the cultural and psychological representative of society at large.

No person is ever completely authoritarian or completely demo-cratic, just as no human being is ever an utter devil or a perfect angel. In each case it is a question of quantity and degree, although differences of quantity eventually become differences of quality. Although there has been no major fascist mass movement in the United States so far, it is a matter of record that some Americans looked upon German and Italian fascism in the 1930's as the "wave of the future" (as it was called in a book of that title) and that others sympathized with Argentine fascism in the 1940's and 1950's.

Dependence and submission in a totalitarian society—fascist or communist—give a person the security for which he hungers but deny him self-expression and self-assertion, the needs for which are as deeply embedded in human nature as the desire for security. Thus denied, these drives turn into repressed hostility and aggres-sion, for the expression of which fascism provides two channels, one for the ruling class, one for the ruled. Within the apparatus of the dictatorial party and government, there is the pattern of the cyclist: crouching before the superior above, pressing down on the subordinate below. Only the leader need not crouch before any-one—he only presses down. Below the top leader—"Big Brother," as Orwell called him in *1984*, the classic fictional portrait of totali-tarianism—although each member of the party and government hierarchy must kowtow to someone above him, in return he may tread on those below him.

Persons outside the ruling class, however, have no one to com-mand; they can only obey. How can they express their hostility and aggressiveness? Since the vast majority of the people in a totalitarian state form the group of those who can only take, but not issue, commands, this is a serious problem for every dictatorship. Although officially the dictator claims that he is universally beloved, he knows that there is much repressed hatred and hostility directed (or capable of being directed) toward him and his regime.

The answer of totalitarian dictatorships is to *direct this latent hostility of the people against real or imaginary enemies.* For the communist, the enemy may be the bourgeoisie, Trotskyites, Titoites, or Wall Street. Hitler first chose the Jews as the target of German aggression; once given a direction for their savagery, the Germans were not satisfied until they had sent six million Jews to the gas chambers. Later new enemies took the place of the Jews: Britain, the United States, Churchill, Roosevelt, Bolshevism, the churches. When they felt that the end was close, Hitler and his cohorts unleashed their vengeance on the Germans themselves; if they had to go down, the German people had to be destroyed with them. In a more recent fascist regime, Peronist Argentina, American imperialism and international finance were the chief targets of fascist hate propaganda.

To men who cannot be masters of their own lives, fascism promises mastery over other people; and if fascism cannot deliver the triumphs it promises, the hatred of the people may turn against their leaders, as it did against Mussolini, who was tried before a partisan committee in northern Italy in April 1945, executed, and then publicly hung from a lamp post in Milan. Having taught his people violence and hatred, he reaped himself what he had sown.

The psychological interpretation of totalitarianism—fascist or communist—is of particular value where the prevailing cultural pattern is not authoritarian, where it takes some personal deviance to break with the democratic pattern of the environment. Thus, in societies like Britain or the United States, the psychological analysis of people who have embraced communism or fascism is of great value because from such an analysis emerges a definite pattern of personality factors that is typical in many American fascists or communists.

Yet it would be futile to explain the historical strength of fascism in Germany or Japan, or of communism in China or Italy, by means of personal psychology. It may be argued that an American or an

Englishman who embraces communism or fascism is not well adjusted, comes from a broken home, or has had an unhappy childhood, but the same can hardly be said of 17 million Germans who voted for Hitler in 1933 or of the many millions of Frenchmen and Italians who have persistently voted communist since the end of World War II. Where totalitarianism assumes the proportions of a mass movement, the main avenue of analysis must be that of the great social, economic, and cultural forces and traditions of a nation.

Whereas the cure for an American fascist or communist may be found on the psychoanalyst's couch, the cure for millions of Italians who vote communist is more take-home pay every Saturday and a more decent life all around. Similarly, the origins of fascist totalitarianism in Germany, Japan, and Argentina lie deeper in the collective lives of those nations than can be revealed from a study of individual personalities. There was plenty that was wrong in Hitler's personality as viewed through non-German eyes, but to the 17 million Germans who identified themselves with him in the election of March 1933, he must have been an admirably adjusted personality.

ELEMENTS OF FASCIST DOCTRINE AND POLICY

Although fascism, like communism, is a movement that exists everywhere, it has no such authoritative statement of principles as communism has; moreover, no one country, at present, is directing a fascist world conspiracy. During the Nazi regime (1933–1945), Germany was the most powerful fascist state in existence, and world fascism was very largely directed, financed, and inspired by German brains and money. Since the defeat of the fascist Axis (Germany, Japan, Italy) in World War II, however, there has been no really major fascist state; Argentina never possessed anything like the worldwide influence that Nazi Germany had until 1945.

The absence of a universally recognized, authoritative statement of fascist principles is not total. Hitler has left in *Mein Kampf* (1925–1927) a trustworthy guide to his thought, and Mussolini's *The Doctrine of Fascism* (1932), a moderate statement of fascist principles, expresses the Italian brand of fascism. The latter has served as a model for most other fascist movements in the world because it is much broader in outlook; Nazism, a specifically German brand of fascism, has proved less suitable for export.

Although there is no *Fascist Manifesto* with undisputed authority among fascists, it is not too difficult to state the principal elements of the fascist outlook:

1. Distrust of reason
2. Denial of basic human equality
3. Code of behavior based on lies and violence
4. Government by elite
5. Totalitarianism
6. Racism and imperialism
7. Opposition to international law and order

1. *Distrust of reason* is perhaps the most significant trait of fascism. The rational tradition of the West stems from Greece and is one of the basic components that have given the West its characteristic culture and outlook. Fascism rejects this Greek root of Western civilization and is frankly *antirationalist,* distrusting reason in human affairs and stressing the irrational, sentimental, uncontrollable elements of man. Psychologically, fascism is *fanatical* rather than reflective, *dogmatic* rather than open-minded; as a result each fascist regime has its taboo issues such as race, empire, the leader, and it is the nature of a taboo issue that it must be accepted on faith and cannot be critically discussed. During the fascist regime in Italy (1922–1945), Mussolini's picture was shown in every classroom in the country over the caption "Mussolini is always right."

The communist states have the taboo issue of Marxism-Leninism, a set of final truths that must not be questioned. In addition, there are the more passing taboo subjects as defined by the top party leaders in Russia, China, or Yugoslavia.

As a matter of basic principle, *democracy recognizes no taboo issue:* there is no subject that cannot be questioned or challenged, not even the validity of democracy itself. In practice, of course, democracies do not always live up to that ideal. Thus, it was argued by some in the 1950's that in the United States the question of the validity of democracy was on its way to becoming a taboo issue, especially since the Supreme Court's 1951 decision upholding the constitutionality of the Smith Act of 1940 (under which the advocacy of the duty, desirability, necessity, or propriety of revolution is a criminal offense).

The individual, too, may have taboo issues, dark corners in his heart or mind that must not be pulled out and subjected to rational examination. The mentally healthy individual has few or (ideally) no taboo issues because he is able to face reality as it is and does not insist on living in a dream world in defiance of reality. Psychologically, the existence of taboo issues in the individual or in a group, party, or nation is due to a sense of insecurity or guilt, or both.

Under conditions of stress and strain, the individual as well as the collective group may take refuge in the temporary shelter of the taboo, postponing the facing of reality but unable to shut it out forever. Since totalitarian regimes operate in a permanent state of high tension and crisis, the taboo is part and parcel of their normal environment. Democracies succumb to the temptation of the taboo, and its false security, only in periods of exceptional strain; it is significant that the Supreme Court's decision on the Smith Act took place in 1951, at the height of the Korean war. In the 1960's, a more tolerant and reflective mood prevailed, and the Supreme Court has greatly liberalized its views on the constitutionality of revolutionary propaganda and organizations.

2. The *denial of basic human equality* is a common denominator of fascist movements and states. True enough, democratic societies do not always live up to the ideal of human equality, but they at least accept equality as the long-term goal of public policy. By contrast, fascist societies not only accept the *fact* of human inequality but go further and affirm inequality as an *ideal.*

The concept of human equality goes back to the three roots of Western civilization. The Jewish idea of one God led to the idea of one mankind, since all men, as children of God, are brothers among themselves. The Christian notion of the inalienability and indestructibility of the human soul led to the ideal of basic *moral* equality of all men. Finally, the Greek-Stoic concept of reason led to the oneness of mankind on the basis of reason as the most truly human bond that all men have in common.

Fascism rejects this Jewish-Christian-Greek concept of equality and opposes to it the concept of inequality, which can most simply be spelled out in the contrast of superiority and inferiority. Thus, in the fascist code, men are superior to women, soldiers to civilians, party members to nonparty members, one's own nation to others, the strong to the weak, and (perhaps most important in the fascist outlook) the victors in war to the vanquished. The chief criteria of equality in the Western tradition are man's mind and soul, whereas the fascist affirmation of inequality is based ultimately on *strength*.

3. The fascist code of behavior stresses *violence and lies* in all human relations, within and between nations. From the democratic viewpoint, politics is the mechanism through which social conflicts of interest are peacefully adjusted. By contrast, the fascist view is that politics is characterized by the *friend-enemy relation.* Politics begins and ends, in this fascist way of thinking, with the possibility of an enemy—and his *total annihilation.* The democratic antithesis to the friend is the *opponent,* and in democratic nations the opponent of today is considered the potential government of tomorrow. (The opposition in the British Parliament is officially called "Her Majesty's Loyal Opposition," and the leader of the Opposition receives a special salary to do his job well.) The fascist knows only enemies, not opponents, and since enemies represent evil incarnate, total annihilation is the only solution. This doctrine applies to domestic as well as to foreign enemies; thus, the Nazis first set up concentration camps and gas chambers for German citizens and later used them for non-Germans.

Contrary to common opinion, *concentration camps* and *slave labor camps* are not incidental phenomena in totalitarian systems like fascism and communism but are of their very core. It is in the concentration and slave labor camps that totalitarian regimes seek to destroy the legal and moral person in man and to deprive him of the last residue of individuality. The technique of brainwashing used by fascists and communists deliberately seeks to break a man's mind to the point where he will publicly confess to crimes he did not commit and perhaps could not have committed. After a period of brainwashing, the victim no longer has a mind of his own; he merely plays back, like a record, what is expected of him.

By institutionalizing organized mass murder in concentration and slave labor camps, totalitarian regimes demonstrate to the entire population what is in store for anyone in disfavor with the men in power, and at the same time they provide the shock troops of the regime with a peacetime outlet for savagery and fanaticism. Immediate death is often considered too humane a penalty by such regimes; moreover, the slow death of concentration or slave labor camps has a greater demonstration value than the clean, old-fashioned method of the execution squad or the gallows.

4. *Government by elite* is a principle that fascists everywhere frankly oppose to the "democratic fallacy" that people are capable of governing themselves. The concept that only a small minority of the population, qualified by birth, education, or social standing, is capable of understanding what is best for the whole community, and of putting it into practice, is not an invention of twentieth-century fascism. Plato, one of the founders of Western political philosophy, strongly believed that only one class, the "philosopher-kings," are fit to rule society. The contrary belief, that the people as a whole are capable of self-rule, is of relatively recent origin and has successfully worked only in limited areas of the globe.

Although the fascist idea of government by a self-appointed elite (a fascist government usually shoots its way into power) is undemocratic, such a government does not always lack popular approval. Strange as it may seem to the democrat, people throughout history have frequently approved of autocratic governments. Approval alone, however, is no evidence of democracy. What makes a government democratic is that it always depends on popular consent given frequently in free elections. In fascist regimes, even when the government enjoys popular approval, it is carried on independently of popular consent, without free elections, a free press, or a freely functioning opposition.

The fascist *leadership principle* expresses the extreme form of the elite concept. It fully reflects the irrational nature of fascist politics; the leader is considered infallible, endowed with mystical gifts and insights. In a conflict between popular opinion and the fascist leader, the will of the leader prevails; he represents the public interest, the way all people would think if they knew what was best for the whole community (Rousseau's "General Will"), whereas the people express only individual whims and desires not necessarily in harmony with public good (Rousseau's "Will of All").

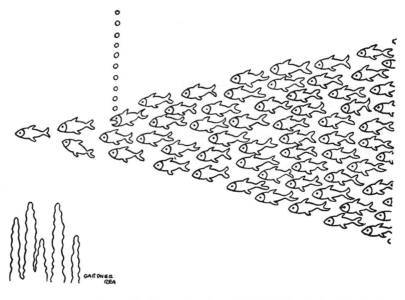

"GOD KNOWS WHAT WE'D DO
IF ANYTHING SHOULD EVER HAPPEN TO HIM!"

The emphasis on leadership is contrary to the fascist enforcement of orthodoxy and conformity. Hitler, Mussolini, and Perón grew up in nonfascist societies with considerable free competition. So far it has been impossible to appraise the leadership qualities of a generation born and bred under fascism. The German, Italian, and Argentine brands of fascism did not last long enough to supply conclusive evidence on the matter.

5. *Totalitarianism* in all human relations characterizes fascism as a way of life rather than as a mere system of government. There are many dictatorships, particularly in Latin America, in which the authoritarian principle is applied only in government. If the people do not make any trouble politically and do not interfere with the rule of the dictator and his henchmen, they can lead their own lives pretty freely. Education, religion, business, and agriculture are not

touched very much by the political dictatorship. By contrast, fascism is totalitarian; it employs authority and violence in *all* kinds of social relations, whether political or not.

With regard to women, the largest discriminated-against minority of the world, fascism is antifeminist. Women should stay in their place, said the Nazis, and their concern should be the famous three K's—*Kinder, Küche, Kirche.* Since women are considered unable to bear arms, they are automatically second-class citizens according to the fascist view, and they are excluded from leadership positions in government or party. They have the right to vote, but since this right in fascist countries means only the right to be enthusiastic about the leader and his party, it is not much of a practical asset. Within the family the father is the leader, and his wife and children get a strong taste of domestic authoritarian government, which has more effect on their everyday lives than the operations of the remote political government in the capital. In the extreme case of modern fascism, Nazi Germany, the contempt for women was finally demonstrated in the official ridicule of the institution of marriage as a false Jewish-Christian prejudice, and German women were encouraged to produce children for the fatherland outside of wedlock.

Fascist countries also make a point of refusing to employ women extensively in schools. From the fascist viewpoint, schools are to teach discipline and obedience, specifically to prepare the boys for military service and the girls for related domestic activities. In a program of such importance, fascist educators feel women teachers have no place.

Thus it can be seen that fascist totalitarianism, unlike the old-fashioned dictatorships of Latin America, is *totalitarian in its objective:* to control all phases of human life, political or not, from the cradle to the grave. It begins the control even before the cradle, by pushing definite population policies, and has been known to reach into the grave, so to speak, to decide whether a dead person should have a burial at all and, if so, in what form.

But fascism is also *totalitarian in its means.* It will use any form of coercion, from verbal threats to mass murder, in obtaining its ends. By contrast, the classical authoritarian dictatorship was, and is, more restrained in its means and resorts to murder only on a limited scale. Thus, whenever a Latin American dictator is ousted, he is usually permitted by his opponents to assemble his family and peacefully depart to a foreign country.

6. *Racism and imperialism* express the two basic fascist principles of inequality and violence as applied to the society of nations. Within the nation, fascist doctrine holds, the elite is superior to the rest and may impose its will upon them by force. Similarly, between nations the *elite nation* is superior to others and is entitled to rule them. German fascism went furthest in its racist and imperialist policies. A straight line led from the theories of the superiority of the German-Nordic "race" to the mass murder of millions of people. The German objective of world domination included the elimination of some nations through genocide and the enslavement of the rest. After the expected defeat of Britain and Russia, the United States was to be next on the list. The Japanese race theories found their practical imperialist expression in the concept of "co-prosperity," under which Japan would prosper by exploiting Asia and the Pacific.

Italian fascism was for a long time (from 1922 to 1938) remarkably free of exaggerated race theories; early Italian propaganda in this general field concentrated on the idea of reviving the old Roman empire. In 1938, however, Mussolini discovered that the Italians were a pure and superior race, and he became more closely tied to Hitler's Germany.

In Argentina, the Perón government strongly emphasized the mission and destiny of Argentina and accompanied this doctrine of Argentine superiority with a deliberate policy of imperialism. Peronist imperialism, probably out of respect for the tremendous power of the United States in the western hemisphere, which makes any fascist territorial ventures highly dangerous, limited itself to economic, political, and ideological expansion; but Argentina built up a vast armament industry, and her neighbors could not help wondering against whom this Argentine war potential was to be used. Only the overthrow of the Perón dictatorship in 1955 removed these fears of Argentine imperialism.

Racism and imperialism are not an exclusive monopoly of fascism. During World War II, the Soviet Union annexed Estonia, Latvia, and Lithuania. After the war, it helped itself to portions of Germany, Czechoslovakia, Poland, Finland, and Romania. Also, Russian leadership in the multinational Soviet Union has been increasingly stressed, differing only in degree from the Great Russian superiority concept as it was officially held in tsarist Russia. More recently, China has made use of the propaganda argument of race and color in her struggle with Russia for supremacy in the communist world and for leading the developing countries—mostly inhabited by non-whites—toward communist revolution.

Baldy in The Atlanta Constitution

" . . . SURE WE'VE COMPLIED, HERE'S OUR NEGRO!"

In the democracies too, there is a tradition of racism; in the United States, for example, racial discrimination has seriously corroded the vitality of democratic ideals. Called (by the Swedish social scientist Gunnar Myrdal) "the American dilemma," the race issue may ultimately decide the fate of democracy in the United States. Britain, with a much smaller proportion of nonwhites in its population (two percent, compared with twelve percent in the United States), has also been beset by racial tensions in the 1960's. While the issue of race is less burning in Britain than in the United States, it has brought to the fore latent prejudices and popular sentiments that sharply contradict the British liberal tradition of the last hundred years. If communists have skillfully exploited American and British racialism in their propaganda in the largely nonwhite developing nations, they have been able to do so because there is enough substance to validate much of that propaganda.

7. *Opposition to international law and order* is the logical outcome of the fascist belief in inequality, violence, racism, imperialism, and war. Whereas nonfascists (with the exception of nonresisting pacifists) accept war as a tragic fact, which should be abolished, fascists raise war to the level of an ideal, because, as Mussolini put it, "war alone brings up to their highest tension all human energies and puts the stamp of nobility upon the peoples who have the courage to meet it."

Any type of international organization assumes some form of government by consent, which is directly contradictory to the fascist principle of *government by force*. Also, equality of states before the law of nations is a basic principle of international order. The fascist concept of the elite leads, as we have seen, to the leadership of one nation over the society of nations as it does to the leadership of one man within the nation's government. Fascist states, therefore, shy away from international organizations in which they are expected to abide by majority decisions and in which government is carried on by methods of discussion rather than by force.

The fascist regimes of Italy and Germany had no use for the League of Nations; Germany withdrew in 1933 and Italy in 1937. In the United Nations, Peronist Argentina consistently played a lone wolf role. In the Organization of American States, she did all she could to prevent effective cooperation between the United States and the Latin American republics—a policy that was later faithfully copied by Cuba under Castro.

In West Germany, neo-Nazi groups merged into the National Democratic Party (NDP) in 1964. In addition to taking a hard line on communism and law and order, the NDP has particularly stressed a strongly nationalist position on issues affecting Germany's relations with other nations. Thus, the NDP favors German withdrawal from all supranational bodies, such as the Common Market, NATO, and the special agencies of the United Nations, since in the view of the NDP there must be no outside interference with German sovereignty. The NDP also takes a belligerent stand on the issue of the lost German territories in the East after World War II, and favors the use of German armed forces for strictly nationalist objectives.

In sum, it can be seen that fascist theory and practice of international politics are not so different from those of communism. Both accept force and conflict as the vehicles of resolving differences.

For the communist, the concept of *class* plays the dominant role in the struggle, whereas fascism sees in *race* and *nation* the key concepts in the dynamics of change.

In practice, communism and fascism lead to similar results, although their theoretical starting points differ. When Germany and Russia finally clashed in 1941, the reason was not ideological but practical; they could not agree on the division of the spoils. Since Russia was not satisfied with German proposals for dividing up the world, Germany attacked Russia as an obstacle on its path to world dominion.

FASCIST ECONOMICS:
THE CORPORATE STATE

The corporate state applies fascist principles of organization and control to the economy. The fascist economy is subdivided in state-controlled associations of capital and labor, and each association has a monopoly in its trade or occupation. *The one-party state is the ultimate arbiter of conflicts between capital and labor.*

The philosophy of the corporate state rests on two assumptions. First, man (except for the small ruling elite) should not be politically articulate as a citizen but only as a worker, entrepreneur, farmer, doctor, or lawyer; general political problems are assumed to be too complicated for the mass of the people, who are only expected to understand issues that bear directly on their vocational or professional work. Second, members of the small ruling elite are supposed to understand broad problems that affect the whole society, and they alone are therefore qualified to govern the community. This conception is Platonic in origin, and in modern times antidemocratic thinkers like Burke and Hegel have supported it against the claims of the democratic theory.

The democratic conception rejects this corporate approach to economic and political organization for several reasons. In the first place, it is not always easy to separate economic from political aspects. Tariffs seem to be a purely economic issue, yet they directly affect political and diplomatic relations with other states. Immigration seems at first sight to be an economic problem, yet delicate psychological and diplomatic issues are involved in it. Economic aid to other nations, as the United States has learned in the last 25 years, has profound military and political aspects as well as economic effects.

Second, the democratic theory holds that only the man who wears the shoe knows where it pinches—the mystic knowledge and insight of the ruling elite are no substitute for the experience of the ruled—or, as Aristotle put it, the guest is a better judge of the meal than the cook. Fascists insist that the cook not only ought to be the final judge of his product but also should impose his judgment on the guests, by force if necessary.

Finally, the democratic theory rejects the fascist assumption that members of one particular class are superior in judgment to the rest of the people and are therefore the nation's natural rulers. Formal education can supply knowledge only, not judgment. Judgment is not something that can be learned in fascist schools for leaders; it is the result of character, intelligence, experience, and personal philosophy. Formal training and education in leadership, party doctrine, public administration, history, and politics do not necessarily add up to true leadership. Jesus did not obtain a Ph.D. in religion, Socrates did not attend a school of education, Lincoln did not major in political science, and Churchill never went to college at all.

The kind of wisdom and moral courage that make up the essence of leadership may be greatly aided by formal education, but the two should not be confused. The democratic theory thus rejects the assumption of fascist doctrine that only a small elite has insight into the public good. From the democratic viewpoint, only God has a perfect understanding of Truth with a capital T, but every man is capable, at least partially, of seeing truth with a small t.

What the one-party state with secret police and concentration camps is to the political side of fascist regimes, corporatism is to fascism's social and economic aspects. Just as in the political sphere fascism replaces the pivotal concept of individual liberty with unlimited state authority, so in the economic sphere it rejects the conception of a free welfare economy—be it capitalist, socialist, or middle-of-the-road. The objective of the corporate state is the *power of the state* rather than the welfare of the individual. More specifically, the ultimate objective of the corporate organization of the economy is the preparation of a *permanent war economy*, because aggressive imperialism is the ultimate aim of fascist foreign policy.

The Italian fascist regime set up a corporate state that was to show the Italians and the world that fascism was not mere reaction, directed against liberal capitalism and socialism, but a new creative principle of social and economic organization. The economy was divided into syndicates of workers, employers, and the professions. Only one syndicate was recognized in each branch of business or industry, and although membership in a syndicate was not obligatory, the payment of dues was. The officials of the syndicates were either fascist politicians or persons of reliable loyalty to the fascist regime. In effect, these associations of workers and employers were nothing but instruments of state policy, with no will or life of their own. Since each syndicate had a monopoly of organization in its field, state control was made that much easier.

To make this method of control more nearly complete, the fascist government established *corporations* which were administrative agencies in a given industry designed to unite and control the associations of *workers and employers* in that industry. According to law, the syndicates were autonomous; in fact, however, they were run by the state. The corporation, supreme instrument of fascist economic organization, made no pretense of autonomy, being as it was nothing but an administrative agency of the state and in no way different from the prisons and the other tools of fascist government by force and propaganda.

Despite the same name, the fascist corporation is, of course, not to be confused with the business corporation in the United States. They have nothing whatever in common. The fascist corporation is a government agency, whereas the American business corporation is a company of limited liability, owned by private citizens and engaged in business.

In the final analysis, the much advertised corporate state was no new principle of social and economic organization, but merely a sign of the fact that in the totalitarian system of fascism economic relations, like all other aspects of society, could not be left to the free interplay of the competitive liberal society. In Mussolini's own words, the essential bases of the corporate state were a *single party,* a *totalitarian government,* and an atmosphere of *strong ideal tension.* The Fascist party provided the first two essentials of the corporate state, and the strong ideal tension was brought about by the ceaseless propaganda of expansionist imperialism.

The first real test for the corporate state in Italy, the best developed historical example so far, came with that country's entry into World War II in June 1940. Fascist Italy revealed itself to be wholly unequal to the task of fighting a major war, not only from the military and political viewpoint, but also from the standpoint of economic efficiency. For 20 years the corporate state had sacrificed the welfare and happiness of a poor people to the dream of a powerful empire and the megalomania of a would-be conqueror of continents. Yet when the first real test of battle came, Italian fascism failed on the economic front even more than on the military front. The economic legacy of the corporate state was not wealth and empire, but the loss of the colonies, poverty, and destitution.

After the execution of Mussolini in the spring of 1945, the Italian people destroyed whatever vestiges were left of the corporate state and embarked upon a new chapter of economic rehabilitation, based on a mixture of economic liberalism and political democracy. In the last analysis, much of the economic ruination of Italy wrought by fascist corporatism was ultimately paid for by the American taxpayer, as the United States poured billions of dollars into Italy after World War II to help her stand on her own feet again. Since 1950, the Italian economy has been one of the fastest growing economies in the world and has provided standards of living undreamed of during the fascist era. During the 1960's Italy doubled her gross national product.

In the western hemisphere, Colonel Perón, speaking for the fascist regime in Argentina just after the successful coup of June 1943, declared his admiration for the fundamental conceptions of the corporate state at the very moment when Italian fascism, the model and inspiration of Argentine fascism, had reduced Italy to ashes and ruins. To Argentina as to other nations, the corporate state under Perón brought inflation and meatless days—meatless days in a country that formerly had been the largest exporter of meat in the world. Above all, corporatism in Argentina (called *justicialismo*) meant the end of free labor unions and their replacement by government-sponsored puppets. The employing class, too, was put under the control of the government. Finally, the Peronist regime followed the corporate systems of other fascist states by dedicating the economy to the hasty development of heavy industry and the manufacture of armaments. Thus, *justicialismo*, which set out to defend justice against both capitalism and socialism, ended up the servant of an imperialistic dictator and his political machine, until both were overthrown in 1955.

PERONISM:
THE CASE OF ARGENTINA

The defeat of the Axis in World War II has by no means removed the threat of fascism forever. In terms of military security, to be sure, there has been no major threat of fascist aggression since the defeat of the great fascist powers, Germany and Japan. As an attitude of mind, however, and as a reflection of social and political authoritarianism, fascism has shown that it can survive temporary defeats; only a few years after fascist regimes led Germany and Italy to disaster and humiliation, neo-fascist organizations in both countries resumed operations.

The case of Argentina is more complex, and it proves that the western hemisphere is not immune from the virus of fascism. In 1943, a group of discontented younger officers overthrew the existing democratic regime, which was far from being perfect but which nevertheless was democratic. The officers were under the leadership of Colonel Juan Perón, who in several years in Italy as a military attaché had become a fervent admirer of Mussolini and of fascist ideas. As soon as the Peronist clique took over, Argentine foreign policy became openly hostile to the democratic nations in World War II and friendly to the fascist powers. On March 27, 1945, when the war was practically over, Argentina, in order to be admitted to the San Francisco Conference under the terms of the Yalta agreement, declared war on Japan, and on Germany "in view of the character of the latter as an ally of Japan." Thus the pro-fascist and pro-Nazi sentiment of the Peronist regime was manifested in the wording as well as the timing of its declaration of war.

Perón at first stayed in the background but then took over the ministries of war and labor. The war ministry gave him control over the armed forces, with which he could supplement the deep affection in which the people allegedly held him. Control over labor removed, as in other fascist states, any threat of organized mass action. The radio was completely subordinated to the government, and the opposition was deprived of access to it. In the newspaper field, Perón leveled his sights at *La Prensa*, one of the five or six great newspapers in the world, having an old and revered tradition of independence. First the Peronist government tried to cajole and harass *La Prensa* into submission by administrative subterfuges rather than by open action. When all pressures and threats failed, Perón seized *La Prensa* early in 1951 and converted it to the pro-government, fascist line. *La Prensa*'s owner, Dr. Ezequiel Paz, obliged to flee to the United States to save himself from prison, was the most famous Argentine refugee; but he was just one of many who sought asylum in the other American republics and in France and England.

In most of its policies, the Peronist regime followed the techniques and aims of Hitler and Mussolini. Yet in one respect—and a very important one—Perón showed intelligence considerably superior to that of his models and masters. Without exception, all the other fascist dictators—like all communist dictatorships—abolished political parties other than the ruling party; and since there could be no regular elections without opposition candidates, fascist elections became plebiscites in which the voters were presented with a major issue and asked to vote yes or no. The votes in fascist elections were usually announced to be somewhere in the neighborhood of 99.6 percent in favor of the dictator.

It is at this point that Perón improved on Hitler and Mussolini. Perón apparently had too much of a sense of humor to announce to the world that 99.6 percent of his people insisted on his leadership. He was satisfied with considerably less. In the presidential elections of 1946 Perón was elected by a majority of only 55 percent, a figure that gave the election the appearance of having been fought under conditions of free campaigning. Nothing was further from the facts, for early in 1944 all political parties had been abolished. This measure hurt the opposition parties more than the government, and it was only shortly before the elections, in late February of 1946, that political parties were reconstituted. Much of the election campaign was conducted in a state of siege, a favorite measure in Latin American dictatorships, under which the government can legally suspend all rights of individual civil liberty. The opposition parties and their leaders were subjected to physical terror from a mob that operated under government protection. In many cases, the police itself used violence against anti-Peronists, and there were numerous murders in the campaign.

In 1949, Perón had the Argentine Constitution of 1853 changed because under it immediate reelection of the president was illegal. A modest man, Perón claimed he did not wish to run for the presidency again, but as a patriotic Argentine he finally gave in to the mounting pressure from all sides and allowed himself to be drafted. The election of November 1951 gave Perón a victory of over 60 percent, still way below the 99.6 percent victories of the other fascist dictators.

In the 1951 election, terror against opposition parties was practiced even more openly than in 1946. Hundreds of candidates were jailed during the campaign for no worse crime than daring to run against the existing regime, and conditions were so chaotic that two presidential candidates were out of the race even before the campaign was over. The Socialists withdrew from the campaign altogether when it became apparent that the whole thing was a farce. Their candidate for the presidency had been imprisoned, as were hundreds of leaders of other parties, six weeks before the election. In typically fascist fashion, the government declared that it had discovered a subversive plot, and a state of siege was once again proclaimed, so that ruthless terror could be legally employed. In the congressional elections of April 25, 1954, the Peronist slate obtained two-thirds of the popular vote. Every radio station was compelled to broadcast Perón's speeches, and the opposition was unable to get any radio time for its candidates. This monopoly of the government was supplemented by many other forms of discrimination, and occasional terror, against the opposition. It was remarkable in the election of 1954, as in 1946 and 1951, that so many Argentines still dared to vote against the Peronist regime.

Late in 1954 Perón started his campaign against the Roman Catholic church; this was the beginning of his undoing. After persisting in that campaign for several months, he was excommunicated by the Vatican on June 16, 1955. On that same day, the Argentine air force and parts of the army staged an armed uprising, but it failed. Three months later, provincial units rebelled again, and this time Perón's fate was sealed when the entire navy went over to the rebels. Only four days after the outbreak of the revolution, on September 19, 1955, Perón quietly slipped away in a Paraguayan gunboat, fleeing eventually to Spain. Since there was virtually no resistance to the revolutionary forces, Perón had to escape in a hurry.

What he left behind came as a shock to the Argentine public. Many were aware that agriculture and industry were in a mess, that public finances were in chaos, that graft was widespread, that Perón's nearest relatives were among the leading grafters, and that honesty and integrity had just about disappeared from public life. But few people knew much about Perón the man, as distinct from Perón the dictator.

In his several homes were found stacks of Argentine currency totaling millions of dollars; boxes of gold money and valuables made of gold and silver; fabulous jewels of his late wife, Eva Perón, and foreign bank books. It was estimated that his deposits in foreign banks must be worth many millions of dollars. Since Perón had always posed as an anticapitalist and friend of the poor, the extent of his private wealth and grafting came as a shock to many of his followers.

The transition from Peronism to constitutional government was not easy. Although direct experience with fascism—as with communism—has an immunizing effect, Argentine democracy missed the opportunity provided by the downfall of the Peronist dictatorship. Mentally still living in the nineteenth century, the opponents of Peronism, particularly in the professional and upper classes, thought that constitutional government could endure without social and economic reforms on a broad scale. The new regime thus failed to win over the labor unions, which had previously been wooed by the Peronist regime. As a result, only a few years after Perón's ouster the Peronists were able to become the largest single party, deriving their strength mainly from working-class and lower-middle-class voters.

In 1962, the Peronists won about one-third of the popular vote, thus constituting a serious threat to democratic government. President Frondizi, who had shown little ability in coping with the renewed pressure of Peronism, was removed from office by the military. In the presidential elections of 1963, a moderate, Arturo U. Illia, was elected, while Peronism suffered a sharp decline. Yet this decline proved very short-lived. In the congressional elections of 1965, the Peronists emerged again as the strongest single party, winning almost 30 percent of the popular vote. The administration of President Illia showed itself unable to solve the political problems of Peronism, the social problems of poverty, and the economic problems of inflation.

In 1966, constitutional government was abolished by a military coup, whose victorious leaders proclaimed their intention of staying in power as long as would be necessary for the "rehabilitation" of Argentina. Constitutional government following the ouster of Peronist fascism thus lasted for only eleven years. The present military dictatorship is of the more traditional Latin American authoritarian type rather than fascism, but—like Peronism—it would not have come to power if the Argentine democratic forces had shown themselves more alert to the causes, rather than the symptoms, of fascist or authoritarian dictatorship.

The military dictatorship installed in Argentina in 1966 was no novelty in Latin America or in Argentina itself. Authoritarian political dictatorships have come and gone in Latin America, but the Peronist regime was the first example in the western hemisphere of a full-fledged fascist state, totalitarian in objectives and means. The Peronist era of 1943 to 1955 proved a poor schooling for constitutional government. The future will tell whether the military regime set up in 1966 will throw Argentina back into the older patterns of authoritarianism with some respect for the rule of law or whether it will move in the direction of fascist dictatorship.

IS FASCISM STILL A THREAT?

Is fascism still a threat in the leading democratic nations? The tendency now is to say, emphatically, no. On balance, this may be the right answer, but to say that fascism is unlikely to take over the government of the United States, for example, is not to say it may not be a serious menace. To the extent that an *anti-intellectual tendency* exists in this or any other democracy, it undermines faith in rational processes; whereas such a tendency need not lead straight to fascism, it prepares the mentality without which there can be no effective fascist movement. Intellectuals themselves may, and do, contribute to this corrosion of faith in reason by identifying with doctrines of violence on the extreme right or left, as has happened in the United States and elsewhere in recent years. Intellectuals who abandon their commitment to rational processes and advocate violence as a legitimate means of social change will find that such advocacy is more likely to lead to a rightist reaction and possible fascist repression than to a more genuine democracy and human liberation.

Racism is another important source—some think the most important source—that feeds the fascist potential in the United States, as in other democracies. Democracy as known before no longer exists in South Africa, for example: racism and democracy just do not mix.

While South Africa still has a multiparty system and a mild (and harassed) opposition press, it has steadily moved in the direction of the fascist police state. It practices such methods as imprisonment without trial, confinement of "dangerous" persons to specific localities, forced residence of millions of blacks in assigned reservations, and censorship of books, movies, and radio according to racist concepts. The racism that started out in South Africa against blacks and Indians later turned into chauvinism against English-speaking whites, nearly one-half of the white population.

South African racial policy has been based on the concept of *apartheid*, or separation. Under this policy, nonwhites are forced to live in separate areas and are also kept apart from whites socially, culturally, and politically. The danger of separation of whites and nonwhites in the United States has become very real. The *Report of the National Advisory Commission on Civil Disorders* (1968) states as its basic conclusion: "Our nation is moving toward two societies, one black, one white—separate and unequal." Should this trend continue, the threat of fascism or of a fascist type of government will be very serious, since such separation and inequality could not be maintained by the traditional processes of constitutional government. As South Africa officially justifies its racist policies as measures against communism, racist-fascist forces in the United States will also feed on anticommunism, as they have done in the past. In addition, black separatists—still only a small minority in the black community—are convinced that the trend toward separation is inevitable in the United States, and they demand the setting up of a separate black nation in the territory of five southern states. *Apartheid* in the United States would be no more reconcilable with democracy than it is in South Africa.

The *cold war* with communism has been another contributing factor in the revival and renewed respectability of fascism. Because fascism and democracy are both opposed to communism, some have concluded that the two are natural allies, overlooking this important distinction: whereas fascist governments favor—as do the major communist states—international change by force, democratic states are committed to international change by peaceful methods. In their domestic policies, the incompatibility between fascist and demo-

**"YES, SON, THIS IS WHAT HAPPENS TO A COUNTRY
WHEN THE EGGHEADS TAKE OVER."**

cratic societies is even clearer, since the goals and practices of fascism aim at the eradication of democracy and constitutional government.

Possibly the most dangerous softening up of democratic resistance to fascism is the destruction of democratic habits and institutions, not by outside attacks, but within the citadel of democracy itself. If there is any fascist threat to democracy today—and there is— it no longer comes from Berlin, Rome, and Tokyo. It derives its parasitic strength from the inertia and apathy of the citizens of a democracy, because without such civic diseases there can be no support for demagogues and fear-mongers who seek to aggrandize themselves at the expense of the whole body politic.

The danger in a democracy like the United States is not outright fascism on the German, Italian, or Argentine patterns, but the insidious and unnoticed corroding of democratic habits and institutions by prefascist and profascist attitudes. Huey Long, who as governor of Louisiana in the early 1930's set up the nearest thing to a fascist dictatorship in the United States, once jokingly said that if fascism ever came to the United States, it would be under the slogan of 100 percent Americanism.

Long was right. The open, self-confessed fascist will not get a sympathetic hearing in the United States because the verbal symbols of fascism are identified too profoundly with evil in the American mind; the fascist fellow traveler, the crypto-fascist, the proto-fascist, the prefascist, and the profascist are more dangerous than the plain unhyphenated fascist. By publicly declaring himself to be what he is, the fascist cannot work under the mantle of respectability. A politician with fascist leanings who denies that he is a fascist and who emphasizes his patriotism can do much more harm than the admitted fascist, who is not permitted to work within the institutional framework of public life. The danger of not recognizing this prefascist attitude is that, should it become full-fledged fascism (as it well might in an economic depression or in some other disaster of the sort that periodically shakes men's faith in democracy), recognition of it as a threat may come too late for those whose earlier judgment was too lenient.

FOR FURTHER READING

Adorno, T. W., and others. *The Authoritarian Personality.* New York: Harper & Row, 1950.

Arendt, Hannah. *The Origins of Totalitarianism.* New ed. Harcourt, Brace & World, Inc., 1966.

Aron, Raymond. *Democracy and Totalitarianism.* New York: Praeger, 1969.

Baumont, Maurice, and others. *The Third Reich.* New York: Praeger, 1955.

Bell, Daniel (ed.). *The Radical Right.* Garden City, N.Y.: Doubleday, 1963.

Bettelheim, Bruno. *The Informed Heart: The Human Condition in Modern Mass Society.* New York: Free Press, 1960.

Blanksten, George I. *Perón's Argentina.* Chicago: University of Chicago Press, 1953.

Bullock, Alan. *Hitler: A Study in Tyranny.* New York: Bantam Books, 1955.

Chabod, Federico. *A History of Italian Fascism.* London: Weidenfeld & Nicolson, 1963.

Cohen, Elie A. *Human Behavior in the Concentration Camp.* New York: W. W. Norton, 1953.

Ebenstein, William. *Fascist Italy.* New York: American Book Company, 1939.

———. *The German Record.* New York: Holt, Rinehart & Winston, 1945.

———. *The Nazi State.* New York: Holt, Rinehart & Winston, 1943.

———. "National Socialism," *International Encyclopedia of the Social Sciences,* XI (New York, 1968), 45–50.

Eisenberg, Dennis. *The Re-emergence of Fascism.* New York: A. S. Barnes, 1968.

Forster, Arnold, and Benjamin R. Epstein. *Danger on the Right.* New York: Random House, 1964.

Fromm, Erich. *Escape from Freedom.* New York: Holt, Rinehart & Winston, 1941.

Gilbert, G. M. *The Psychology of Dictatorship.* New York: Ronald Press, 1950.

Halperin, S. William. *Mussolini and Italian Fascism.* "Anvil Books." Princeton, N.J.: Van Nostrand, 1964.

Hoess, Rudolf. *Commandant of Auschwitz.* New York: Popular Library, 1961.

Kirpatrick, Ivone. *Mussolini: A Study in Power.* New York: Hawthorn Books, 1964.

Laqueur, Walter, and George L. Mosse (eds.). *International Fascism: 1920–1945.* "Harper Torchbooks." New York: Harper & Row, 1966.

Mosse, George L. *The Crisis of German Ideology: Intellectual Origins of the Third Reich.* New York: Grosset & Dunlap, 1964.

Nathan, Peter. *The Psychology of Fascism.* London: Faber & Faber, 1943.

Orwell, George. *1984.* "Signet Books." New York: New American Library, 1950.

Payne, Stanley G. *Falange: A History of Spanish Fascism.* Stanford: Stanford University Press, 1961.

Shirer, William L. *The Rise and Fall of the Third Reich.* New York: Crest Books, 1962.

Stern, Fritz. *The Politics of Cultural Despair: A Study in the Rise of the Germanic Ideology.* "Anchor Books." Garden City, N.Y.: Doubleday, 1965.

Viereck, Peter. *Metapolitics: The Roots of the Nazi Mind.* New York: Capricorn Books, 1961.

Warren, Robert Penn. *All the King's Men.* "Modern Library." New York: Random House, 1953.

Weber, Eugen. *Varieties of Fascism.* "Anvil Books." Princeton, N.J.: Van Nostrand, 1964.

Woolf, S. J. (ed.). *European Fascism.* "Vintage Books." New York: Random House, 1969.

the
democratic
way
of life

part two

democratic capitalism

chapter three

TWO CONCEPTIONS OF DEMOCRACY

George Bernard Shaw once proposed that, in order to eradicate misunderstanding and confusion about the meaning of democracy, the leading scholars and thinkers of the world be convened and the issue be settled once and for all. Unfortunately, the root of the trouble lies deeper. Disagreements about the concept of democracy are not semantic, but reflect differences of a more fundamental nature.

When a representative of the United States, Britain, or France talks about democracy, he assigns to it a meaning that is different from what a Russian or Chinese communist has in mind when he uses the same term. Thus at the end of World War II, when the United States, Britain, France, and the Soviet Union occupied Germany, one of their chief objectives was the democratization of Germany. At first all four powers wholeheartedly agreed on the objective, but it soon became evident that the Russian concept was entirely different from the Anglo-American-French understanding of democracy.

The Western powers took the view that bringing democracy to Germany meant free elections; a free press; freedom of political association; freedom of religion, thought, and speech; equality before the law; the right to oppose the government; the right to choose one's job; the right to form free trade unions; the right to move freely within one's country, go abroad temporarily, or emigrate permanently.

Above all, *freedom from fear* is basic in the Western concept of democracy. No society can be called free unless its citizens feel safe from unwarranted intrusion into their affairs by governmental authorities, particularly the secret police.

The communist conception of democratizing Germany was entirely different from the Western. It meant the destruction of capitalism and the setting-up of a state-owned economy in Germany. When a communist speaks of democracy, he has in mind, not government *of* the people, nor government *by* the people, but, as a leading Soviet philosopher puts it, "whether this or that policy is carried out in the interests of the people, in the interests of its over-whelming majority, or in the interests of its minority" (G. F. Alek-sandrov, *The Pattern of Soviet Democracy,* 1948).

Which doctrine reveals whether government is carried out *in the interests of the people?* Marxist-Leninist doctrine. Who interprets the doctrine correctly? The Communist party. Who in the Communist party determines the party line? The Politburo, a group of a dozen men or so. Who in the Politburo determines its general policy? The top communist leader who controls the party, army, and police. If the leader loses control over any one of these key elements of power—as happened to Khrushchev in 1964—he is removed and becomes an "unperson."

Communists call the essentials of democracy—freedom of speech, press, and association, equality before the law, and all the other fundamental democratic rights and liberties—*formal* democracy, as compared with the *real* democracy of communism, in which the means of production are owned by the state. In this communist conception, the traditional democratic freedoms assume a new meaning.

Freedom of the press? By all means, provided the newspapers function "in conformity with the interests of the toilers" (article 125 of the Constitution of the Soviet Union). Freedom of speech? Completely and unqualifiedly, provided the speaker's words support the communist cause. When an American told an acquaintance in Moscow that he could criticize and lambaste the President of the United States near the White House in Washington, D.C., the Soviet citizen sardonically replied he could do the same: he, too, could go to the Kremlin in Moscow and publicly lambaste the President of the United States. In 1968, when a handful of Russians tried to express in Moscow their public disapproval of the Soviet occupation of Czechoslovakia, they were quickly arrested, tried, and sentenced to stiff prison and labor camp sentences.

Two criteria determine, in communist thinking, whether a government deserves to be called democratic: first, the nature of the economic system it operates and, second, the kind of foreign policy it pursues.

The case of Germany illustrates the importance of the economic system. In the elections of West Germany in 1953, only 2.2 percent of the vote was for the Communist party. Outlawed in West Germany in 1956, the party remained legal in West Berlin. In the West Berlin city elections of 1958, the communists obtained 1.9 percent of the vote, and in the elections of 1963 only 1.3 percent. Yet from the communist viewpoint, West Germany is a dictatorship because the *interests* of its population are not determined by the one party that knows what is best for the Germans, the Communist party. In particular, as long as capitalism exists in Germany there can be do democracy there, the communists say, because capitalism is by definition a dictatorship of the wealthy over the poor, even though a majority of the latter may vote in its favor. From the communist viewpoint, West Germany today could be called a democracy only if the Communist party, supported by 2.2 percent of the popular vote, ruled Germany, because only the Communist party could rule in the interests of the German people.

By contrast, in the Soviet view East Germany is a true democracy, because it has abolished capitalism and operates a state-owned and state-run economy. The fact that a communist one-party dictatorship rules East Germany in dependence on Soviet military force stationed in its territory, the fact that this artificial regime has to keep its population imprisoned behind frontiers of barbed wire and concrete walls to prevent mass flights into West Germany, the fact that political prisons and "correctional" labor camps have been set up—all this is irrelevant to the communist proof of democracy.

The second criterion which, in communist political thinking, determines whether a government is democratic is foreign policy. In the view of Chinese communists, for example, Albania is a true democracy, because it sides completely with China on foreign policy (and particularly so in the Chinese campaign against the Soviet leadership). For this very reason, Albania is—in Soviet eyes—not a democracy, but a "deviationist, power-mad oligarchy." Should the Albanian communist government tomorrow switch sides and line up with Moscow against Peking, it would become a shining example of democracy in the Soviet judgment, although Albania might continue its internal system of extreme totalitarianism, more Stalinist than that of any other European communist state.

**DEMOCRACY
AS A WAY OF LIFE**

From these illustrations the principal characteristics of the Western concept of democracy as a way of life clearly emerge:

1. Rational empiricism
2. Emphasis on the individual
3. Instrumental nature of the state
4. Voluntarism
5. The law behind the law
6. Emphasis on means
7. Discussion and consent in human relations
8. Basic equality of all human beings

   1. *Rational empiricism* is perhaps the most important single element in the free way of life. It is based on confidence in reason and in the applicability of reason not only to physical nature but also to human relations. Dogmatists *know* what the truth is; for communists the concept of class is the ultimate in truth, where as to fascists race and nation are the last repositories of truth. Since the dogmatist is so sure that he knows, he need not inquire further; his aim is to strengthen what he knows already, and he brands whoever questions his knowledge guilty of intellectual subversion. The psychological and historical relation between dogmatism in philosophy and authoritarianism in politics is clear: absolute certainty of knowledge leads to fanatic enthusiasm in sentiment, which in turn leads to intolerant repression in government.

   In contrast, empiricism, first fully developed by John Locke (1632–1704), is based on the idea that *all our knowledge derives from experience.* In this conception, truth (with a small *t*) is tentative, changing, and subject to constant checking and verification.

   Since the history of both physical science and social thought is full of truths that turned out to be wholly or partly untrue, the rational empiricist refuses to believe, as the dogmatist believes, that mankind ever has arrived, or ever will arrive, at final answers. One of the most paradoxical puzzles of the progressive enlargement of knowledge is that, as our understanding and knowledge of a particular problem or field increase, the awareness of our ignorance increases at an even faster rate. Many a problem solved—in the physical as in the social sciences—creates more new problems than existed before the solution.

It takes a lot of knowledge and inquiry to know what one does not know. The man who was first aware of his ignorance was probably, in the evolution of human thought, the first scientist; for, aware of *what* he did *not* know, he set about finding an answer. Without Newton's "solution" of the problem of gravity, there would have been no new world of physical phenomena unlocked by Einstein. Without the "solution" of the problem of government by the democratic method in the modern world, there would have been no Tocqueville discovering in his *Democracy in America* (1835) the new world of political problems created by the democratic solution.

The rational empiricist therefore views truth, in the study of nature as much as of man, as an endless process and considers the knowledge or truth of today no more than a *probability*, to be changed if new facts are brought to light. Bertrand Russell writes in his *Philosophy and Politics* that the genuine liberal says not "This is true," but "I am inclined to think that under present circumstances this opinion is probably the best."

Science and democracy also share the emphasis on procedure, on *how*, not what, answers will emerge as the result of the quest for true knowledge. The main justification of freedom of expression in both science and democracy is broader than the mere satisfaction of individual persons' desires for self-expression and self-fulfilment, defensible as that criterion alone may be. In science, the whole scientific community depends on, and feels entitled to, the free gathering and communication of all possible data and ideas. Similarly, the political community of democracy depends for its very existence on the unhindered expression of the widest range of facts and opinions before a decision is made.

Ideally, a legislative body in a democracy acts like a judge who renders his decision after he has listened to all sides presenting arguments that may be material or immaterial, important or unimportant. In fact, the oldest legislative body—the British Parliament—began, and functioned during the first few centuries of its existence, as a

Drawing by Steinberg; © 1969 The New Yorker Magazine, Inc.

High Court: and even now the upper house of Parliament, the House of Lords, serves as Britain's supreme court. To this day, all democratic legislatures follow the British parliamentary procedure originally developed in a framework of judicial proceedings.

What most distinguishes a democratic from a totalitarian legislature is therefore not the final product, what laws are made in either institution, but what procedures are followed. Above all, democratic procedure requires, as do the judicial and scientific procedures, that *all sides of an issue be heard.* From this basic procedural requirement stem the essential democratic liberties of speech, publication, assembly, and association.

It is probably no coincidence that rational empiricism and democracy have developed more or less simultaneously in England, France, and the United States. In British thought for example, John Locke, the founder of empiricism, is still the most persuasive exponent of philosophical liberalism. In the United States, empiricism has been the dominant school of thought, culminating in John Dewey (1859–1952), whose application of rational empiricism to philosophy and politics has been a lasting contribution to the American liberal heritage.

In the mass society of contemporary capitalist democracy, the liberal commitment to critical rationalism has been confronted with several serious threats. In the revolution of communications media, the picture, with its powerful appeal to emotion, increasingly replaces the printed word, with its appeal to reason and reflection. Advertising techniques in the capitalist market have been refined to the point where the sales appeal is to unconscious and subliminal drives rather than to consciously felt needs and desires. In politics, too, some have argued, the rational orientation toward issues has given way to the emotional appeals of leaders and would-be leaders, and as a result of television the leader, too, has been replaced to a considerable extent by the *image* of the leader, by what he *appears* to be to the irrational response of the voters rather than what he really is in the light of cold reflection and sober reasoning. Finally, the revolution in communications media has produced the problem of "sensory overload." The individual is constantly bombarded by sensations, enticements, threats, and packaged bits of information and misinformation that demand immediate response or satisfaction —and such instant reactions are basically incompatible with the slow and plodding methods of critical rationalism.

2. *Emphasis on the individual* sharply separates liberal democracy from both fascist and communist totalitarianism. In the eyes of the liberal democrat, no social or political institution, be it a local boy-scout group, a party precinct, or the state, has a purpose other than to serve the individual.

In the totalitarian doctrine, the state is the master, the individual the servant. Hegel, the intellectual ancestor of both fascism and communism, says in his *Philosophy of Law* (1821) that the individual finds his liberty in obeying the state and the fullest realization of his liberty in dying for the state. Only when the individual dies for the state does he lose the last trace of any personal whimsicality and uniqueness and become completely a part of the state.

By contrast, Locke sees the indestructible essence of man in resisting, rather than in blindly obeying, the state. The liberal principles of life, liberty, and the pursuit of happiness are thus the exact opposite of the authoritarian concept of citizenship as duty, discipline, and death for the state.

Thomas Jefferson, one of the greatest liberal individualists of all time, remarked in a letter to Colonel William Stephen Smith, dated November 13, 1787, that "the tree of liberty must be refreshed from time to time with the blood of patriots and tyrants." The Declaration of Independence, too, states that life, liberty, and the pursuit of happiness are among the unalienable rights of man and that "whenever any form of government becomes destructive of these ends, it is the right of the people to alter or to abolish it, and to institute new government, laying its foundations on such principles, and organizing its powers in such form as to them shall seem most likely to effect their safety and happiness."

The historical roots of individualism are three: first, the Jewish concept of one God leads to the idea that all men, as children of God, are brothers to each other. Second, the Christian doctrine of the indestructibility of the human soul maintains that whatever social, economic, and political inequalities may exist, all men possess a spiritual equality and uniqueness that no earthly power can override. Third, in the Stoic view, the one principle of action that governs all things is *to be at one with oneself,* to know oneself, and to act in conformity with one's rational principles and purposes. The true self of man, according to the Stoics, is not his flesh or bones, but the faculty that uses them, his *reason,* the part of man that more than anything else characterizes him as human.

At no time, of course, has this individualism been fully accepted, and the counterforces of totalitarianism always threaten it. At the present time, in particular, the threat of all-destructive thermonuclear warfare leads to a strengthening of anti-individualist attitudes, stressing the idea of "let's close ranks" rather than "let each man decide what is right or wrong and act accordingly."

Apart from the pressures of international tension and conflict, there have been other forces that have threatened, and still threaten, traditional liberal individualism. Above all, there is the emergence of the *group* as the decisive factor in government and the economy. In politics, the individual can be effective only to the extent that he joins a political party or pressure group. The framers of the Constitution did not mention political parties in it and were strongly suspicious of them as forces that would dissolve the unity of the nation and lessen the importance of the individual in the process. Yet today the study of democratic politics is dominated by the concept of the group as the decisive force in the political process.

In economics, too, the individual farmer, merchant, or worker of classical capitalism has been largely supplanted by the group. Today, a labor union may bargain on a nationwide basis for an entire industry, the farmer depends on farm blocs in and out of Congress, and the individual businessman has either been replaced by the large corporation or, if he still exists, depends on his trade association to pursue his economic interests. All this does not necessarily mean that individualism is dead, for in a pluralistic society the individual joins a group to defend his individual integrity against threats that issue from other powerful interest groups or from government.

3. The *instrumental theory of the state* views the state as a mechanism to be used for ends higher than itself. Both Plato and Aristotle, the founders of Western political theory, conceived of the state as an organic entity, with a life and purpose of its own, superior to the purposes of the individual. Plato and Aristotle thought of the state as the *highest moral good*, the source of moral values and spiritual enrichment for the individual.

From the Jewish-Christian viewpoint of religion, the instrumentalist theory of the state maintains that the highest values in man's life relate to God and that no earthly law can claim to supersede God's. The function of the state is to maintain peace and order, so that men can pursue their activities devoted to higher ends. From the rational-humanist viewpoint, the instrumentalist theory of the state affirms that the ability of the individual to use his reason in discovering what is right and wrong is the ultimate test of political authority and that the state therefore cannot turn evil into good or wrong into right solely because it possesses the means of physical coercion.

The liberal doctrine stresses society far more than the state; in the classical liberal doctrine *society is considered basically self-sufficient,* and *the state is to step in only when the voluntary efforts of society fail.*

The instrumentalist theory of the state thus relegates the state to a supplementary position. As long as individuals can get along without the state, the liberal bias is against the state, even if the state could do the same thing a little better. In the totalitarian state, the assumption is always in favor of the state. The totalitarian state organizes and controls not only the sensitive areas of the economy, education, and religion, but even chess players and Sunday afternoon hikers.

4. By contrast, the democratic theory sees in the principle of *voluntarism* the very lifeblood of a free society. Fellowship can be experienced most deeply in small, voluntary groups. Such groups were first formed in seventeenth-century England on a religious basis, and to this day the English-speaking world abounds with thousands and thousands of religious sects that are small in size and entirely voluntary in nature.

Later, the principle of voluntary association was applied in the field of politics (parties), education (private schools), and economics (labor unions and employees' associations). In charity, the Red Cross and local community chests testify to the fact that there is still a strong sentiment for retaining voluntary activity. Even in England, which has national health and social security programs covering every person from the cradle to the grave, there has been a reassertion of the importance of voluntary organization in social welfare, supplementing the governmental programs.

The bias of the principle of voluntarism is for the smaller community and against centralized government. For long, this originally liberal principle was adopted by conservatives and states'-righters in defense of conservative policies. Yet recently the protest against centralism has also been taken up by others: blacks who demand community control over schools and police in their areas in large cities, and white liberals who want to restore the importance of state and local governments through revenue-sharing with the federal government.

5. The concept of *the law behind the law* flows directly from the *federal* view of state and society in classical liberalism. Society is conceived as an aggregate of diverse voluntary associations, and the state itself is looked upon as an essentially voluntary body because its authority is derived from the consent of the governed.

Whenever authority is organized on a federal basis, there has to be a higher law defining the relationships of the parts among each other and of each part to the whole. Classical liberalism, therefore, has always adhered to the idea that the relations between state and society, between government and individual, are ultimately defined by a law higher than that of the state. In fact, classical liberal thought in Britain and the United States assumes that the *law is not the product of the state, but precedes it.* The function of the state in relation to man's basic rights is to protect and define such rights, not to create them.

In the United States, in particular, the concept of the law behind the law has never been challenged as the foundation of American political thought and experience. The Declaration of Independence specifically recognizes it, and the Constitution has also recognized that no legislative body can make laws without due process or laws that otherwise violate basic principles of reason. The very existence of the United States is, of course, due to the insistence that above the law then ruling, the law of imperial Britain, there was a higher law to which the revolutionary colonists pledged allegiance.

Opponents of democratic government have charged that this concept of a higher law, making government dependent upon the consent of the governed, opens the door to rebellion and anarchy. In his *Two Treatises of Government* (1690), John Locke answers this charge with three counterarguments. First, Locke concedes that the democratic theory of government admits of the possibility of rebellion, but he denies that it does so more than any other theory. When the people are made miserable, they will rebel under any form of government; let the governors be "sacred and divine, descended or authorized from heaven, give them out for whom or what you please, the same will happen." Second, Locke says, men do not rebel "upon every little mismanagement in public affairs," or "for light and transient causes," as the Declaration of Independence puts it. Third, and here Locke moves from the defensive to the offensive, government by consent coupled with the right of the people to rebel is "the best fence against rebellion."

Locke could only guess in 1690 whether his arguments would be proved by experience, because democracy was then still a thing of the future. Yet experience has proved him perspicacious. Although democratic systems of government, based on the Lockean-Jeffersonian principle of the people's right to rebel, have periodically experienced civil disorder, riots, and violence, they have proved themselves comparatively stable in the long run. By contrast, where the concept of the higher law has been rejected in the name of law and order, the political results have been blood purges, conspiracies, plots and counterplots, and violent swings from one extreme to another—the political record, specifically, of communist and fascist dictatorships.

6. The *emphasis on means* in democratic life is based on the realization that ends lead no existence apart from means but are continually shaped by them. The totalitarian makes a clear-cut distinction between means and ends. He is absolutely certain of what the ends are, and possessing this certainty, he pays little attention to the nature of the means. Thus, communists believe in universal brotherhood and cooperation as their officially professed end, yet they fail to realize that the means employed in bringing about communism—secret police, "correctional" labor camps, thought control, denunciations, repression of dissent—increase hatred and misery rather than diminish it.

One of the main difficulties in separating means from ends is the fact that *in most practical situations a means is simultaneously an end.* Thus, education is for some an end in itself; for others, it is but a means to an end—to a degree, for example. Yet, a degree may again be only a means to the end of a happier, fuller life, or a better job. Again, a better job is not necessarily an end in itself; it is likely to be a means to some higher end, such as expressing a sense of craftsmanship or serving society.

The central position of means in free societies is entrenched in their historical experience. Magna Carta, habeas corpus, and jury trial, to mention but a few roots of liberty in the English-speaking world, are originally all procedural devices, means; and the history of liberty may aptly be described as a history of procedure. In representative assemblies too, it is not the legislative product that distinguishes a democratic body from a nondemocratic one, but the difference of procedure. In the one case, procedure aims at the fullest and fairest guarantee of the right of the minority to be

Drawing by John A. Ruge; © 1968 Saturday Review, Inc.

**"I DON'T EXPECT THE CHINESE TO BEHAVE EXACTLY AS WE DO
HERE IN WILTON—BUT THERE MUST BE A HAPPY MEDIUM."**

heard; in the other, procedure aims at silencing minorities and
bringing about the loudest possible volume of cheers for the
dictator.

At present, the danger in democratic societies lies in the possible
waning of this awareness that differences over means are the heart
of the difference between democracy and totalitarianism. In opposing a totalitarian system like fascism or communism there is a
natural tendency to imitate their means, and because the tendency
is natural, special efforts must be made to guard against it. In
defending democracy, some persons are willing to use means that
are bound to destroy the very thing they seek to defend.

7. *Discussion and consent* are the means by which a democratic
society typically settles divergent viewpoints and interests. It is
the democratic view that, since no one possesses absolute truth,
both sides to an argument may make a contribution to the best
possible answer and that the only way to get that answer is to
marshal all the available evidence.

The independent voter in a democracy typifies the person who is not willing to commit himself unconditionally to one party, either because he knows too little or (less often) too much about politics, or simply because—whatever his level of political information—he does not expect much from government in any case. The importance of the independent voter can be clearly seen in many elections. In 1952 the Republican party elected Dwight D. Eisenhower over Robert A. Taft as its presidential candidate, mainly for his wider appeal to independent voters. In contrast, Goldwater's defeat in the presidential election of 1964 was attributed by many to his relatively weak appeal to independent voters. In 1968, Nixon attracted many independent voters who voted Republican for the presidency and Democratic for other offices.

In the theory of the democratic society, governments derive "their just powers from the consent of the governed" (Declaration of Independence). If the state becomes oppressive and unmindful of the rights of the people, then the democratic theory, as was pointed out earlier, upholds not only the right but the duty to revolt against such government. This right to rebel can be claimed only where the methods of discussion and consent are blocked by tyrannical despotism; where the channels of discussion are open, as in a democratic state and society, a democrat cannot claim the right of rebellion against the state.

The communist or New Left revolutionary who today claims the right to revolution as a general democratic privilege bends this concept for his own purposes. From the democratic viewpoint, *the democrat has the moral right, and duty, to rebel against the totalitarian system, but the totalitarian possesses no such right against the democratic system.*

8. The *basic equality of all human beings* is a point of democratic doctrine and policy that is frequently misunderstood. No democrat has ever said that all people are identical but only that in basic respects they are equal. The very uniqueness of each and every person creates a kind of equality that is important in the democratic outlook. From the religious viewpoint of the Jewish-Christian tradition, all people are equal before God; God's challenge to every human being is the same, although men's response to it varies enormously. From the rationalist-humanistic viewpoint, all people share, over and above differences of race, sex, religion, nationality,

and class, one common trait: the ability to reason. In this sense, all people are citizens of the world rather than of a particular, distinctive group, and their basic equality derives from what they have in common rather than from what separates them.

The equality that men receive at birth, according to democratic theory, is not in the nature of an outright gift or grant but an *opportunity*, a *challenge*. The Jeffersonian phrase "pursuit of happiness" admirably expresses the thought that man does not have the right to happiness, in the sense that the state or his family or friends owe him happiness, but only in the sense that he has the right to *pursue* happiness, unhindered by unreasonable obstacles.

However, equality does not mean, as Plato charged it meant, "dispensing a kind of equality to equals and unequals alike." The contrary is true, of the ideal democracy at least. In practice it is not easy to ascertain when equals are still equal and when they become unequal. Thus, to take an illustration: the most common interpretation of democratic equality is "equality of opportunity." A grave difficulty arises immediately. If all men were endowed with the same talents and abilities, and were born into the same homes, and received the same schooling, giving all an equal opportunity would be a fair solution. Yet people differ in native talent and even more in background and education.

Legislative action cannot equalize the I.Q. of the population, and there will always be differences of ability, drive, and motivation, but laws can make equality of opportunity more real by trying to equalize conditions before the race starts: increased inheritance taxes lessen the impact of inherited wealth, progressive income taxes favor the lower-income groups, and free education (from nursery school to university) benefits the indigent more than the affluent. In other words, equality of opportunity, if it allows ability alone to operate, quickly establishes and perpetuates a meritocracy of inequality. *Need*, too, must be considered; it adds to the principle of efficiency that of happiness.

Of all principles of the democratic way of life, equality has proved the hardest to translate from ideal into reality. Social and economic inequality has for long existed in political democracies, although the range of inequality has been gradually narrowed by means which the democratic political process provides. Racial inequality

—in the United States as well as in some other democracies throughout the world—has proved itself less amenable to the processes of
democratic politics. Yet in the long run democratic societies will
have to realize that democracy and racial inequality do not mix,
and that either one or the other will have to go.

CONDITIONS
OF POLITICAL DEMOCRACY

Of all the aspects of democracy, the political has top priority.
Although political democracy is not identical with democracy as a
way of life, the instinct of those who tend to identify the two is not
wholly unsound. Experience has shown that political democracy,
if practiced over any length of time, leads to the extension of the
democratic principle to social, economic, and international problems. So far, there is less evidence that social or economic democracy leads to political democracy. Precisely because political democracy merely defines "the rules of the game," it is more far-reaching
than social or economic democracy, which is concerned with one
particular substantive area of problems.

The first characteristic of democratic government is the maintenance of a political climate in which *political liberty* can thrive. In
every society, those who uphold the orthodox views may freely
express them. *Political liberty begins at the point where unorthodox
opinions may be freely presented, without legal, social, or economic
penalties.*

The political liberty of a society can best be measured by the
margin of unorthodoxy that is *tolerated* in that society. This yard-
stick enables us to go beyond the crude classification of dictatorship
and democracy, which is valid only on a general level. Examining
first the totalitarian states by this criterion, we find the least margin
of unorthodoxy in China today, in the Soviet Union under Stalin,
and in Nazi Germany under Hitler; a much wider margin in the
Soviet Union under Khrushchev or in Yugoslavia under "national
communism," and the relatively largest unorthodoxy in some traditional Asian, African, and Latin American dictatorships. By comparison with the ideological dictatorships of either the fascist or

Drawing by Donald Reilly; © *1967 The New Yorker Magazine, Inc.*

"NO, NO, SWEENEY! IDENTIFY! EMPATHIZE!"

communist type, the nonideological military dictatorships, such as were set up in Brazil (1966), Nigeria (1966), or Peru (1968), tolerate a considerable degree of unorthodoxy so long as the authority of the military rulers is not challenged.

Measuring the margin of unorthodoxy in democratic societies, we find Britain, France, Scandinavia, the Netherlands, Australia, and New Zealand on the top of the list, while the United States trails behind. Needless to say, the positions are never fixed, and the range of unorthodoxy constantly changes; by general agreement there is less uniformity and conformity of thought in the United States today than ten years ago, and there may be more again ten years hence.

Common agreement on fundamentals is a second condition indispensable to the successful working of political democracy. The most important agreement, and the one no written constitution can by itself guarantee, is the common desire to operate a democratic system. Where there is no written constitution, as in Great

Britain, there is no protection of political minorities or individual nonconformists other than the decency and restraint of the majority. Legally, the British Parliament could outlaw the opposition and introduce a totalitarian state overnight. But the government is not doing that because it is party to an unwritten agreement to abide by democratic principles.

By the same token, written constitutions are not necessarily a protection. Fascism developed in Italy, Germany, Japan, and Argentina despite written constitutions, and the existence of a democratic constitution in Czechoslovakia after World War II did not restrain the communists from destroying it.

Even in the United States, the written Constitution is, in itself, no last line of defense of political democracy. There have been times when the Congress, the executive, or the judiciary—or all three—have shown little respect for political liberties; and there have been other times when the spirit as well as the letter of the Constitution have been faithfully respected. Throughout these ups and downs of American democracy, the Constitution remained the same; the variable was the greater or lesser determination of the people to defend liberty at all cost.

The lesson of all this historical experience is simple: *the strength of a democracy is never greater than the will of the people to uphold it.*

Where agreement on fundamentals is lacking, political democracy suffers from stresses and strains that may well become fatal. An irreconcilable division on fundamentals between major parties may lead to civil war or dictatorship. Such a situation existed in the United States in 1860 when there was no agreement on the basic issue of slavery. In 1930, the German political system was a democracy as far as the paper constitution was concerned; but two-thirds of the electorate wanted to set up totalitarian dictatorships of either the communist or fascist type, and the fascists finally won out in 1933. Obviously, no constitution, however perfect on paper, can save a democracy if the antidemocrats outvote the democrats two to one. A democratic constitution *assumes*, but *cannot in itself create*, the will to maintain democratic institutions.

The Fourth Republic of France (1945–1958) provides another

example. During its existence, the forces favoring or tolerating republican government based on an omnipotent parliament mustered just a little over one-half of the electorate. On the extreme left, the communists, dedicated to the principle of revolutionary dictatorship, were supported by one-fourth of the electorate. On the extreme right, supported by about one-fifth of the electorate, there were groups that either sought to set up a new republican regime based on a strong executive or that aimed at doing away with democracy altogether.

Such disagreement on fundamentals could not work, and it did not work. The Fourth Republic ended in 1958, and the new Fifth Republic was centered on the personality of Charles de Gaulle. A new equilibrium of forces has emerged; the communists, with about 20 percent of the popular vote, remain the only force opposed to any form of democratic government. Eighty percent of the popular vote (Socialists, Catholic Democrats, Radicals, Gaullists, and Independents) are united on the formula that French republicanism can be saved only by a strong executive as proposed by de Gaulle. Time will tell whether the Fifth Republic under de Gaulle and his successor since 1969, President Pompidou, reflects a new French agreement on fundamentals or whether it is but another makeshift solution covering up the absence of such basic agreement.

Is agreement on economic policy a necessary condition of political democracy? A generation ago, this question was answered more often in the affirmative than today. Conservatives frequently expressed apprehension lest the new socialist principle of public ownership undermine the whole fabric of institutions. In contrast, socialists frequently expressed the fear that conservatives would be unwilling to adhere loyally to democratic principles if socialist parties were given a chance to change the economic organization of society by constitutional means and that the propertied classes would put property above constitutional democracy.

Experience has shown that both sides have been wrong. In theory, the disagreement on basic economic policy between conservatives and socialists looked bigger than it has worked out in practice. The conservatives have abandoned much of their old economic laissez-faire position, and the socialists, having considerably modified their economic philosophy, are now satisfied with a program consisting of welfare state legislation and the socialization of only a few basic industries.

The very nature of the democratic process makes the choice of extreme programs very unlikely. Since elections are generally decided by the floating independent vote, which by definition is middle-of-the-road, no extreme program has a chance of being accepted.

Government by more than one party expresses the democratic principle, borrowed from the law, that "the other side must also be heard" (*audiatur et altera pars*). The democratic viewpoint holds that different men perceive different aspects of truth, mainly in the light of their lives and experiences, and that there will be at least two sides to any major question.

The communists say that the two-party system is a product of capitalism; that the opposing interests of capitalists and workers must be represented in opposing parties; and that, since capitalism has been abolished in the Soviet Union, there is no need for an opposition party to the Communist party.

This line of argument has serious flaws. In the first place, it wrongly assumes that property is the only line of political party. In Europe, party loyalties are frequently based on religious or ideological loyalties; in the United States the regional factor is often important. Also, the communist argument exaggerates the impact of property on party. Only about 60 percent of the British working class vote Labour, and in the United States the correlation between income and vote is equally indecisive. If income were the only decisive factor, political prediction would be much easier than professional pollsters have found it to be.

Even if capitalism could be abolished in the most democratic manner, there would still be need for more than one party. Assuming a classless society in which all productive property is owned publicly and in which incomes too are relatively equal, there would still be questions of vital concern to the community, questions admitting more than one answer. For example, every state, whether democratic, fascist, communist, socialist, or capitalist, has to decide each year what portion of its national product is to be consumed and what portion is to be saved and invested. Another typical question that every community has to face is how much to spend on social welfare and which groups should be favored—the claims of the old compete with those of the young; education may compete with health. The answer to such questions cannot be found in the form of economic organization.

After all, even when there was no capitalism in the modern sense, there was a multitude of parties. When suffrage was limited to the propertied classes, as it was in most countries until about one hundred years ago, the existing parties were divided not on the basis of rich and poor, but along other lines—town versus country, secularism versus clericalism, states' rights versus centralism, free trade versus protection, republicanism versus monarchism, slavery versus freedom, to name but a few.

PSYCHOLOGICAL ROOTS OF DEMOCRACY

Man has lived for about a quarter-million years on this planet, yet he has had some knowledge of democratic ideas and practice for only about twenty-five hundred years. Even today, democracy as a way of life exists only imperfectly in a relatively small portion of the world. Democracy, then, can scarcely be called "natural." On the contrary, the democratic way of life is the most difficult of all; it does not emerge spontaneously and by accident but is the result of deliberate thought, seeking to correct what is natural, all too natural, in human behavior. Because it is so difficult, democracy is nowhere more than a goal, a commitment only partly realized.

Just as the behavior of the child is more natural than that of the adult, the behavior of the authoritarian is more natural than that of the democratic personality. The process of growth and development from childhood to maturity is natural only in the biological and physiological sense, not in the social and cultural sense. Socially and culturally, the transformation of the child into the mature adult demands much forethought, planning, and hard work.

Politically, the authoritarian personality is fundamentally the grownup who has never become mature, the ostensible adult who still accepts the dependency and security characteristic of childhood. By contrast, the democratic personality is ideally the emotionally and intellectually mature adult, the person able to stand on his own feet and shape his life for himself. The mature adult does not need security provided by an external authority; he possesses security within himself. The price of this emotional and intellectual independence is high, since to attain it a person must face responsibilities and make decisions by himself, without being able to blame anyone afterward if his decisions are wrong.

There is no growing up without making mistakes, and the overprotected child *can* make no mistakes—his father will see to that! Similarly, in a dictatorship the system prevents the individual from experimenting and acting on his own, so that (in theory, at least) he always does the right thing. By contrast, the process of growing up, of moving away from supervision to personal responsibility, implies the possibility of choosing the wrong thing, of making mistakes; in this sense, *democracy may be defined as the right to make mistakes.*

Implied in this concept is not the desirability of erring for the sake of erring, but the recognition that freedom implies choice between alternatives and that no one can grow to maturity, no one can be truly democratic, without learning to make choices and without occasionally making the wrong choice.

The 200-percent-American defenders of democracy who want to make it a crime for anyone ever to think or act wrongly are trying to have a democracy with authoritarian personalities, people who think and do only what authority has allowed them to think or do.

The attitude of the democratic personality toward the leader is markedly different from that of the authoritarian personality. The latter regards the leader of the nation with a mixture of loyalty and reverence resembling the emotions he first felt toward his parents, particularly his father. The traditional reference to a chief of the state as the "father of the country" is the linguistic expression of a profound psychological tie; the adult in such a society has really never outgrown the father-child relationship.

By contrast, *the democratic personality puts more emphasis on the group than on the leader.* This feeling goes back to that of the rebellious child, who joins with his brothers in a league of equals to destroy the authority of their father. "Liberty, equality, fraternity," the three ideals of the French revolution, express the attitude of the democratic personality against authority. For this reason, democracies frequently act with deep suspicion whenever a great leader appears. Churchill was opposed in England before World War II because he was "too clever," not average enough, and therefore potentially dangerous. Clemenceau was removed from French public life after World War I because he was too much of a leader. Many American voters who cast their ballots against Franklin D. Roosevelt were to some extent motivated by the fear that he was not Mr. Average American. For this reason alone—there are others, too, of course, such as the perennial shortage of great leaders—democratic electorates often put mediocrities into high offices. However, a democratic political system proves its maturity and stability if it can safely survive mediocrities as presidents and prime ministers.

It is for this reason, too, that impersonal factors like constitutions, charters, and congresses play such an important part in democratic states; leaders come and go, but the institutions continue unimpaired. In contrast, the authoritarian personality thinks in terms of allegiance to a particular person. In Spain and Latin America, for example, political loyalty revolves around the phenomenon of *personalismo;* the political attachment and allegiance are to one particular person rather than to a party, program, or constitution. Even democratic parties in such countries usually are split into various factions, each led by one man, to whom his group owes allegiance. But this is even more true, of course, of anti-democratic movements: thus we speak of Hitlerism, Peronism, Stalinism, but not of Churchillism, Trumanism, or Nixonism.

The formation of the democratic personality is first determined in the *family*. It was Sigmund Freud who emphasized that the first five years are probably the most decisive years of life as far as basic attitudes are concerned. In the early years of life, the home is school, church, and government all rolled into one. In some societies, parents are accorded absolute power over their children; in such societies the family resembles a miniature absolutist state, in which the fiat of the absolute ruler, the father, is the law. In contrast, democratic family relations give the child the first experience of democracy long before he has ever heard that word. The degree of authoritarianism inherent in the family structure of a society is only one of the factors that impinge upon the character of its political system, but it is an important factor. Conversely, the degree to which a political system is authoritarian has a direct effect on the authority structure of the family. Thus, during the authoritarian and totalitarian eras of Germany and Japan the strongly authoritarian pattern of the family in both countries was often noted. Although this authoritarian family pattern drew on many other sources beside the political heritage of both nations, the destruction of political totalitarianism in Germany and Japan, through their defeat in World War II, had as one of its by-products a loosening of rigid male and paternal domination in the family.

One of Germany's leading child psychologists, Kurt Lewin, came to the United States in 1932 and stayed here until his death in 1947. In a paper on "Some Social-Psychological Differences between the United States and Germany" (reprinted in his *Resolving Social Conflicts*, 1948), he makes the following observations:

> To one who comes from Germany, the degree of freedom and independence of children and adolescents in the United States is very impressive. Especially the lack of servility of the young child toward adults or of the student toward his professor is striking. The adults, too, treat the child on a much more equal footing, whereas in Germany it seems to be the natural right of the adult to rule and the duty of the child to obey. The natural relation of adult and child in the United States is not considered that of a superior (*Herr*) to a subordinate (*Untergebener*) but that of two individuals with the same right in principle. The parents seem to treat the children with more respect.

Even a society with a comparatively unauthoritarian family structure may have a wide range of differences based on religion, region, or social class. Thus, empirical research in the United States has found that "lower-status child-rearing practices foster compliance to authority; upper-status socialization places a much greater emphasis on self-expression and individual aspiration" (Fred I. Greenstein, *Children and Politics*, 1965, p. 155).

The *school* is, next to the home, perhaps the most important single source of a child's basic psychological attitudes. What children learn formally in school is much less important than what they pick up unconsciously from the way in which the school in fact operates. Democratic educational theory requires that the teacher help the child learn *how to think* rather than *what* to think. A teacher, therefore, who shows in his behavior and relations with his students that he (or she) is authoritarian and domineering will find that his best prepared lectures on the democratic faith of Jefferson or Lincoln will be of no avail, because the meaning of democracy in the context of the school can only be conveyed through living experience. Similarly, a school board or principal who treats classroom teachers like perpetually compliant subordinates will find that such administrative behavior has its indirect and direct impact on the way in which children learn the meaning of democracy. Mechanisms for self-government of students in high schools and colleges can become an important experience in democratic awareness, provided such mechanisms are not controlled and operated from the front office of the administration.

The autonomy of states, communities, and school districts is one of the few surviving elements in the American federal system. While this freedom has at times resulted in schools of poor quality in some regions of the country, it has been defended on the ground that local autonomy is a more fundamental value than a potentially better educational system run by the national government—as, for example, exists in France.

The existence of private schools in democracies is a further expression of freedom in education. In totalitarian societies, the state generally abolishes all private schools since there is only one pattern that is right and the state knows what it is and has the means to enforce it. In democratic societies, many important educational innovations have been given their first trial in small experimental schools; if successful, such advances then spread to the public school system.

The attitude toward *women* sharply differentiates the democratic from the authoritarian personality. The authoritarian generally desires to keep women "in their place"; his scale of values is oriented strongly toward masculine traits and preferences. Many legal codes officially recognize the superior position of the male by declaring him to be the head of the family and by subordinating his wife to him in matters of property and other basic issues.

Feminism is not only the creed of women who wish to assert their equality, but also the feeling of democratically inclined men who resent the treatment of women as inferiors just as they resent the treatment of any other human being as an inferior on the basis of race, for example, or religion, or nationality. As in other cases of intolerance and inequality, the democratic personality is keenly aware of the fact that *unfair and arrogant treatment is harmful not only to the person so treated, but also to the person who metes it out.* This aspect of racial segregation was recognized by the Supreme Court when it declared racial segregation in public schools unconstitutional in its historic decision of May 17, 1954.

The Civil Rights Act of 1964 prohibited discrimination in private employment on grounds of sex (as also on grounds of race, color, or religion). Despite this important progressive piece of legislation, women still have a long way to go before attaining genuine economic equality. Women's pay generally ranges from one-half to two-thirds of men's pay in the same occupational category; in 1967, only 5.2 percent of white American women earned $7,000 or more, as compared with 41.5 percent of white males and 9.5 percent of all nonwhites.

The *range of affection* determines the degree to which a person matures, to which he can be called democratic. The child first knows only himself. Gradually he discovers a world outside his own body and desires—his mother, father, brothers and sisters, neighbors, and classmates. The degree of his maturation and adulthood is in direct proportion to his capacity to enlarge his horizon and make friends with all kinds of people.

The immature personality stops early in this process; he can only identify with his own group and considers others dangerous and hostile. This group-egotism may include the family only, or it may extend to social class, political party, nation, or race. In all these cases, the attachment to the in-group is frequently more an *expression of hatred for the outsider than of affection for the insider.*

By contrast, the democratic personality is always aware of his own imperfections and those of his social class, party, or nation, and this realization makes him tolerant of different people, different races, different religions, different ideas. His capacity to co-operate and love is not a rigid fixation on one particular object, but the expression of a *general capacity to cooperate, to share, to love.*

Love that is exclusively directed at one person or group is usually not love but either masochistic self-abasement or sadistic domination. Love and cooperation in the democratic sense imply freedom, equality, and integrity, not exclusiveness and domination. When St. Paul said that there was "neither Jew nor Greek, neither bond nor free," he gave expression to a conception of human relations in which there was no in-group and no out-group, but only one humanity.

The strength of the democratic personality is proportionate to the strength of democratic institutions and practices in the society in which he lives. To the extent that persons are given leeway to develop and to act freely and spontaneously, they will experience less frustration, rage, and hatred.

Aggression is generally the *result of frustration,* although the causal relationship does not always appear immediately. Many persons are able to repress temporarily their aggressive impulses following frustration; such delays and repressions do not destroy the aggressive reaction, but merely postpone, exaggerate, and distort it. The democratic society seeks to minimize frustration by removing its sources as much as possible. Thus, in a democracy, the citizen has the right to criticize any political leader, the government, or any idea.

This *freedom of expression serves as a safety valve,* preventing resentment and hostility from being repressed and transformed into aggression and hatred. As everybody knows from his own experience, once he has told somebody off he feels better. Freedom of expression is a psychological catharsis, in which the soul keeps itself from accumulating resentment and hostility.

The cathartic function of freedom of expression as a safety valve is of essentially short-term political utility, however. In the long run, free speech must do more than merely provide temporary release from tension: if social stability and peace are to be secured, free speech must lead to a change of the social relations that have resulted in conflict. If free speech degenerates into a mere ceremonial testifying to the existence of democratic procedures without producing the necessary remedial action, the respect for free speech may be easily undermined. Once a significantly large group of people loses faith in the function of political dialogue to resolve social conflicts, once the suspicion spreads that free speech is merely a device to maintain the status quo, direct action and violence may replace the more rational methods of the dialogue.

It is generally agreed that the democratic personality is more tolerant and more cooperative than the authoritarian personality. But the question is often raised whether these human gains are not paid for by the loss of efficiency. Controlled experiments with children and adults have shown that the efficiency of a group can

Drawing by Herbert Goldberg, © 1966 Saturday Review, Inc.

**"IS THAT THE TRUTH, HOPGOOD? YOU REALLY
LIKE ME FOR MYSELF?"**

be raised by substituting a democratic group decision for a lecture, request, or command from the top. In industry, management is increasingly using democratic group discussions to raise efficiency. This is still a new field of experimentation, but there is certainly no evidence that the autocratically run group produces more efficient individuals.

In the field of education too, schools and colleges are trying to get away from the lecture method, by which the teacher tells the student that such and such is so and so—period. The advantage of the discussion method over lecturing is that the teacher no longer functions as a little god issuing the law from Mount Sinai but is more in the nature of an umpire who sees to it that the rules of debate are properly observed; the discussion itself has to be carried forward by the students, and whatever conclusions they arrive at are the product of their own group thinking, not of superior authority. Discussion, of course, assumes equality; superiors do not discuss with inferiors, but tell them what to do.

The *feeling of being wanted is one of the strongest driving forces of action and allegiance;* nothing can produce that feeling better than the democratic process of consultation, discussion, and free exchange of ideas. With love, greater things can be accomplished than with hatred. This old religious truth is also borne out by psychology, politics, and history.

INDIVIDUAL FREEDOM
AND NATIONAL SECURITY

The best introduction to the problem of individual liberty is still John Stuart Mill's essay *On Liberty* (1859). Mill wrote his essay at a comparatively civilized time, when there seemed to be little need for it. Yet he foresaw that illiberal forces would gain in influence, and he hoped that men would then turn to *On Liberty.* Though Mill modestly disclaimed originality other than that which "every thoughtful mind gives to its own mode of conceiving and expressing truths which are common property," the essay has grown in stature as time goes on, because many of Mill's predictions have come true, and much that he has to say is still valid today.

As Alexis de Tocqueville had done in his *Democracy in Amer-*

ica (1835–1840), Mill attacked the idea that the evolution of government from tyranny to democracy necessarily solves the problem of individual liberty. *Tyranny can be exercised by one, by a few, or by the majority,* and the latter is potentially the worst of all, since it commands the widest moral support, whereas oppression by one or a few is mainly physical. The power of public opinion in a democracy often exercises more restraint and repression against dissidents than a dictator exercises by physical means in a dictatorship. Protection against political tyranny is therefore not enough. It must be supplemented by protection against social tyranny, which leaves fewer means of escape, "penetrating much more deeply into the details of life, and enslaving the soul itself."

Mill sees that the natural tendency of man is not to be tolerant and open-minded, but to impose his views on others, and that lack of power is frequently the major cause of tolerating dissent. It makes little difference how numerous the dissenting minority is: "If all mankind minus one, were of one opinion, and only one person were of the contrary opinion, mankind would be no more justified in silencing that one person, than he, if he had the power, would be justified in silencing mankind."

Silencing an unorthodox opinion is not only wrong but harmful, because it robs others of an opportunity to get acquainted with ideas that may be true or partly true. "All silencing of discussion," Mill argues, "is an assumption of infallibility." Therefore Mill states that, unless *absolute freedom of opinion*—scientific, moral, political, and theological—is guaranteed, a society is not completely free.

No individual can grasp more than a fragment or portion of truth; no society can speak for all mankind; finally, whole eras are no more infallible than individuals. History is full of opinions held by one age as the last truth, only to be considered false and absurd by subsequent ages.

Just as liberty is not complete unless it is absolute, so discussion must be completely unhampered, and free discussion must not be ruled out when "pushed to an extreme," because the arguments for a case are not good unless they are good for an extreme case. Mill is aware of the argument that some opinions are so useful and important to society that they must be excluded from public discussion and criticism, but he answers that the "usefulness of an opinion is itself a matter of opinion."

Mill does not accept the "pleasant falsehood" that truth inevitably triumphs over persecution; history "teems with instances of truth put down by persecution." In the history of religion in the West, for example, there are numerous sects and churches that have been successfully suppressed, and Mill therefore concludes that "persecution has always succeeded, save where the heretics were too strong a party to be effectually persecuted."

Moreover, *the greatest harm of persecution is inflicted not on those who dissent from established beliefs, but on those who do not,* because the mental development of the latter is stifled by the fear of expressing unorthodox or dissenting views. In an atmosphere of cowed uniformity there may be a few exceptional great thinkers but not an intellectually active people. "No one can be a great thinker who does not recognize that as a thinker it is his first duty to follow his intellect to whatever conclusions it may lead."

Moreover, dogmatism robs truth of its vigor and vitality and is more likely to destroy truth than keep it alive. For its own health, truth needs to be "fully, frequently, and fearlessly" discussed. If possible at all, the opposing opinion should be expressed by someone who really believes in it. Only in the constant process of being challenged can truth grow and remain healthy. "Both teachers and learners go to sleep at their posts, as soon as there is no enemy in the field."

The necessity for the fullest expression of opinion may be based on three grounds. First, the silenced opinion may be *wholly true,* in which case its suppression is wholly unjustified. Second, the silenced opinion may be *partly true and partly false,* as most opinions tend to be, in which case "it is only by the collision of adverse opinions that the remainder of the truth has any chance of being supplied." Third, even if the silenced opinion be *wholly erroneous,* it should not be suppressed, because its very challenge of truth prevents the latter from degenerating into dogma and prejudice.

The purpose of individual liberty is personal self-development. It is the privilege of every person to interpret experience in his own way, and his moral faculties can only be brought into play when he is obliged to choose between alternatives. A person who merely follows custom and tradition makes no choice, nor does he who lets others make his decisions for him. *Different persons should be permitted to lead different lives;* the principle of liberty thus inevitably implies that of variety and diversity.

It should be noted that the progress of industrial civilization does not make it easier for men and women to remain individual personalities, because increasingly "they now read the same things, listen to the same things, go to the same places, have their hopes and fears directed to the same objects, have the same rights and liberties, and the same means of asserting them." People who do the same things tend to think the same thoughts.

This standardization has progressed enormously in the last hundred years; the radio, television, and movie industries have added new dimensions of prefabricated opinion. The number of daily papers is steadily declining in Britain and the United States (there are hundreds of cities and towns with only one daily paper) and the number of newspaper readers is constantly increasing, so that more and more people are reading fewer and fewer papers. Moreover, standardization has now reached the point where not only is identical news coverage published in thousands of papers, but even editorials, purporting to present the viewpoint of the local paper's editor, are actually "canned," prepared in a New York or Washington agency and then "farmed out" all over the country.

Mill reminds those who are willing to repress individual liberty for the sake of a strong state that the worth of a state is no more than the worth of its individual citizens. When the state "dwarfs" its men and reduces them to docile instruments, it will find that "with small men no great things can really be accomplished."

Mill is still the best guide to liberty based on reason. Yet *On Liberty* is more than a century old, and it cannot be expected to give clearcut answers to the problems that baffle us today. In particular, Mill did not deal with the problem of revolutionary movements in a democracy.

In the United States, the curbing of revolutionary movements by legal means is based on the Smith Act of 1940, Section 2 of which makes it unlawful for any person knowingly or willfully to "advocate, abet, advise, or teach the duty, necessity, desirability, or propriety of overthrowing or destroying any government in the United States by force or violence, or by the assassination of any officer of such government." In 1948, eleven communist leaders were indicted for violation of the Smith Act. The trial, one of the most important political trials in American history, lasted more than nine months and required almost 16,000 pages to record. Finally, the Supreme Court took up the case and decided against the communist leaders on June 4, 1951.

The main constitutional issue involved was *whether the Smith Act violated the First and Fifth Amendments.* The First Amendment provides that Congress shall make no law "abridging the freedom of speech, or of the press; or the right of the people peaceably to assemble, and to petition the government for a redress of grievances." Under the Fifth Amendment, no person "shall be deprived of life, liberty, or property, without due process of law." By a majority of six to two, the Supreme Court held the Smith Act constitutional.

A central concept in the conflicting opinions of the Court was the *clear and present danger* doctrine, as expressed by Mr. Justice Holmes in 1919: "The question in every case," Holmes wrote, "is whether the words used are used in such circumstances and are of such a nature as to create a clear and present danger that they will bring about the substantive evils that Congress has a right to prevent. It is a question of proximity and degree."

Writing for the majority in the case of the communists, Chief Justice Vinson declared that the communists *did* create a clear and present danger in recommending the overthrow of the government by force and violence. Chief Justice Vinson even went beyond the "clear and present danger" doctrine by accepting a narrower concept of *probable danger:* "In each case [courts] must ask whether the gravity of the 'evil,' discounted by its improbability, justifies such invasion of free speech as is necessary to avoid the danger." In a concurring opinion, Mr. Justice Jackson denied that the clear-and-present-danger doctrine could properly be applied to the case; otherwise communists plotting a revolutionary conspiracy would be protected during its period of incubation, and the government could move "only after imminent action is manifest, when it would, of course, be too late."

In his dissenting opinion, Mr. Justice Black emphasized that the communist leaders were not charged with any nonverbal acts designed to overthrow the government and that the outlawry of verbal expressions of revolution constitutes a drastic qualification or complete repudiation of the clear-and-present-danger doctrine. Mr. Justice Douglas, in his dissenting opinion, conceded that "the freedom to speak is not absolute," and accepted, in general, the Holmesian principle. However, whereas Holmes left the meaning of his principle rather vague, Douglas quoted approvingly Mr. Justice Brandeis in *Whitney* v. *California* (1927) that "no danger flowing from speech can be deemed clear and present, unless the incidence of the evil apprehended is so imminent that it may befall before there is opportunity for full discussion." Following Brandeis, Douglas argued that free speech *has* destroyed communism in the United States and that it is "inconceivable" that advocates of communist revolution in the United States would have any success. Under the Brandeis doctrine, it might be one thing to preach publicly against conscription when there is ample opportunity to rebut pacifism in public debate and quite another thing to preach pacifist doctrine outside a draft board, when such opportunity to rebut does not exist.

The Brandeis doctrine was expressed much earlier by Thomas Jefferson, who was willing to "tolerate error so long as reason is left free to combat it." In his first inaugural address Jefferson said that "having banished from our land that religious intolerance under which mankind so long bled and suffered, we have yet gained little if we countenance a political intolerance as despotic, as wicked, and capable of as bitter and bloody persecutions." Going into the fundamental question of how to deal with those who advocate basic change, Jefferson had this to say: "If there be any among us who would wish to dissolve this Union or to change its republican form, let them stand undisturbed as monuments of the safety with which error of opinion may be tolerated where reason is left free to combat it."

Jefferson was willing to allow even antirepublican (or antidemocratic, as we would say today) doctrines, not only on the basis of rational argument but also because he had tremendous faith in a free America, "the strongest government on earth." It is possible that our present wavering with regard to the Jeffersonian doctrine coincides with something deeper: a loss of self-confidence in the strength of liberty and the growing fear that antidemocratic propaganda, if unchecked, might gain too many converts.

There are indications of a return to more traditional American concepts. Virtually reversing its position of 1951, the Supreme Court ruled on June 17, 1957, in the case against fourteen west coast communist leaders that a distinction must be made "between advocacy of forcible overthrow as an abstract doctrine and advocacy of action to that end," and that "mere membership or the holding of office in the Communist Party" did not constitute sufficient evidence of the intent to overthrow the government by force. While this decision did not explicitly invalidate the constitutionality of the Smith Act, it marked, at least, a return to the clear-and-present-danger doctrine that had been strongly modified, if not abandoned, in 1951. In any case, the 1957 decision of the Supreme Court reestablished the traditional democratic concept under which all doctrines, including revolutionary ones, may be lawfully advocated and propagated. In other words, the validity of democracy is no longer a taboo issue that must not be challenged.

Under the Internal Security Act of 1950 (known as the McCarran Act), the Communist party was required to register with the government. In 1961, the Supreme Court held that this requirement was constitutional, but in 1964 and 1965 it effectively nullified the practical value of this position, for it ruled that neither the Communist party nor individual party members could be compelled to register, since this would be compulsory self-incrimination forbidden by the Fifth Amendment. The net effect of these (and other) decisions since 1957 has been to allow the Communist party to come out into the open more and more. In 1966, the party held its eighteenth national convention—the first since 1959. Yet despite the considerable freedom enjoyed by communists in recent years—due mainly to the liberal interpretation of existing laws by the courts and law enforcement agencies—the membership of the Communist party has remained stable at the low figure of about fifteen thousand. Above all, the party has failed to make any significant progress in penetrating its three prime targets: Negroes, Mexican-Americans, and labor unions.

In the protection of traditional liberties, the judiciary has held up best in the contemporary crisis. In 1955, for example, the United States Court of Appeals upheld the "natural right" of American citizens to travel abroad, thus denying the Department of State the authority to decide arbitrarily who may undertake such travel. Since that decision, upheld in a similar case by the Supreme Court in 1958, the government can deny the issuance of a passport only after due process of law, whereas until that time it could, and did, make such vital determinations on its own discretion. Although the Fifth Amendment does not specifically mention the right to travel, the Supreme Court held in 1958 that it is part of the "liberty" protected by the Fifth Amendment against infringement without due process of law. In 1964, the Supreme Court declared unconstitutional the provision of the McCarran Act under which Communists were forbidden to apply for passports. The court ruled that the government has the right to restrict travel under special circumstances on grounds of national security but that it could not forbid all Communists from traveling to all countries where passports are required. The government must show in each specific case why denial of a particular trip to a particular Communist is required by considerations of national security. In 1967, the Supreme Court ruled that a person could not be denied employment in a defense plant solely on the ground of membership in the Communist party.

In education too, the Supreme Court has had to reconcile individual liberty with national security. In 1957, the Court dealt with an important aspect of academic freedom. Professor Paul Sweezy, after lecturing at the University of New Hampshire on economics, was questioned by the state's attorney general about his political activities and beliefs. He denied the charge that he had ever been a member of the Communist party but refused to give any information about his teaching or his political opinions and associations. As a result, he was held to be in contempt by the New Hampshire Supreme Court. The United States Supreme Court decided that Professor Sweezy's conviction was invalid and added the warning that government should be "extremely reticent" to tread in the areas of academic freedom and political expression: "No one should underestimate the vital role in a democracy that is played by those who guide and train our youth. To impose any strait-jacket upon the intellectual leaders in our colleges and universities would imperil the future of our nation."

THE BRITISH APPROACH TO CIVIL LIBERTY AND LOYALTY

Britain no longer occupies the position of the leading great power which it held in the nineteenth century. Yet it is still the nation with the longest experience in constitutional government, or freedom under law, and its way of dealing with a basic problem of modern democracy—how to reconcile civil liberty with national security—may be of interest to other democratic nations.

The main problem posed in civil liberty is that of public policy toward the revolutionary movements of communism and fascism. The British position is clear, unhedged by any ifs and buts: there are no legal restrictions on advocating communist or fascist doctrines or on organizing such parties. Only acts are punished. Espionage, for example, is a punishable crime, but a communist who spies for the Soviet Union or for China is punished for the crime of spying and not for being a communist.

The definition of what constitutes an act is not always easy. Under the Public Order Act of 1937, for example, the wearing of political uniforms (generally indulged in by fascists rather than communists) is forbidden. This prohibition, however, is based on the reasoning that the wearing of a political uniform is more than an expression of a political conviction. It is, in itself, an act of intimidation, particularly when thousands of uniformed party members march in paramilitary formation through main thoroughfares. Nearly all countries of whatever political persuasion forbid the unlawful wearing of official uniforms, since the uniform symbolizes the governmental monopoly of power and force. A private political army of uniformed men easily gives the impression to the public that it is on a par with the police and armed forces. Totalitarians in Britain may still display their political ideals in an outward manner clearly visible to the public, provided it is not done through uniforms.

The Public Order Act also forbids private political organizations to train their members in the use of firearms. After the assassination of President John F. Kennedy in 1963 and of Martin Luther King and Senator Robert F. Kennedy in 1968, many Americans were shocked to learn how easy it is for anybody in the United States to buy guns—from mail order houses, sporting goods stores, and from a thousand and one other sources of supply. In Britain, strict control of firearms is not confined to political organizations. Weapons can be bought and owned only by holders of a special license. The unlawful possession of firearms is a serious crime. Even policemen are unarmed, on the supposition that no self-respecting criminal would think it cricket to attack an unarmed policeman with a deadly weapon.

All these restrictions lie in the area of action, and they in no way affect the teaching of revolutionary doctrines or the organizing of revolutionary parties. In Britain, there is no special legislation against communist or fascist groups, no House of Commons Committee on Un-British Activities, no Internal Security Act, no Subversive Activities Control Board, and no restrictions on the right of communists or fascists to run for public office. Both parties have put up candidates for many elections, but their poor showing has done them more harm than if they had been prevented by law from running. The fascists, for example, have never been able to elect a single member of the House of Commons. The communists had one member in the Commons in the 1930's, and two were elected in 1945; but since that time not a single communist (out of 630 members) has been elected. Moreover, the communists not only lost in all elections since 1950, but their defeats were embarrassing and humiliating to them as a result of the extremely small communist vote. Part of this communist failure was due to a consistent policy followed by the Labour party.

The British labor movement has at no time approved of any cooperation with communists. In the middle 1930's, when communists in many countries sponsored Popular Fronts and United Fronts of all antifascist forces against the Berlin-Rome-Toyko Axis, the British labor movement forbade its members to have anything to do with such efforts, on the grounds that its integrity would be jeopardized by association with communist aims. Members of the Labour party who violated the ban by cooperating with communists in front organizations or appearing with communist speakers on the same platform were ousted from the party. At the time, the Labour party's policy of not getting tangled up with communists was markedly different from that of antifascist parties, both socialist and nonsocialist, in other countries, and the Labour party was attacked for being hypocritical, sanctimonious, intransigent, and dogmatic. The passage of time, however, would seem to have vindicated fully the consistent policy of British socialism to have no dealings whatsoever with communism.

In 1945, the Labour government surprised many people by allowing the fascists in Britain to reorganize as a political movement, although a number of fascists had committed treason during the war. The socialists in Britain took the view that the fascists had a right to engage in political propaganda as long as they did not violate any laws; further, they felt that the effectiveness of fascist propaganda depended rather on the common sense of the people than on prohibitory laws. Above all, British socialist leaders saw that if fascism lacks the protective coddling of extreme right-wingers and conservatives, it has no way of permeating larger groups of people.

In most other nations, the political left fought fascism, whereas the right concentrated on communism; the division of labor was exactly the opposite in Britain. *Fascism was destroyed by the Conservative party* and *communism by the Labour party.* Both major parties clearly understood that the issue of democracy versus totalitarianism must not be poisoned by partisan arguments and that it is too big an issue to be dragged into the mud of election campaigns. As a result, there are few (if any) countries in the world in which both fascism and communism are as dead and ineffectual as in Britain.

Moreover, this fight against totalitarianism was primarily carried on by the British people through their party organizations rather than through the strong arm of the government. In the United States, the House Committee on Internal Security (known until 1969 as the Committee on Un-American Activities) and the attorney general of the United States periodically publish lists of subversive organizations and publications for the information of law-enforcement officers as well as interested citizens. In Britain, the Labour party from time to time issues lists of communist or communist-dominated organizations which no member of the Labour party is permitted to join. This policing of the communist movement and its network of front organizations by the Labour party is probably more effective than if the same job were done by the government because it uses publicity, a weapon the communists do not like, rather than the authority of the state.

Often confused with the problem of civil liberty is that of loyalty and security. They are related but distinct. In civil liberty, the individual encounters the state as a *citizen;* in loyalty and security programs, the individual encounters the state as a *government employee.* Loyalty and security problems are thus much narrower than those of civil liberty: whereas all citizens may be affected by matters involving civil liberty, loyalty and security impinge only on a segment of the citizenry, that is, public officials. Also, whereas civil liberty pertains to a wide range of relations between the individual and the state, loyalty and security are limited to the employer-employee relation between government and the individual.

Yet, in spite of this narrower range, loyalty and security programs have aroused much interest and controversy in the last two decades. Both Britain and the United States adopted such programs in 1947, when it became clear that the hoped-for cooperation between the Soviet Union and the Western nations did not materialize. In the American approach, every federal employee is subject to a general check before being hired. In "sensitive" positions (relating to national security or secret scientific research) there is a particularly stringent investigation, and the government may bar persons of doubtful background from such employment.

The British approach is different. From the very beginning of its security program in 1947, only applicants for, or holders of, sensitive positions are investigated with respect to political background or other personal traits that may make an individual unsuited for a position of high trust and responsibility. In the case of nonsensitive jobs, there is no political check at all, since in the British view the state has no right to inquire into a person's political views if the position he holds or applies for is not related to national security. In this approach, a communist would be barred from any work— even janitorial—in the Air Ministry or the Atomic Energy Commission but could work—except on the very highest levels, where some information might be confidential—in the Ministry of Agriculture or the Ministry of Health.

The main differences between the British and the American methods of dealing with revolutionary movements are twofold. First, the British allow less violence, preparation of violence, or intimidation than is the case in the United States, but they allow more freedom of speech, propaganda, and organization of revolutionary groups than is afforded in the United States. The greater

Drawing by David Langdon, © Punch, *London*

"YES, IT'S SUPPOSED TO ACT AS A SORT OF SAFETY VALVE, OTHERWISE THEY'D ALL BE SITTIN' HOME OR GOIN' TO THE PICTURES, OR SOMETHIN'."

acceptance of violence in the United States than in Britain goes beyond politics and constitutes one of the general differences between the two countries. For example, in proportion to its population Britain has only about one-tenth the number of homicides committed annually in the United States.

Second, there is a broader and more basic difference between the American and the British approaches. Since the passage of the Smith Act in 1940, a tendency has grown up in the United States, often (but not always) restrained by the Supreme Court, for government to act as a philosophical and moral teacher who determines which political ideas may be taught or may be the goal of organized groups. By contrast, the *British approach is to look at revolutionary movements from the viewpoint of the policeman on his beat.* Policemen are not philosophers or ideological experts, and their sole job is to prevent breaches of the peace here and now. If a public speaker causes a disturbance or an interference with the free flow of traffic, the policeman has the duty to restore order. He is not concerned with what the speaker says, but only with the breach of peace.

Although there has been no restraint on the freedom of speech and association of communist and fascist groups in Britain, they have been less influential than revolutionary and extremist groups in the United States, where legislative, executive, and judicial restraints have been employed for many years. It is a moot question whether the British approach, if used in the United States, would produce the same results as it has done in Britain. The British experience shows at least that in a democracy freedom can be a more effective weapon than repression in the struggle against revolutionary totalitarianism.

CLASSICAL CAPITALISM

Capitalism developed historically as part of the movement of *individualism*. In religion, that movement produced the Reformation; in learning, the growth of the physical sciences; in human relations, the social sciences; in politics, democratic government; and in economics, the capitalist system. The concept of *capitalist civilization* is therefore a legitimate one; it suggests that capitalism is more than a particular type of economy, that it is a whole social system. It first developed in eighteenth-century Britain and later was transplanted to northwestern Europe and North America. A few basic traits have characterized it from the beginning.

In the capitalist system, *ownership of the means of production* (land, factories, machinery, natural resources) *is held by individuals, not by the state.* This does not exclude public ownership of natural monopolies or basic public services (post office, public utilities), but such cases are considered the exception rather than the rule. Government may also own land. In the United States, the federal government owns one-third of all land, mostly in Alaska and the West.

The bias of the capitalist civilization in favor of private ownership of the means of production is based on two considerations. First, ownership of productive property means power over the lives of other people; from the democratic viewpoint, it is preferable that such *power* be *diffused among many property owners* rather than held by one owner, the state. Moreover, the economic power of private property owners can be curbed by the popularly elected government; were the state to own all productive property, economic and political power would coincide, and the outlook for personal economic liberty would be uncertain. Second, the assumption of capitalist thinking is that *technological progress* is more easily attained when each person minds his own business and has a personal incentive to do so.

The second principle of the capitalist system is that of the *market economy.* In the precapitalist era, the economy was generally local and self-sufficient; each family produced just about what it needed, supplementing its simple needs with some barter or exchange operations in a primitive local market. *Division of labor* was barely known, and each family had to do many jobs that nowadays are spread among hundreds of various crafts and specialties. Also, the type of occupation a person was in and the price he could charge for his goods and services were largely predetermined for him by custom and usage. In contrast, the market economy of the capitalist system is based on specialization of labor. Each person supplies only a very small part of his needs through his own skills and labors. The products or services are designed not for the producer's own household, but for the market. As to prices, supply and demand are the determining factors—to the extent that competition is not distorted by monopolies, oligopolies, or "price leadership" of dominant companies in a particular business or industry.

As to planning in the economy, the government under fascism and communism tries to plan the whole economy. But in doing so it runs up against the difficulty of the limitation of the span of control. No human being can anticipate all the possible contingencies in an intricate economic system, encompassing many millions of persons and operated by economic decisions running daily into tens of millions. As we saw earlier, the Soviet leadership has abandoned, since the middle 1960's, the concept of rigid central planning, and has decentralized the process of economic decision-making by giving the managers of the individual plant more discretion in adapting to the changes of the market. In the capitalist market economy, each decision-maker has to watch over a much smaller area, and his span of attention and control is more limited and therefore more manageable.

The comparatively unregulated operation of supply and demand is the most fundamental aspect of the market economy. Neither communism nor fascism believes in it; in fascism, ownership of the means of production is formally still in the hands of private individuals, but this is not too important, because fascism does away with the market economy and substitutes for it the *command economy*. The state may tell individuals where to work, what jobs to choose, what to produce, what prices to charge, and how to invest savings and profits. Communism abolishes private ownership of the means of production and the market economy. The communist economy, too, is a command economy, in which economic decisions are made by the state. In contrast, the market economy is an economy in which individuals may make their own economic decisions in the light of their interest, experience, and intelligence.

The tremendous political implications of the market economy have finally been recognized by socialist economists. W. Arthur Lewis, a socialist economist, examines this question in a book written for the Fabian Society, *The Principles of Economic Planning* (1949). As a socialist, Lewis is opposed to the orthodox concepts of laissez faire, as are most nonsocialist economists today.

The real issue, Lewis argues, is not between planning and no planning, but between *planning by direction* and *planning by inducement*. In the former, the government (as under fascism or communism) tries to get the right things done by direct control and regulation of output, prices, and wages. A government agent watches every step in the plan, and those workers or managers who fail to fulfill their quota may be punished as saboteurs, although neglect or incapacity rather than willful disregard may have been the cause of their failure.

In a democratic state, the government indirectly stimulates certain economic activities through the budget, taxation, interest rates, and other policies of planning by inducement, thus avoiding the two main defects of planning by direction: bureaucratic centralization and economic inefficiency. Far from rejecting the free market as the normal mechanism of economic adjustment, Lewis holds that "our aim should be to preserve free markets wherever possible." It is also of no little interest that Lewis, in accepting the principle of the market economy, is driven to the conclusion that the nationalization of all industry is undesirable because of the usual reasons against monopoly: inefficiency, lack of initiative, and concentration of power.

Thus, the *function of the free market as a mechanism of political liberty* is now increasingly being recognized by socialists, and it gradually dawns on them that the question of ownership is less important than the question of whether economic decisions are made by independent individuals or corporations on the one hand, or by the state on the other.

The distinction between the command economy and the market economy thus reflects in the economic field the more basic political distinction between totalitarianism (fascism and communism) and liberalism (socialism and capitalism).

The most important specific liberty in the market economy is consumer sovereignty: the consumer not only has the freedom to choose between the goods offered for sale, but he ultimately determines through such free choice what and how much is to be produced. In a market economy the government does not determine how many automobiles or television sets are to be produced—as is still the case after the economic reforms of the sixties in the Soviet Union—but this determination is cumulative, made by the individual choices of millions of consumers. Even in a market economy, the government may indirectly influence the level of production: in a period of inflation and an "overheated" economy, for example, the government may increase the rate of interest, thus hoping to discourage corporations and individuals from borrowing at high interest rates. But such governmental intervention by inducement is basically different from the authority of the government to determine, in a fascist or communist command economy, how much of a particular item is to be produced regardless of the desires of the consumers.

Another essential characteristic of the market economy is *competition*. In the precapitalist economy, custom and usage dictated what goods and services were worth, and there were many persons who could not compete at all, because they were excluded from some occupations or trades. In the modern economy, the alternative to competition is either the private monopoly or the legal monopoly of the state. In both cases, arbitrary determination of the prices of goods and services by a de facto authority (as in the case of private monopoly) or a legal authority (as in that of the state) takes the place of the free interplay of buyers and sellers.

In industry, *research* has become one of the keenest areas of competition. Research today means cheaper and better products tomorrow, and the vitality of competition is seen in the fact that companies are spending an increasingly larger share of their budget on research. In 1930, research expenditures in the United States amounted to $160 million; in 1968, they exceeded $24 billion. About two-thirds of this outlay comes from the federal government, most

WHERE 140 MAJOR DEVELOPMENTS OF THE LAST 20 YEARS WERE STARTED

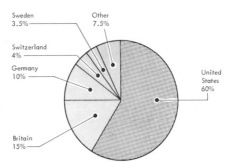

Sweden 3.5%

Other 7.5%

Switzerland 4%

Germany 10%

United States 60%

Britain 15%

of the rest from private industry. Research, by accelerating the rate of change in the economy, promotes competition at an early stage, long before the product or service reaches the market. Research is also an important factor in the competition between whole economies. The United States spends a higher proportion of its gross national product on research and development than any other nation, and American technological leadership is greatest in areas where research expenditures are very high: computers, jet aircraft, artificial fibers, and miracle drugs, to mention but a few.

The *profit* principle is another basic principle that characterizes the capitalist system. So far, no historian has been able to show that before capitalism the profit principle was absent—the merchant in ancient Greece, for example, did not stay in business for his health.

Yet there is one tremendous difference between capitalism and precapitalist systems: the capitalist economy provides more opportunity for profit than any previous economy because it guarantees three freedoms that were not commonly found in precapitalist systems—freedom of trade and occupation, freedom of property, and freedom of contract. Obviously, where the institution of slavery exists, the slaves cannot enter the profit system. Their economic fate is determined by their social positions; not possessing any of the other three basic economic freedoms, they have no access to the profit system.

In the Middle Ages, products were made by guilds and sold at prescribed prices. The profit system was thus doubly limited. Only a member of the guild could enter the process of production; furthermore, prices were defined not by freedom of contract between buyer and seller, but by the authority of custom, the church, or the state.

Even in modern states like Germany and Japan, American occupation authorities after World War II were amazed to find how many professions and trades were virtually closed to outsiders, and they found it no easy task to induce the German and Japanese lawmakers to allow easier entry into more trades and occupations.

Moreover, whenever the capitalist system is described as a profit system, it is frequently forgotten that the other side of the medal is equally important—capitalism is also a *loss* system. Although it is true that never have so many made so much profit as under capitalism, it is equally true that in no other system have so many lost so much as under capitalism. In American economic development, losses, bankruptcies, and failures were very heavy in the early mining, railroading, and automotive industries. In the more recent field of television, a pioneering company like the Radio Corporation of America lost many millions of dollars when it first introduced color television; the initial stages of black and white television were also loss operations.

These are not isolated instances. In a typical year, about four out of ten corporations report net losses. Out of ten business firms started in an average year, five end within two years, and eight within ten years—lack of success being the main reason.

STRESSES AND STRAINS IN MODERN CAPITALISM

The theory of capitalism approximated reality most closely in its classical period, roughly from the middle of the eighteenth to the end of the nineteenth century. In the twentieth century, capitalism has had to face stresses and strains—some internal, such as technological developments of industry itself; others external, such as wars.

The separation of ownership from management and financial control was made legally possible by the invention of the *corporate form of business:* each shareholder in a corporation is liable only to the extent of the shares he owns, no more and no less. In the precapitalist economy, a partnership involved full personal responsibility of each partner for the operations of the business. Partnerships tended to be relatively small, and each partner had a sense of personal involvement, financial and moral, in the business. In a big modern corporation, where fifty million or one hundred million shares are owned by more than half a million shareholders, the link between the individual shareholder and the corporation, of which he is part owner, is very tenuous. The corporation may be located thousands of miles away from most of the shareholders, and in most corporations only a small fraction of shareholders, generally less than one percent, attend the annual meetings in which officers are elected and other important business is transacted.

Management draws up the list of officers to be elected, management presides over the elections, management explains why its proposed policy decisions should be adopted, management decides the salaries of management, management finally submits all its proposals to a vote: the vote is normally between 95 and 99 percent in favor of management. This is a comfortable majority, as compared with average majorities of 52 to 55 percent in political elections. "Like a stockholders' meeting" is a common phrase used to describe any perfunctorily run meeting.

In fact, whenever there is a real fight between management and a strong opposition, as there was over the New York Central Railroad in the 1950's and the Chrysler Corporation in the 1960's, the controversy makes the front page. When the unusual happens and the opposition manages to acquire control, a new cycle of one-party rule starts again for an indefinitely long period. According to a recent study of 500 large corporations, the probability of a serious struggle for control in a big corporation is, on the average, once every 300 years!

The essence of the problem is simple. In government, democracy has established the principle that *those who wield power must be accountable to the public.* The people are the principal, the government their agent. Political power in a democracy must not be held for the benefit of the rulers; it is a trust, the purpose of which is to protect the interests of the people.

In the economic realm, on the other hand, a constitutional situation prevails that runs counter to the basic concept of democracy: corporation managers wield far-reaching power over stockholders and employees, and they constantly make decisions affecting the public interest without any clearly defined responsibility to the public. Whereas in a capitalist democracy political policies are arrived at through processes of consent that begin at the bottom and end at the top, in corporate business economic policies are made from the top and passed on to the bottom. The character of modern industrial organization is hierarchical, founded on discipline and obedience. Recently, however, the traditional pattern in industry has been considerably modified by organized labor, legislation, public opinion, and the growth among businessmen of some sense of responsibility toward the community.

Drawing by Joseph Mirachi, © 1962 Saturday Review, Inc.

**"AND THERE, GENTLEMEN, IS MY OPINION
FOR WHAT IT'S WORTH."**

The more capitalism succeeds, the more it destroys—paradoxically enough—its original institutional and ideological character by collectivizing the framework of business. The first collectivists in the capitalistic era were not its critics, but the most successful capitalistic entrepreneurs—men like Andrew Carnegie, John D. Rockefeller, and Henry Ford, who created vast industrial empires.

Like other empires, industrial empires tend to become bureaucratic and conformity-minded, to follow routine and precedent, and, above all, to transform personal initiative and enterprise into impersonal rules of administrative routine. Whereas the original individual capitalists were men of bold, daring adventurousness, the bureaucratic administrators of the new, vast industrial empires tend to put security above everything else. If risk-taking was one of the most characteristic traits of original capitalists, large corporate business has tended to shy away from risk-taking investments and stick to "safe bets."

The danger is that, as business becomes bigger, the free-enterprise system may gradually become a "safe-enterprise" system. Psychologically, there is *less difference between large-scale capitalist enterprise and large-scale socialized enterprise on the one hand than between small-scale capitalist enterprise and large-scale capitalist enterprise on the other.* It is for this reason that such defenders of capitalism as Justice Brandeis and President Wilson were afraid that the "curse of bigness" might eventually destroy not only big private enterprise, but private enterprise itself. Again, this problem of bigness is not peculiar to the economic institutions of liberal capitalism; in politics too, there is the threat of "big government" destroying the very elements that give life and color to democracy.

Who owns American business? Until recently, there were only guesses on this question, but now the facts begin to come to light. About 60 percent of all corporate stock is owned by individuals, the rest by investment companies, insurance companies, foundations, and institutions. On the positive side, there has been a substantial growth in the number of persons owning stock: from 6.5 million in 1952 to 24 million in 1968. On the negative side, there is the fact that in 1963 fewer than 0.1 percent of the taxpayers owned 19.5 percent of all individually held stock, and those with incomes over $25,000 (about one percent of all taxpayers) owned 48 percent of all individually held stock. While concentration of stock ownership has been slightly declining in recent years, the present degree of concentration is high enough to suggest that the American economic system still has a long way to go before it can rightfully be called "people's capitalism."

To get some idea of the role of big business in the American economy: in 1968, the 500 largest industrial corporations accounted for 64 percent of total U.S. industrial sales, for 74 percent of all profits in industry, and for 69 percent of employment in all industrial corporations. The trend toward bigness has continued throughout the last two decades. In 1948, the 200 largest manufacturing corporations held 48 percent of the assets of all manufacturing corporations; in 1967, the share of the largest 200 went up to 59 percent. Much of this move toward bigness has been the result of mergers growing in numbers at a rapid rate. In 1950, the number of mergers was 219; in 1968, 2,268. More important still, the number of large companies (with assets of ten million dollars or more) acquired in mergers has also risen constantly. In 1950, four large companies were acquired in mergers, with total assets of $173 million. In 1968, the number of acquired large companies was 193, with total assets of $12.6 billion. About half of the 1,200 large companies involved in mergers in 1949–1968 were taken over by the largest 200 corporations.

The phenomenon of concentration can be illustrated by a giant corporation like General Motors, the largest manufacturing company in the world. In an average year, General Motors produces half or more of all passenger cars in the United States and is also the largest manufacturer of buses and locomotives. It employs about two percent of the whole labor force in manufacturing, and its after-tax profits amount to about seven percent of all corporate after-tax profits in manufacturing. Its annual sales in the United States alone exceed the gross national product of more than 100 countries.

Yet there is another side to the picture. In the first place, the small businessman has by no means disappeared from the American scene. In fact, the number of business firms has risen at a faster rate than the population. In 1900, there were 21 firms per 1,000 persons; in 1960, the figure was 26 firms per 1,000 persons. Retail trade and services have provided the largest opportunities for small business. Often, expanding big business is accompanied by a simultaneous growth of many new small businesses. For example, as people buy more cars, there are new opportunities for small manufacturers of parts, and gas stations, garages, motels, restaurants, and all the other services and trades connected with automobile travel.

Secondly, there is *no hereditary aristocracy in big business.* Of the 100 largest industrial corporations in 1909, only 31 were among the 100 largest in 1960. Of the ten largest corporations in 1909, only two were in the same category in 1960. Moreover, the competition is not only between individual firms in this top group; changing conditions of the economy entail keen *competition between whole industry groups.* Steel, coal mining, and textiles were relatively much more important in 1909 than in 1960, whereas the petroleum, chemical, and electrical equipment industries rose sharply in their relative importance in the top 100 corporations. This rapid change in the composition of the top group during five decades further illustrates the point that bigness is not to be identified with monopoly.

Defenders of big business maintain that a big country and a big market need big business. Individual security, too, has a better chance in big business, they argue, than in small enterprises, because the former can do a better job in long-term planning of production, stability of employment, and the provision of services like pension and sickness benefits. In the field of labor-management relations, the greatest progress has been made in the mass production industries, like steel and automobiles, in which big business predominates; by contrast, labor unions have made little progress in agriculture and retailing, where the small unit prevails.

In research, too, big business carries most of the work and responsibility. Occasionally, important inventions are still made in small laboratories; then it takes the resources and organization of larger corporations to translate the inventions into economic realities. More and more, however, industrial research is carried out by big corporations because it requires large financial resources and many years of effort.

Concerning the impact of big business on competition, it is argued that the two are not incompatible. Big business produces a new kind of competition—internal competition. Not only is there competition between General Motors and Ford, but within General Motors itself the Chevrolet competes with the Pontiac, the Oldsmobile with the Buick. Moreover, there is competition in passenger transportation between the automobile and the airlines.

The problem of competition in the changing American economy is the key issue in *American Capitalism: The Concept of Countervailing Power* (1952), by John Kenneth Galbraith. In classical economics, competition was conceived in terms of many sellers, each with a small share of the market, and restraint of excessive private economic power was provided by competing firms on the same side of the market. Galbraith concedes that this classical model of competition has largely disappeared, since many markets have come to be dominated by a few firms and since there is frequently tacit collusion among these firms on major policy decisions. The most famous recent case of such collusion was revealed in 1961 in the successful prosecution for price-fixing of the major companies in the electrical industry.

Yet Galbraith does not conclude from the widespread disappearance of traditional competition that there is no longer any restraint of private economic power left. In fact, new restraints have taken the place of the old competitive mechanism, and these restraints—termed by Galbraith "countervailing power"—are the very product of concentration and bigness.

These new factors of restraint appear not on the same side of the market but on the opposite side, not with competitors but with customers and suppliers. The concentration of industrial enterprises not only has led to a relatively small number of sellers but also has brought about the predominant position of a few buyers. Galbraith explains the growth and expansion of retailers like Sears, Roebuck or the A&P in terms of countervailing power; by contrast, the absence of a few large firms in the housing industry has meant more traditional competition and less efficiency, since the many small enterprises in the housing industry are unable to use countervailing pressure against labor unions and suppliers of materials.

In the field of labor too, Galbraith is impressed by the fact that strong unions have developed mainly when faced by strong corporations, as in the steel, automobile, and electrical industries. In contrast, there is no major union in the retail business or in agriculture, the closest approaches in the United States to pure competition. Galbraith concedes that countervailing power is not universally effective as a restraint on private economic power and that it fails to operate during inflation when relative scarcity of demand disappears and too many buyers compete for available goods and services. If supply is small in relation to demand, the seller need not surrender to the bargaining power of the buyer, who thus loses his capacity to function as a countervailing power.

The weakness of the concept of countervailing power lies in the fact that, though the power of the large seller may be checked by that of the large buyer, the resulting benefit need not be passed on to the consumer. Monopoly benefits may be amicably split between the large buyer and the large seller, or between the large corporation and the large union, at the expense of the consumer. In substituting the few giant competitive units of the twentieth century for the many small ones of the eighteenth, the theory of countervailing power still assumes that a socially fair market equilibrium may be obtained without the intervention of the community in defense of the public interest. In a sense, therefore, the concept of countervailing power, illuminating and provocative as it is, is essentially a sophisticated restatement of the doctrine of the self-regulating market of classical economics, imaginatively adapted to the economic facts of today.

SOURCES OF STRENGTH
OF CAPITALIST DEMOCRACY

Capitalism, it has been said by a close student of the subject,

. . . during its rule of scarce one hundred years, has created more massive and more colossal productive forces than have all preceding generations together. Subjection of nature's forces to man, machinery, application of chemistry to industry and agriculture, steam-navigation, railways, electric telegraphs, clearing of whole continents for cultivation, canalization of rivers, whole populations conjured out of the ground —what earlier century had even a presentiment that such productive forces slumbered in the lap of social labor?

The author goes on to say that capitalism "has accomplished wonders far surpassing Egyptian pyramids, Roman aqueducts, and Gothic cathedrals; it has conducted expeditions that put in the shade all former migrations of nations and crusades." This eulogy of capitalism was written, not by the research director of the National Association of Manufacturers or of the United States Chamber of Commerce, but by Karl Marx, in the *Communist Manifesto*. Few students of capitalism have been as aware as Marx of the fact that capitalism is a *revolutionary way of life*, creating a new material world as well as new values. To cite but a few facts about the United States, the most representative example of capitalism: with six percent of the world's population, the United States accounts for one-third of the world's industrial output. With seven percent of the earth's surface, the United States has more than one-third of the world's surfaced roads, two-fifths of the world's trucks, and nearly three-fifths of its automobiles. In the air, about one-half of all miles flown by civil aviation are American. One-third of the world's college students and professors and one-quarter of the world's institutions of higher learning are in the United States.

The abolition of slavery, the broadening of suffrage, education for all, the doubling of longevity within a century, the highest increase of population on record—all coincide with the development of capitalism and could hardly have been accomplished by a civilization motivated solely by greed. In the world today, the great charitable foundations are to be found primarily in the capitalist nations, particularly in the English-speaking world, not because there are no wealthy people in Asia or Latin America, but because wealthy persons in precapitalist or early capitalist societies have not accepted the concept that the possession of wealth entails obligations toward the community.

In the United States, there are more than twenty thousand private charitable foundations, with assets totaling more than $20 billion. Their annual gifts exceed $1.5 billion. The Ford Foundation, the largest of them all, has assets of more than $3 billion, and since 1936 has spent about $2.5 billion. Currently, it spends more than $200 million annually at home and abroad. Educational television alone has received about $200 million from the Ford Foundation, and has thus been kept alive. Yet philanthropy in the United States is not predominantly based on a few wealthy individuals or foundations. Two-thirds of all foundations are small, with assets of less than $200,000 and with annual grants of under $10,000. Also, most of the charitable funds are contributed by many millions of individuals. In 1967, Americans contributed almost $15 billion to charitable purposes; the bulk of this sum, over $11 billion, was donated by individuals, the rest by foundations, corporations, and charitable bequests. In the academic year 1967–1968 private support for American colleges and universities reached $1.6 billion, about four times the amount received a decade earlier.

Since the middle 1960's, foundations have increasingly gone beyond the traditional goals of philanthropy, which are education, health, and religion. A growing proportion of foundation money is being devoted to alleviating poverty, helping black community organizations, and fighting urban decay. In some instances, foundations—particularly the Ford Foundation—have been criticized for entering controversial areas. In the long teachers' strike in New York City in 1968, the Ford Foundation gave financial and moral assistance to experimental public schools under black community control, and the teachers' union charged that the Ford Foundation was trying to undermine it and tamper with the public school system by using its vast financial resources. In general, the main criticisms against the leading foundations have been not that they are too conservative but that they are too liberal in their orientation and too willing to finance those who seek to change the status quo.

Economic doctrines critical of capitalism need not hide, in the

Drawing by Ed Fisher, © *1969 Saturday Review, Inc.*

"BRIEFLY STATED, OUR PROBLEM IS HOW TO RAISE ENOUGH PHONY-LIBERAL MONEY TO DEFEAT PHONY LIBERALISM!"

United States, in secret, illegal sheets, but are taught at private and public colleges and universities endowed by large capitalist fortunes or maintained by state legislatures. Conservatives' suspicion of social science—an important beneficiary of foundation support— is not wholly unfounded; their frequent confusion of social science with socialism is not quite as obtuse as it may appear to the reformer, since social science, by digging up the facts, may well lead to the social changes the conservatives most fear.

American philanthropy has not been limited to the United States. The United States government and private American foundations gave India, in the years 1952–1969, about $8 billion. About half this sum was an outright gift, and the other half was in loans. A large portion of the loans is repayable in rupees rather than in "hard currency" such as dollars. Since the United States returns most of these rupees to India for development purposes, the bulk of the loans are gifts in all but name. This program substantially aided India in such major areas as farming, industry, community development, education, and health. The progress in health, largely due to American assistance, has perhaps been the most dramatic. In 1953, for example, India had 75 million malaria cases, of which one million died. In 1962, fewer than 2,000 malaria cases were reported.

Yet this attitude is not new and is not a product of the cold war; it was practiced on a large scale long before communism existed. The Rockefeller Foundation, set up in 1913, spent over $500 million in the first forty years of its existence; most of this money was spent on education, much of it abroad. The Carnegie group (Carnegie Corporation, Carnegie Endowment, and Carnegie Foundation) has been active in the field of education and international cooperation. None of these major charitable foundations confine their benefits to American institutions or individuals; they all had their own "foreign aid" programs long before the government stepped into the picture after World War II.

The political implications of the market economy can now be clearly seen: first, *individual risk-taking*, the desire and capacity to assume responsibility and make decisions that affect one's life. This applies not only to the businessman who plans to set up his own business or move it to another place, but also to the worker, who can move freely from New York to California to look for better opportunities—without having to get permission from the government. Risks thus taken often fail, but without such motivation there can be no democracy, and historically there has been no democracy without it.

Logically, it is conceivable that democracy may develop in the future without this economic background, but so far it has not happened that way. The capitalist economy developed before democratic government. Persons who constantly faced danger, risk, and responsibility in their economic affairs were ultimately unwilling to accept authoritarian government from kings and aristocrats, and when the capitalist middle classes could not obtain their objectives peacefully, they resorted to revolution: the English civil war in the seventeenth century, and the American and French revolutions in the eighteenth century.

In fighting for itself, the capitalist middle class appealed to the universal principles of human liberty, the rights of man, and natural law. Later, organized labor and socialist movements in democratic societies appealed to the same principles in seeking to modify the capitalist system or change it altogether.

The second principle of capitalism that directly affects government is the *diffusion of decision and power*. Instead of one central authority's laying down the law of the market, thousands of little decisions hold each other in balance. Many of these decisions are based on erroneous facts and bad judgment, but such defects are preferable to the big errors made by a central authority, particularly if the central authority is subject to no political checks. Every type of democracy seeks to diffuse power by various devices in order to avoid the abuse and corruption that follow the concentration of power. To the extent that a capitalist economy can maintain diffusion of power in the economic area in the face of monopolistic tendencies, it supports one of the key principles of political democracy.

Taking a larger, worldwide view, it should be remembered that capitalist civilization, as represented primarily by Britain in the nineteenth and the United States in the twentieth century, revolutionized the underdeveloped continents. The masses of Asia, Africa, and Latin America learned from their contact with capitalism the appreciation of more and better material things. Asian communism owes its existence partly to Western ideas and promises that Western capitalism made but failed to carry out. Marx gathered his ideas, not in the steppes of central Asia or Siberia, but from German philosophy, English political economy, and French revolutionary politics.

WHY SOCIALISM HAS NOT SPREAD IN THE UNITED STATES

The question is often asked why socialism has not been able to gain a strong foothold in the United States. According to socialist writers, the United States as the leading capitalist country in the world was bound to develop the "inner contradictions" out of which socialist mass movements would develop. Yet nothing of the sort has happened. Is it because socialism is European? There are strong socialist parties in Canada, Australia, New Zealand, Chile, Japan, and other countries outside of Europe. Why the failure in the United States?

The Socialist Party of the United States was founded in 1901. In the presidential elections of 1904 and 1908 it polled about 400,-000 votes. In the presidential election of 1912, it polled nearly 900,000 votes. This was six percent of the total vote, the highest percentage ever polled by it in any election. It maintained its absolute voting strength of about 900,000 votes in the elections of 1920 and 1932, receiving much fewer votes in the intervening years of prosperity. The great depression of the 1930's filled the Socialist party with hope of further growth. Yet 1932 was the last election in which the party made any impact. After that year, things went badly for it. In 1932, Franklin D. Roosevelt was elected president, and after four years of vigorous New Deal policies, the Socialist party obtained only 187,000 votes. This downhill trend accelerated in subsequent elections; in the 1952 election, the party obtained only 18,000 votes—a big drop from 903,000 in 1932. In 1956, the party received only 2,000 votes—and in the light of this abysmal showing it decided to stop putting up candidates in presidential elections.

Even in the heyday of its popularity, in the election of 1912, the

Socialist party was relatively strongest in the agricultural states of the west, and not—as in Europe—in the industrial areas of the east. In these agricultural states—Arizona, California, Idaho, and a few other states of the west—the Socialist vote represented not the outcry of the "oppressed industrial proletariat" against capitalism, but the protests of farmers against low prices for farm products, high interest rates, and corrupt politics.

Socialism bases its appeal on two main issues: (1) *social equality* and (2) the *abolition of poverty.*

As to social equality, one of the driving forces of European socialism has been the protest against the inequality of social classes that Europe (and part of the extra-European world) has inherited from its feudal past. By contrast, the *United States is a nation without a feudal past* and has therefore developed without the legacy of the inequality of classes. In public opinion polls, the vast majority of Americans consider themselves middle class; psychologically, at least, there is little class consciousness in the United States. Social mobility is very great, mainly because higher education is available to more persons than anywhere else in the world. An American has about eight times as good a chance to get a college education as has a Briton. A black American's chance for a college education is several times higher than that of a white Briton, German, Frenchman, or Italian.

If social inequality in the United States has not been a major disruptive force in the American political process, racial inequality has been the persistent and pervasive form of inequality that has characterized American society from colonial days. Unlike the inequality of classes which affects the majority of the people in other countries, racial inequality affects only 12 percent (about 11 percent blacks and one percent other nonwhites). Yet this comparative numerical advantage is more than compensated by the depth of racial tensions, since inequalities between social classes are generally not as strongly felt and resented as racial inequalities, particularly when they are historically based on slavery.

Whereas the issue of capitalism versus socialism is relevant to the problem of social inequality, it has little bearing on racial inequality. Some capitalist societies are more racist than others, and the same is true of socialist and communist states. Problems of racial harmony exist in all continents whether the majority is white, black, or brown, and in each case the degree of racial inequality is determined not by one but by many factors. In the United States, the main thrust of the black response to racial inequality has not been in the direction of socialism. There have been a few black leaders, such as Bayard Rustin and A. Philip Randolph, who are socialists and who have favored a coalition between blacks and labor unions. In recent years, however, the influence of socialist opinion has decreased in the black community in favor of more militant leaders who stress black racial solidarity and black power rather than the ideology of interracial and international socialism. There is also a small minority of black revolutionaries, the Black Panthers, who see in Fidel Castro, Che Guevara, and Mao Tse-tung the models of revolutionary guerrilla warfare, but the overwhelming majority of the black community rejects Maoism or Castroism even more than democratic socialism.

As to the second promise of socialism, the abolition of poverty, socialist groups in the United States have not been able to make poverty a major popular issue. Early in this century, Werner Sombart, the noted German economic historian, studied the American labor movement and predicted that socialism in the United States would founder on the abundance of "roast beef and apple pie." As the American historian Frederick Jackson Turner saw in the nineteenth century, the frontier provided the American poor with an escape from poverty and class war—a phenomenon which did not, and could not, exist in overcrowded Europe. When the frontier was closed around the turn of this century, economic opportunity in the expanding economy and the migration to the west replaced the agricultural frontier as the means of escaping poverty.

Poverty in the United States has dramatically declined in recent decades. In 1947, 32 percent of Americans were poor, as compared with 13 percent in 1968 (the poverty line for a family of four being defined as an annual income below $3,553 at 1968 prices). Yet there is the undisputable fact of growing concern about poverty in the United States. The richest nation in the world, enjoying the highest living standards and suffering from less poverty than any other major country, the United States shows more public concern about poverty than anywhere else. There are two reasons for this paradox.

First, as the production of wealth in the United States increases and as poverty declines, the sensitivity to the still remaining poor segments of the population also deepens, since the ultimate goal of abolishing poverty altogether seems so close at hand. In India, poverty is no news, but in the United States it is. In the United States itself, poverty is more discussed today than it was twenty or thirty years ago when it was much more widespread.

The second reason for the explosive elements in American poverty is that poverty is closely tied to the issue of race. In absolute numbers, the number of poor whites is about double that of poor nonwhites. But the *incidence* of poverty is much higher among nonwhites than among whites. Among whites, 12 percent were poor in 1968, as compared with 33 percent among nonwhites. Unemployment, an important cause of poverty, is also characterized by a persistent bias along racial lines: in depression and prosperity, the rate of unemployment is always about twice as high among blacks as it is among whites.

Incomes of blacks have gone up faster in recent years than those of whites—but not fast enough to bridge the gap. Thus, looking at the income group of $7,000 and over (in constant dollars), we find that the percentage of white families achieving this income level rose from 21 to 55 in 1947–1966, whereas the percentage of nonwhite families reaching that income group rose from 6 to 28 in the same period. In those twenty years, the percentage of nonwhite families in the income group of $7,000 and over had thus increased 4.5 times, as compared with the increase of 2.5 times for white families. Yet, despite this faster relative improvement of nonwhite families, the fact is that the percentage of white families in this income group in 1966 was still twice as large as that of nonwhite families.

Looking at the problem in a broader, international perspective, we find again that it is one of race and not of socialism versus capitalism. In 1968, among black American families the median income—that is, half had more and half had less—was $5,360, which was higher than the median family income in Britain, one of the wealthiest nations in the world. Yet blacks in the United States are understandably more concerned with the fact that the median income of black families in the United States in 1968 was only 60 percent the figure for white families.

Intelligent foreign socialists are gradually realizing that the socialist-capitalist controversy is not very relevant in the United States. Thus a leading British socialist economist, C.A.R. Crosland, writes in *The Future of Socialism* (1957), the most searching analysis of socialism in the last twenty years, that in Britain a leftist would be a socialist, whereas in the United States he would be much less concerned "to promote social equality or material welfare, of which plenty exists already, than with reforms lying outside the field of socialist-capitalist controversy" such as civil liberties, racial equality, juvenile delinquency, and foreign policy. With respect to inequality of wealth—a key theme in traditional socialist argumentation—Crosland points out that "in the United States, property is more equally distributed than in Britain" (*The Conservative Enemy*, 1962, p. 39). In Britain in 1953, the top three percent owned 49 percent of all wealth, and the top ten percent owned 76 percent; in the United States, the top three percent owned 33 percent of all wealth, and the top ten percent owned 56 percent. In both top groups of wealth-holders, the figures are considerably lower in the United States than in Britain (Robert J. Lampman, *The Share of Top Wealth-Holders in National Wealth, 1922–1956*, 1962, p. 215).

THE NEW PLURALISTIC ECONOMY

The controversy of socialism versus capitalism has also been rendered obsolete by profound structural changes in the economies of the most advanced Western nations. The public attention which the constant political tug of war over specific economic issues receives conceals the long-term forces that are at work.

Increased public responsibilities for social and economic welfare, for example, are not primarily the result of moral conversion or of partisan struggles between rugged individualists and do-gooders, but of increasing output of goods and services. Some of the more democratic developing nations have set up very elaborate schemes of welfare state policies—but in many cases these schemes exist on paper only, since the nations are too poor to pay for the desired welfare. By contrast, where economic levels are high enough to permit welfare policies, as in most advanced Western nations and increasingly in some communist states, there is at least a realistic foundation for such schemes.

A second structural change of capitalism has been the relative growth of the *not-for-profit sector*. Traditional economic analysis and popular economic thinking still concentrate on the private, profit-seeking sector of the economy while neglecting the economic importance of *government* and *private nonprofit* institutions, which together constitute the not-for-profit sector of the economy. In fact, the not-for-profit sector of the economy is growing at a faster rate than the profit-seeking sector. In 1929, for example, the not-for-profit sector accounted for 12.5 percent of the gross national product. In the late 1960's, the share rose to about 30 percent. In 1929, employment in the not-for-profit sector was about ten percent of the civilian labor force. In the 1960's, employment in this sector stood at over 20 percent of the labor force. Government in 1929 employed seven percent of the labor force, as compared with 15 percent in the 1960's. The fastest growth has not been in federal government, as is commonly believed, but in state and local government.

However, the economic impact of the not-for-profit sector is even larger if one adds its indirect contribution to the economy. These indirect effects derive mainly from the goods and services it buys, such as defense contracts of the federal government or laboratory equipment bought by colleges and universities, private or public. In 1929, these indirect effects of the not-for-profit sector were responsible for about five percent of the civilian labor force. In the 1960's, the share rose to about 12 percent. Combining the more than 20 percent of direct employment in the not-for-profit sector with the 12 percent of indirect employment generated by it, we find that the not-for-profit sector is responsible for at least one-third of the civilian labor force. According to a pioneering study in this field, it is more likely that the not-for-profit sector of the economy directly and indirectly accounts for about 40 percent of the labor force (Eli Ginzberg and others, *The Pluralistic Economy*, 1965, p. 209).

What are the reasons behind the growth of the not-for-profit sector of the economy? In the expansion of government, defense (on the federal level) and education, health, and welfare (on all levels of government) have been the main areas of growth. Private nonprofit institutions have also enlarged their activities, mainly in education and health. The cost of protecting the security of the United States, as expressed in expenditures on defense and international affairs, was below one percent of gross national product in 1929 and about ten percent of gross national product in fiscal 1968. In education, private and public, expenditures were 3.1 percent of gross national product in 1929 and 6.8 percent in 1968. Annual expenditures on health, both private and public, also doubled: the increase was from about three percent of gross national product in 1929 to over six percent in 1968.

Finally, the growth of the not-for-profit sector is due to an inherent tendency in advanced economies which has nothing to do with capitalism or socialism. As an industrial economy advances, more and more labor goes into the rendering of services rather than into the production of goods. Since the scope of the not-for-profit sector includes services—such as education, community services, health services, social welfare—rather than goods, its role in the economy is likely to grow as the shift from goods to services persists.

So far, there has been little tampering with the traditional concept of leaving the production of goods to private enterprise working for profit, and this pattern is likely to continue. Even socialist governments in Scandinavia or Britain have concentrated their socialization programs on services (health, pensions, education) rather than on industrial production. As an economically advanced nation progressively increases its wealth, there is more demand for public provision of services which are considered essential but which many people cannot buy in the open market, such as old-age pensions, health insurance, education, urban renewal, clean air, or cheap transportation in metropolitan areas.

Increasing wealth also makes it possible for private nonprofit institutions to enlarge their activities. Pension funds of labor unions or endowments of private colleges and universities run into many billions, and these vast funds had to be produced first in the profit sector of the economy before they could be channeled into the not-for-profit sector.

Because the not-for-profit sector of the economy plays such an important part in services, its labor force share in services is about one-fourth of the total. In the decade of the 1950's, for example, one out of two new jobs in the entire American economy was in the not-for-profit sector, not surprising in the light of the fact that the bulk of new jobs are created in service industries rather than in goods-producing industries.

The profit sector and the not-for-profit sector are not antagonists engaged in a deadly struggle for supremacy. In health and education we see an interesting mixture of private profit, private nonprofit, and government. Most physicians are self-employed and are part of the private profit sector of the economy. Most hospitals are private nonprofit institutions. The largest general health insurance program is carried on by Blue Cross and Blue Shield, private and nonprofit, although there are also private, profit-seeking insurance plans as well as government health insurance programs (such as federal medicare for the aged and similar state programs since 1966). The federal government increasingly contributes to the building of hospital facilities and, since medicare, pays for medical costs of the aged.

In education too, there is cooperation between the private profit, private nonprofit, and government sectors of the economy. Harvard University's endowment is worth over $1 billion. Most of this endowments comes from gifts by wealthy capitalists, by nonprofit foundations originally set up by wealthy capitalists, or by individuals who generally earn their living in the private sector. Of its annual budget of well over $100 million, about one-third comes from government sources, the rest from interest earned on endowment funds, from student fees, and from annual gifts. Harvard, a private nonprofit institution, thus receives its funds from all three sectors of the economy: private profit, private nonprofit, and government. Its graduates then return to all three sectors of the economy, the majority working for private business or in self-employing professions.

The traditional socialist charge against the profit motive in capitalism was coupled with the hope that the removal of profit would abolish poverty. Economic reality has worked differently. To the extent that the profit motive has given way to nonprofit service—whether it be private or public—the cause has been, not poverty, but rising wealth and rising expectations of the people. Also, nonprofit does not mean absolute equality or uniformity. There is still room for ambition and even for competition. Labor unions, foundations, colleges are all nonprofit, but their top salaries often compare favorably with executive salaries in private business. Frequently, successful men in any one of the three sectors of the economy move on to the other two. Former government officials, civilian and military, are to be found in important positions in business corporations or nonprofit foundations, and a top executive of an automobile company may become secretary of defense or president of the World Bank. As the number of men and women increases who have had experience in private business, private nonprofit institutions, and government, the result is likely to be a lessening of ideological rigidity.

THE WELFARE STATE

The main principles of the welfare state are relatively simple: first, the recognition that every member of the community is entitled, solely because he is a human being, to a *minimum standard of living;* second, the welfare state is committed to putting *full employment* at the top of social goals to be supported by public policy.

Particularly in the United States, the adherents of the welfare state believe that full employment can be attained without having recourse to nationalization. Taxation properly adjusted to periods of prosperity and depression, interest rates determined by governmental decision according to economic needs, fiscal policies designed to redistribute purchasing power in harmony with the best interests of the nation, investment incentives in times of contracting business, public works for direct unemployment relief, government credits to builders or buyers of homes—these are but a few of the measures the government can adopt in stabilizing the economy without changing its foundations.

In the United States, the great depression of 1929–1939 undermined faith in the orthodox philosophy of laissez faire, according to which the disequilibrium of the market would eventually be restored to a new equilibrium without any interference from the outside. When the American economy reached the stage in which one out of every four employable persons found himself out of work, in which the farmer could not sell his products at reasonable prices, in which more and more business enterprises went bankrupt or were unable to pay wages to their employees or earn profits for their shareholders, something had to be done. The New Deal, starting with the first term of President Franklin D. Roosevelt in 1933, was not so much a set of premeditated philosophical principles to be superimposed upon the American people as a series of emergency measures in response to urgent practical problems.

The Agricultural Adjustment Act (May 12, 1933) attempted to help the farmer by raising farm prices to a level that would enable farmers to buy industrial products as they had been able to do in the years 1909–1914. In order to make such "parity" possible, farmers were to reduce production, in return for which they would receive higher prices (as a result of decreased supply) from the consumer and subsidies from the government. Traditionally opposed, in theory at least, to government interference, the farmers have been content with that part of the welfare state which directly protects their interests.

The National Labor Relations Act (July 5, 1935), commonly known as the Wagner Act, established for the first time full statutory regulation of labor-management relations in the United States. In the preceding half century, the employer in the United States was free to recognize or not to recognize labor unions and to bargain or not to bargain with them. Employers frequently discharged employees for union activities, and if unions became too strong, employers would use various means to break them—company unions, private police, labor spies, lockouts, and professional strikebreakers.

The main purpose of the Wagner Act was to encourage collective bargaining between labor and management, thus substituting peaceful discussion for violence. Although the law did not, and could not, compel both sides to agree, and strikes and lockouts still remained legal, the experience of collective bargaining quickly resulted in a dramatic decline of violence in labor disputes.

Dissatisfaction of management with some provisions of the Wagner Act led to its replacement in 1947 by the Labor-Management Relations Act, commonly known as the Taft-Hartley Act. Though spokesmen for labor voiced deep dissatisfaction with the Taft-Hartley Act, it left the basic principle of the Wagner Act—collective bargaining—substantially unchanged.

The Social Security Act (August 14, 1935) marked another milestone in the movement for social reform in the United States. In modern industry the individual is frequently at the mercy of large impersonal forces over which he has no control. The efforts of the family, private charity, and the local community have all too frequently proved insufficient to protect the individual against the hazards of old age, disability, or unemployment. The passage of the Social Security Act marked the recognition that government, on the local, state, and federal levels, is partly responsible for assuring its citizens of some protection against want and insecurity. Apart from its humanitarian motivation, social security also has important economic effects, since such payments provide people with a minimum purchasing power which contributes to the stability of the economy.

In a historic breakthrough, Congress in 1965 amended the Social Security Act by including health insurance for persons over 65, covering both hospitalization and doctors' bills and going into effect on July 1, 1966. Under this insurance program, popularly known as medicare, the federal government pays the entire cost of illness, apart from small basic fees paid by the insured. Although federal medicare covers only persons over 65, the federal government makes grants to state health insurance programs for families with dependent children whose income and financial resources are insufficient for necessary medical services. Numerous states quickly made use of this federal provision and set up supplementary state programs, known as medicaid. Whereas federal medicare has no means test but an age limit, state medicaid programs have no age limit but a means test, since each state prescribes the income level below which it provides health insurance.

In 1969, President Nixon proposed to Congress a Family Security Plan which, if enacted, will make the United States one of the first countries to adopt a guaranteed annual income for every family. Under the plan, a family of four without income would receive

$1,600 of federal funds a year, to be supplemented by additional state grants. The working poor will also be aided under the plan, such "income supplements" to be provided until the income for a family of four reaches $3,920 a year. The proposal also contained the requirement that recipients of aid who can must learn a skill and accept suitable employment.

The Family Security Plan introduced two new criteria into public assistance for the needy out of general government funds. First, the working poor will for the first time be eligible for assistance. Second, there will be for the first time a uniform nationwide minimum level of income for every needy family. Under the old program of Aid to Families with Dependent Children (AFDC), each state set its own benefit level, which led to huge discrepancies in benefits in the various states. In 1968, for example, a family of four received $55 a month in Mississippi, but more than $300 in Connecticut and New Jersey. Such differentials in benefits drew many migrants into areas with high welfare benefits. In New York City, for example, half a million persons were on welfare in 1965. By 1969, the number went up to over one million, which meant that ten percent of its population and 20 percent of its children were on welfare—during a period of substantial economic expansion throughout the country.

Far from weakening private initiative, public programs seem to stimulate it. For example, private pension funds have grown faster than public pension funds. Public pension funds (Social Security trust funds, state and local government retirement systems) rose from $4.5 billion in 1940 to $70 billion in 1968, but during the same period private pension funds rose from $2.4 billion to $114 billion.

In the field of education, too, 1965 was a turning point in the expansion of the welfare state. Under the Elementary and Secondary Education Act of 1965, the federal government makes direct grants, currently amounting to several billions annually, to individual school districts with children from low-income families. The criteria for eligibility for aid are so liberal that 95 percent of all school districts qualify. Federal aid is also available to children in private (mostly parochial) schools, although the funds are administered by public agencies.

In the Higher Education Act of 1965 the federal government also greatly expanded its role in an area in which it has previously played a less important part. In addition to institutional grants and loans for construction, training, and research, the federal government gives financial help to over two million, out of seven million, students. These programs include work-study aid, grants for "disadvantaged" students, direct federal loans, and federally guaranteed private loans. In the case of such private loans, the federal government guarantees repayment of the loan and pays the interest while the student is at school. After graduation, the student pays the interest and repays the loan in annual installments. Total federal outlay for education rose from $1.5 billion in fiscal 1961 to $7.9 billion in fiscal 1970, or from 1.5 percent of federal expenditures in 1961 to 4 percent in 1970.

The major categories receiving social welfare benefits from federal funds in 1968 included: 24 million retired workers and their dependents and survivors; more than five million veterans and their dependents; 9.5 million receiving public assistance, including 6.1 million persons receiving AFDC aid; and 1.5 million retired federal employees and their survivors. These figures do not include eight million people helped by medicaid, 20 million children receiving school lunches with federal subsidies, three million people receiving federal food stamps, and more than two million college students receiving federal grants, loans, or insured private loans. Omitting the last four categories, about one out of every five Americans receives financial help from federal sources.

Total outlays for social welfare (federal, state, and local) were 8.6 percent of the gross national product in 1955, but over 13 percent in 1968. In relation to all public expenditures, total welfare outlays amounted to 32.2 percent in 1955, and rose to 43.7 percent in 1968. The forecast for the 1970's is that welfare outlays on all levels of government will continue to rise both as a percentage of the gross national product and of all government expenditures, particularly as after the Vietnam war more funds will be available for welfare purposes.

One of the main mechanisms of bringing about greater equality through redistribution is *taxation*. Thus in 1962—a typical year— the top 20 percent of consumer units in the United States received 45.5 percent of all family personal income but paid 60.9 of all income taxes. The top five percent received 19.6 percent of all income but paid 36.1 percent of all income taxes. By contrast, the lowest 20 percent received 4.6 of income but paid only 1.7 percent of income taxes. The proportionate share of the top one percent of income receivers has suffered the most drastic decline. In 1929, the top one percent received 14.5 percent of total personal income, but this share was cut by about one-half after World War II. As to the top five percent of income receivers, their share was 30 percent of total personal income in 1929 but only 15 percent in the late 1960's.

Yet taxation cannot produce wealth; it can merely transfer it from one group to another. The improved material well-being of the American people in the last generation is due primarily to increased production of goods and services. At the same time, a heightened sense of equity underlying the philosophy of the welfare state has brought about more equality in the distribution of incomes than used to prevail in the United States. Incomes have improved both absolutely (in terms of actual size) and relatively (in terms of the distribution among various groups of the population).

These changes are illustrated in the figure on page 232. In it, American families are divided (in terms of constant dollars) into three main groups: low-income, under $5,000 per year; middle-income, from $5,000–$10,000, and high-income, over $10,000. In 1950, 56.2 percent of all families were low income; in 1967 only 25.1 percent, a reduction of over one-half. The percentage of middle-income families rose from 35.5 percent to 40.2 percent, or by one-seventh. The proportion of high-income families more than quadrupled, from 8.4 percent of all families in 1950 to 34.7 percent in 1967. Whereas in 1950 low-income families outnumbered midde-income and high-income families combined by about five to four, in 1967 middle-income and high-income families combined outnumbered low-income families by the higher margin of three to one.

The figure also shows that the absolute and relative position of nonwhite families improved faster in 1950–1967 than did that of white families. In the low-income group, the percentage of nonwhite families decreased at a slightly slower rate than that of white families. But in the middle-income group, the percentage of nonwhite families tripled as compared with a rise of less than one-tenth

FAMILY INCOME LEVELS

(percent distribution of families by income group)

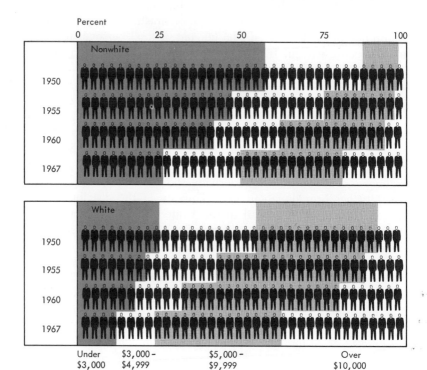

In constant (1967) dollars

Source: U.S. Bureau of the Census

for white families. In the high-income group, nonwhite families increased ninefold, whereas white families only quadrupled. Despite this rapid improvement of the income position of nonwhite families, the overall distribution of income for nonwhite families in 1967 was only slightly better than that of white families in 1950. As long as the relative distribution of incomes of nonwhite families differs significantly from that of white families, it matters little how high the absolute incomes of nonwhites are. What matters politically is that nonwhites as an identifiable group lag behind white families. The income revolution can also be studied in the changing proportions of different sources of income. In 1929, 59 percent of all personal income was derived from wages and salaries; in 1968 the percentage rose to 68. By contrast, income derived from dividends, interest, and rentals dropped from 21 percent in 1929 to 14 percent in 1968. This sharp drop is significant since income from dividends, interest, and rentals is primarily important to high-income groups. Income from transfer payments (public and private pen-

Drawing by Mulligan; © *1963 The New Yorker Magazine, Inc.*

"YOUR MANAGEMENT IS PROUD AND HAPPY TO ANNOUNCE THAT
FOR THE TENTH CONSECUTIVE YEAR, DESPITE OPPRESSIVE
GOVERNMENT CONTROLS AND TAXATION, THE CONTINUING
COST-PRICE SQUEEZE, AND UNENDING AND UNREASONABLE
WAGE DEMANDS, OUR NET EARNINGS HAVE AGAIN TOPPED
ALL PREVIOUS RECORDS."

sions, unemployment relief, veterans' benefits, and other types of assistance) rose from 1.6 percent of all personal income in 1929 to 8.5 percent in 1968. This item is mainly beneficial to the lower-income groups and further illustrates their relative advance. Taking wages, salaries, and transfer payments as one combined major category of income, we find that this item accounted for 60.6 percent of all personal income in 1929, whereas the percentage rose to 76.5 in 1968.

Looking at the whole problem of income distribution in the United States, an outstanding authority in this field comes to the following conclusion: "Do the rich get a larger share of income in the United States than they do in other countries? According to the available evidence this is not the case. The United States has about the same income distribution as Denmark, Sweden, and Great Britain and a much more equal distribution than most of the other countries for which data are shown. There is no evidence that incomes are more widely distributed in any country than they are in the United States" (Herman P. Miller, *Rich Man, Poor Man,* 1964, pp. 11–13).

The evolution of the welfare state in the United States is part of a worldwide trend to make the economy more responsive to the needs of man. The growth of the not-for-profit sector in the American economy—as in other economies—also indicates that profit need not be the sole mechanism of economic progress or of social advance. The welfare state has neither resulted in perfect justice and liberty for all, nor has it led—as its opponents predicted in the 1930's that it would—to the repressive society of authoritarianism or totalitarianism.

In adapting itself to the economic changes brought about by the expansion of the not-for-profit sector and to the social changes effected by the welfare state, the capitalist system has undergone a profound transformation. This new and constantly evolving system is neither capitalist nor socialist, if capitalism means laissez faire, and if socialism means public ownership of the means of production. It is generally called a "mixed economy," combining predominantly private initiative and property with public responsibility for social welfare. Just as the mixed economy of today shows basic changes in relation to the predominantly laissez-faire economy of a generation or two ago, the economy a generation hence may show equally revolutionary changes as compared with the economy of today.

FOR FURTHER READING

Arnold, Thurman W. *The Folklore of Capitalism*. New Haven, Conn.: Yale University Press, 1937.

Berle, A. A. *The American Economic Republic*. New York: Harcourt, Brace & World, 1963.

Berlin, Isaiah. *Four Essays on Liberty*. New York: Oxford University Press, 1969.

Beveridge, William. *Full Employment in a Free Society*. New York: W. W. Norton, 1945.

Carmichael, Stokeley, and Charles V. Hamilton. *Black Power: The Politics of Liberation in America*. New York: Vintage Books, 1967.

Clark, Kenneth. *Dark Ghetto*. New York: Harper & Row, 1965.

Cornuelle, Richard C. *Reclaiming the American Dream*. New York: Random House, 1965.

Dollard, John, and others. *Frustration and Aggression*. "Yale Paperbacks." New Haven, Conn.: Yale University Press, 1960.

Drucker, Peter F. *The Age of Discontinuity: Guidelines to Our Changing Society*. New York: Harper & Row, 1969.

Epstein, Edwin M. *The Corporation in American Politics*. Englewood Cliffs, N.J.: Prentice-Hall, 1969.

Free, Lloyd A., and Hadley Cantril. *The Political Beliefs of Americans: A Study of Public Opinion*. New Brunswick, N.J.: Rutgers University Press, 1968.

Friedman, Milton. *Capitalism and Freedom*. "Phoenix Books." Chicago: University of Chicago Press, 1963.

Fromm, Erich. *The Sane Society*. New York: Holt, Rinehart & Winston, 1955.

Fuchs, Victor R. *The Service Economy*. New York: National Bureau of Economic Research, Columbia University Press, 1968.

Galbraith, John Kenneth. *The New Industrial State*. Boston: Houghton Mifflin, 1967.

Ginzberg, Eli, and others. *The Pluralistic Economy*. New York: McGraw-Hill, 1965.

Harrington, Michael. *The Other America: Poverty in the United States*. Baltimore: Penguin Books, 1963.

Heilbroner, Robert L. *The Limits of American Capitalism.* New York: Harper & Row, 1966.

Heller, Walter W. *New Dimensions of Political Economy.* Cambridge, Mass.: Harvard University Press, 1967.

Lampman, Robert J. *The Share of the Top Wealth-Holders in National Wealth, 1922–1956.* Princeton: National Bureau of Economic Research, Princeton University Press, 1962.

Macpherson, C. B. *The Real World of Democracy.* New York: Oxford University Press, 1966.

Mason, Edward S. *Economic Concentration and the Monopoly Problem.* New York: Atheneum, 1964.

Miller, Herman P. *Rich Man, Poor Man.* New York: Thomas Y. Crowell, 1964.

Mishan, E. J. *Welfare Economics.* 2nd ed. New York: Random House, 1968.

Seligman, Ben B. (ed.). *Poverty as a Public Issue.* New York: Free Press, 1968.

Shonfield, Andrew. *Modern Capitalism: The Changing Balance of Public and Private Power.* New York: Oxford University Press, 1965.

U.S. Department of Labor. *Social and Economic Conditions of Negroes in the United States.* BLS Report No. 332, Current Population Reports, Series P–23, No. 24. Washington, D.C.: U.S. Government Printing Office, 1967.

Wolfenstein, E. Victor. *Personality and Politics.* Belmont, Calif.: Dickenson, 1969.

democratic socialism

chapter four

HISTORICAL BACKGROUND

It is not easy to state when socialism first appears. Some have asserted that the ideal commonwealth in Plato's *Republic* is socialist, inasmuch as its ruling class has no property of its own and shares all things in common. Others have claimed that the Bible, particularly the Old Testament, constitutes the first socialist code, covering as it does the protection of workers, women, and the weak. The early Christians rejected the concept of "mine and thine," and practiced socialism in their everyday lives; and in the Middle Ages numerous sects and movements, mostly religious, attacked wealth and commerce as wicked and incompatible with the Christian life. Such sects frequently withdrew into isolation, living an austere existence and sharing poverty in brotherly love as a protest against the greed prevalent in the world around them.

During the Renaissance and the Reformation, there was a revival of protest against inequality based on wealth. The new arguments increasingly combined the older faith with the newer rationalism, as evidenced, for example, in Thomas More's *Utopia* (1516). In the Puritan revolution of the seventeenth century, there arose, side by side with the main movement of middle-class origin, a more radical group—called "Diggers" or "True Levelers"—that sought to attain communal ownership of land not currently in use. The movement was short-lived, but its radical protest against private landed property was not to be entirely forgotten.

Despite all such illustrations from earlier times, *socialism* as a major political force can properly be said to have originated *as the result of modern industrial capitalism.* To the extent that socialism contains within itself an element of protest against social inequality—and no movement can call itself socialist unless it expresses that kind of protest—it is as old as Western civilization itself. Both Greek and Jewish-Christian thought categorically reject the conception of wealth as the basis of the good life.

Another feature of socialism—the protest against money as the chief tie between human beings—is also not confined to the socialist tradition: many nonsocialists have voiced their disapproval of the "cash nexus." But if we look in history for something more specific and concrete than a vague protest against social injustice, we find that socialism as an effective, organized political movement is the product of the Industrial Revolution.

Just as communism has happened—and is likely to happen—only in countries *before* they have undergone the full impact of industrial revolution, democratic socialism develops only in societies *after* they have experienced considerable industrialization.

Wherever industrialization has taken place in societies without deeply rooted liberal institutions, the political adjustment to the resulting tensions is likely to be either some sort of fascism (as happened in modern Germany, Italy, Japan, and Argentina) or communism (as in Russia and China). Because industrialization in these societies is promoted and controlled by an authoritarian state, its primary purpose is the power of the state.

In contrast, where industrialization has occurred in relatively liberal societies (as in northwestern Europe, North America, Australia, and New Zealand), the purpose of the economy is the welfare of the individual, and the adjustment to the inevitable tensions and conflicts of industrial capitalism assumes some form of democratic socialism or the welfare state, rather than fascism or communism.

This basic distinction between the authoritarian and the liberal society can cut away a lot of confusion. Thus, the question is frequently debated whether a fascist economy is socialistic (because of the comprehensive regulation of economic activity by the state) or capitalistic (because the means of production are left in private hands).

Such discussions are endless and insoluble because they are based on a false premise: that the basic distinction in the world's economic systems is between socialism and capitalism. In actuality, the line of division runs differently: between *free market* or *welfare economies* which operate democratically and aim at individual welfare and *coercive* or *command economies* which operate by command and coercion and aim at the collective power of the state. Both capitalism and socialism fall into the group that is dominated by the concept of welfare economics, whereas fascism and communism fall into the second group, the command economy.

Differences among the species within each major group are important, but they are not crucial. Thus, capitalism and socialism disagree on the best method of bringing the maximum welfare to the people; the former stresses individual property and effort, while the latter puts its faith in collective productive property and effort.

Fascism and communism do not see eye to eye in every detail on how best to operate an economy in the service of the state. Differences between fascism and communism, however, tend to fade into insignificance if it is recalled that the objective—the power of the state—is the same, and that the means—ranging from friendly pressure to slave labor and the concentration camp—are amazingly similar and frequently identical.

In some ways, of course, socialism opposes capitalism, but such opposition is the rebellion of the child against the father, not the total war of stranger against stranger. Just as the rebellious child uses arguments he has learned from his own father, socialism employs, in the controversy with its progenitor, a whole arsenal of capitalist values and attitudes, especially pragmatic utilitarianism.

As to the specific problem of property, socialism inherits from capitalism one basic goal: *to preserve the unity of work and ownership.* In the seventeenth and eighteenth centuries, the early phase of modern capitalism, that unity was a reality. In the England of John Locke or the America of Thomas Jefferson, the average farm, store, or workshop was generally small enough to be owned and operated by one person or family. *Work and ownership coincided.* The chief threat to this unity came from the state, which sought to prescribe, to regulate, to snoop—in short, to play the role of an omniscient busybody in economic matters. This attitude was resented by the individual entrepreneur because he knew that he could run his own business without any unsolicited advice from self-confident state officials.

As the capitalist economy progressed, however, the individual (or single-family) form of ownership and work was gradually replaced, primarily because of technological progress, by an economic system in which large-scale enterprise swallowed up the original capitalist-owner-manager. *As the size of industrial enter-*

prise grew larger and larger, work became more and more socialized, collective, whereas ownership remained private.

In seeking to restore the classical harmony between work and property, the socialist reformer faces two alternatives—(1) the division of large-scale enterprises into small units, so that work and ownership can coincide again in one person or family, or (2) collective ownership.

The former method is feasible in agriculture, where large landed estates can be physically broken up and divided among landless farm workers, as was done in France during her revolution in the eighteenth century, in Mexico and Guatemala during this century, and—on a smaller scale—in Italy after World War II. Whether such a breakup of large landed estates is economically sound or not is highly debatable. In many cases the productivity of dwarf farms created by agrarian reform is lower than that of the original large farm units. A reform government, however, may be willing to pay the price of lower productivity for the greater social benefit of having an independent farm class. In any case, the technology of agriculture is still simple enough so that large units can be broken up, and small units can be operated with relative efficiency.

In industry, this solution is physically out of the question. An automobile or aircraft factory cannot be divided up into 10,000 portions, each to be operated by one worker as his personal piece of property. The technological nature of modern industrial enterprise is such that there is no alternative to collective work and operation. Thus, in facing the task of reuniting work and ownership in industry, collective ownership seems to socialists the logical answer, just as the classical liberal deduced the right to individual ownership from the fact of individual work. In both systems—classical liberal capitalism and democratic socialism—there is the underlying assumption that the *right to property ultimately rests on work, effort, and industry, rather than on formal law, custom, or birth.*

John Locke, the founder of modern political and economic liberalism, based the right to property on human labor, and the value of property on the amount of labor "admixed" to nature's resources. The socialists have accepted the Lockean and capitalist rationale of labor. What has changed since Locke is simply the technological character of labor, not its ethical implications. If the logic of capitalism demands individual property for individual work, the logic of socialism demands *collective ownership* for collective work—*provided collective work is the only possible form of managerial organization.*

Where small property has survived as a technologically efficient unit, as in agriculture, the professions, the arts, and some areas of retailing, servicing, and manufacturing, socialists generally agree with adherents of capitalism that private ownership should be kept and strengthened. Thus, socialist governments have enjoyed long tenure in predominantly agrarian countries like Denmark and New Zealand because farmers in those countries have been sympathetic to the socialist program of maintaining their economic integrity and individualism by cheap credits, guaranteed parity prices, and other policies designed to protect the small farmer against the threat of domination by banks, insurance companies, and wholesalers.

ROBERT OWEN: CAPITALIST-SOCIALIST

The filial link between socialism and capitalism can be illustrated by the fact that the first modern socialist was a wealthy and successful capitalist. Robert Owen (1771–1858), generally regarded as the founder of British socialism, was the first to use the term "socialism." A self-made capitalist, he had made a fortune by the age of forty. He was a man of sound, practical judgment, and he could easily meet one test of experience frequently described by conservatives as essential whenever a reformer comes forth with some new scheme: "Have you ever met a payroll in your life?" Owen had. In his *A New View of Society* (1813), he describes himself as a "manufacturer for pecuniary profit."

His views were the result, not (like Marx's) of study in the British Museum, but of experience in his own industrial enterprises. Owen dedicated his book to His Royal Highness, the Prince Regent of the British Empire; he was no refugee from his own society, as were Marx and Lenin later, but a respectable, wealthy man, as

English as mutton or tea. He considered drink an incentive to crime and a main source of misery, and his list of virtues and vices would have appealed to Benjamin Franklin.

Far from looking upon capitalist Britain as a dungeon of inhumanity, he described the British constitution as being "among the best devised and most enlightened that have hitherto been established." Refusing to believe that evil can be transformed into good in a day, he advocated "progressive repeal and modification" of unjust laws and conditions; strongly rejecting the alleged blessings of revolutionary change, he felt that "the British constitution, in its present outline, is admirably adapted to effect these changes, without the evils which always accompany a coerced or ill-prepared change."

Realizing that love and fellowship cannot be conceived in hatred and born in strife, Owen appealed to "every rational man, every true friend of humanity," and he hoped for cordial cooperation and unity of action between the government, Parliament, the church, and the people.

Owen's rationalism also emerges from the fact that *A New View of Society* discusses one subject more than any other: *education.* Owen believed that the evils of his society were due to circumstances rather than to the depravity of man, and he was convinced that, just as crime and degradation were the result of specific social and economic conditions, education in a new environment could produce human beings endowed with rationality, habits of order, regularity, temperance, and industry.

In his own time, children of six and seven years of age were employed in factories for 12 hours a day and more, and Owen made the suggestion, bold and radical for the capitalist conscience of 1813, that a regular workday of 13 hours from six in the morning to seven in the evening should not be imposed upon *children under 12;* after that age "their education might be finished, and their bodies would be more competent to undergo the fatigue and exertions required of them." Human nature, Owen says, is "universally plastic," and if education is the key to make men more rational and cooperative, "the best governed state will be that which shall possess the best national system of education."

Owen in the true liberal-capitalist tradition looked to society rather than to the state for important change. A century before Keynes and Beveridge, Owen understood the crucial importance of full employment for the maintenance of a civilized society. Yet he was opposed to the dole (cash relief to the unemployed) on the ground that the "industrious, temperate, and comparatively virtuous" should not be compelled to support the "ignorant, idle, and comparatively vicious." Owen clearly saw the human aspects of unemployment; yet he did not want the state to dispense employment, but to provide an educational system good enough to equip every person with the skills wherewith to find employment in the open market.

A believer in the individualist principle of *self-help,* Owen started the cooperative movement and supported the incipient trade union organizations springing up throughout England and Scotland. For Owen, cooperation was more than selling milk to housewives; he believed that *producers' cooperatives* rather than consumers' cooperatives would establish a new social order. He sank much of his fortune in producers' cooperatives in England and spent several years and the better part of his wealth in a cooperative venture in the United States. His best-known experiment, the settlement of New Harmony in Indiana, did not succeed, but his ideas are today more important than ever.

The British experiment of nationalizing selected basic industries and services has raised the fundamental question whether the Owenite method of cooperation outside the formal machinery of the national government is not preferable to nationalization as effected in Britain since 1945. In the British labor movement too, the Owenite bias against the state is still strong; if the labor unions have never been overenthusiastic about nationalization schemes, it is because they dread the growth of the state machinery and the transformation of free labor union officials, responsible to their members, into semi-government officials, responsible to the state.

SOCIALISM AND DEMOCRACY

The link between democracy and socialism is the most important single element in socialist thought and policy. Looking at the history of socialism, it can be quickly seen that *successful socialist movements have grown up only in nations with strong democratic traditions,* such as Great Britain, the Scandinavian countries, Belgium, the Netherlands, Switzerland, Australia, New Zealand, Chile, and, more recently, Israel.

The reason for this parallelism is simple. Where democratic, constitutional government is generally accepted, socialists can concentrate on their extensive economic and social reforms: to create more opportunity for the underprivileged classes; to end inequality based on birth rather than service; to open the horizons of education to all the people; to eliminate discriminatory practices based on sex, religion, race, or social class; to regulate and reorganize the economy for the benefit of the whole community; to maintain full employment; to provide adequate social security for the sick, unemployed, and aged; to replan the layout of towns and cities; to tear down the slums and build new houses; to provide medical facilities for everybody, regardless of the size of his purse; and finally, to rebuild society on the foundation of cooperation instead of competition, incentive, and profit.

All these goals of democratic socialism have one thing in common: *to make democracy more real by broadening the application of democratic principles from the political to the nonpolitical areas of society.*

Freedom of worship and freedom of political association, historically the first liberties to be won, are still the essential foundations of democracy. Where these foundations exist, therefore, socialists can concentrate on the "finer points" of democracy.

In contrast, socialist parties have fought an uphill and generally losing struggle in nations in which democracy is not a living thing, but an aspiration, a hope, an idea yet to be realized. For example, the Social Democratic party in Germany always worked under a heavy handicap. In the Second Reich (1870–1918), political autocracy was a reality, and parliamentary institutions were a cover for the virtual dictatorship of Bismarck and then of Emperor William II. In the 1870's, Bismarck outlawed the Social Democrats as "enemies of the state," and the party leaders who escaped being jailed fled to England, other free nations in Europe, or America.

During the Weimar Republic (1919–1933), the Social Democratic party was paralyzed again by the insecurity of democratic institutions; the main issue of the Weimar Republic was not this or that social reform in which the socialists could take a special interest, but something much bigger: the issue of democratic government itself. Whereas, in nations with long-established democratic habits, socialists could argue over issues *within democracy,* taking the existence of democracy for granted, German socialists constantly had to argue and fight over the *issue of democracy itself.* As fascism grew in the Weimar Republic, the German socialists became more concerned with the defense of republican and democratic institutions than with problems of economic reform.

In Russia before 1917, the situation was even simpler. The despotic tsarist regime did not even make the pretense of democracy or self-government; social and economic reform by peaceful means was thus made virtually impossible, and the door for revolutionary communism was opened.

World War II provides further illustrations of this point. In France, for example, the Socialist party had become the strongest political party by 1936, far stronger than the Communist party. During World War II, however, under the German occupation, the political environment of underground and illegal activity was much more congenial to the communists than to the socialists. Democratic socialists in a country like France function best when they can carry membership cards rather than high explosives. The type of person who joins such a party is stable, probably a family man, in any event a skilled worker or civil servant with a steady job. People of this kind do not readily engage in illegal, terroristic activities such as were necessary in France under German occupation in World War II.

The communists, on the other hand, attract an entirely different type of person, more fanatical, more devoted to the cause, and used to illegality and semi-illegality even in so-called normal times. What the Third French Republic (1870–1940) could never accomplish, four years of German occupation managed to do; at the end of World War II, the communists, polling about twice as many votes as the democratic socialists, emerged as the strongest single party of France. The communists remained the strongest party until the elections of November 18 and 25, 1962, in which, as in subsequent elections, the Gaullist party (Union for the New Republic) heavily defeated them.

In contrast, the socialist vote in the British general election of 1966 was *210 times larger than the communist vote*. The evidence (not only from Great Britain, but also from other democratic countries with strong socialist movements) indicates that fullest civil liberty for all ideas and parties, including revolutionary organizations, seems to be the best antidote against fascism and communism, and that repression is the natural soil for the growth of revolutionary movements.

If one were to rank democratic nations today according to their respect for civil liberty, Great Britain, Norway, Denmark, Sweden, the Netherlands, Belgium, Australia, and New Zealand would be at the top of the list; all these countries are, or recently have been, governed by socialist administrations or by coalition cabinets with strong socialist participation.

The reasons for this parallelism are not too complex. Democratic socialists are keenly aware of the fact that without the opportunities provided by liberal, constitutional government they could not get to first base. Once in control of the government, socialists still maintain the psychology of the opposition, because they know that the possession of political power does not automatically solve the problems of social and economic organization. In other words, before socialists take over the government, they are in opposition to the government *and* to the wealthy classes; after they gain control of the government, the oppositionist psychology, directed as it is against the economic status quo, necessarily persists.

Moreover, even in the purely governmental realm, socialists tend to preserve a certain degree of caution and suspicion after they get into office, because they realize that, though they can gain control of the legislature in an election, the other sources of political power—the civil service and the judiciary—may be hostile to them.

Another factor essential to this discussion is all too frequently neglected. Examining the remarkably high state of civil liberty in nations with strong socialist movements, one tends to overlook *the high respect for civil liberty demonstrated by the opponents of socialism.* After all, if the conservative and propertied classes had shown less respect for the letter and spirit of constitutional government, the chances of socialist growth would have been very slim. From the viewpoint of dollars and cents, the conservatives' genuine acquiescence in socialism meant that they valued their faith in democracy more highly than their pocketbooks and were willing to be heavily taxed even for programs they considered undesirable or unreasonable.

It can thus be seen that both groups took a gamble: the socialists trusted their opponents not to destroy the processes of democratic government in order to protect their financial interests; the propertied classes trusted the socialists not to abuse electoral victories and to act reasonably and moderately when in office.

Where the propertied classes were unconvinced by the Biblical admonition that it is more blessed to give than to receive and were unwilling to pay higher wages to workers and higher taxes for the sake of social justice, the natural response to distrust was more distrust. It is in this kind of political atmosphere that democratic socialism has been pushed back in Italy and France, giving way to the more radical demands of communism.

SOCIALISM VERSUS COMMUNISM

Socialism and communism are not two of a kind, but represent two incompatible ways of thought and life, as incompatible as constitutional liberalism and revolutionary totalitarianism.

There are several points of irreconcilable antagonism between socialists and communists. First, *communists* seek to bring about the end of capitalism by a single act of *revolutionary upheaval and civil war.* Once in power, communists are determined to stay there indefinitely; as we saw earlier, under the Brezhnev Doctrine of 1968 the Soviet Union will not allow any communist government to relinquish its monopoly of power or even to share it with other groups, as was attempted in Czechoslovakia. *Socialists,* on the other hand, adhere to *strict constitutional procedures;* they seek power by ballots rather than bullets, and once in office they know they are not in for keeps but are subject to being voted out in the next election.

Above all, the British Labour party has successfully eliminated communism from its main position of influence—labor unions. *If communists are a negligible factor in Britain today, the main credit goes to the organized labor movement.* It has steadily and quietly fought them whenever and wherever they have tried to gain influence. In open elections, the communists are no menace in most democratic nations, but in labor unions the communist technique of infiltration has often been extremely effective. Because of the communist goal of revolution, it is understandable that socialist parties look upon communists as troublemakers who must be kept out of unions or any other organized working-class activity. And because trade unionists have had the most intimate knowledge of communism—based on everyday contacts rather than on a study of ideology—they have generally proved themselves to be the staunchest opponents of communism in the labor movements. The purely political elements of the socialist parties have not always shown the same steadiness and vigor.

It is understandable why the communists work with such energy for the control of organized labor: they know that no amount of propaganda will convert the middle and wealthier classes to communism. In contrast, the socialists have learned from elementary electoral statistics that parliamentary majorities cannot be obtained by appealing to one class only; a considerable proportion of the working class (in England about 40 percent) does not vote Labour, and if the Labour party is to obtain a majority, it must appeal to other groups. The communists think only in terms of *class* and class antagonisms; the socialists have learned to think in terms of *parliamentary majorities.*

The socialist rejection of Marxist thought applies even to the term "proletariat." As Prime Minister Harold Wilson put it, "The idea of a proletariat is nonsense. I am more interested in people as individuals than in the mass. I am interested in the family, because most happiness is family happiness. I am interested in Saturdays and Sundays and Bank Holidays" (*Manchester Guardian Weekly,* March 17, 1966).

In the crucial issue of public ownership, the gap that separates socialists from communists is unbridgeable. Communists visualize the transition from capitalist enterprise to public ownership as sudden and complete. There is no payment for expropriated property, because communists consider that capitalist ownership of property is no better than theft. In contrast, socialists do not believe that the transition from capitalism to public ownership of the means of production can be either sudden or complete. Most socialists believe in the installment plan. Public ownership of the means of production is to be built up gradually, by installments; if one phase works, then the next will be tackled. Responsible socialists feel

RELATIVE VOTING STRENGTH OF SOCIALIST AND COMMUNIST PARTIES

(as of October 1, 1969)

Country	A: Socialist percent of total vote	B: Communist percent of total vote	C: Relation of A to B
Australia	47.7%	0.5%	95.4
Austria	44	3	14.7
Belgium	35.8	1.9	19
Canada	13.5	0.18	75
Denmark	42.1	1	42.1
Finland	29.8	21.2	1.4
France	20.46	20.03	1.02
Germany (West)	28.8	2.2	13
Great Britain	47.9	0.22	210
India	8.2	9.4	0.87
Israel	50	2.8	18
Italy	19	26.9	0.7
Netherlands	30	2.4	12
New Zealand	41.6	0.11	378
Norway	50.2	1	50.2
Sweden	50.1	3	16.7
Switzerland	26.7	2.6	10

Note: In the period 1946–1969, socialist voting strength generally remained stable. As to communist voting strength, the only major increase was in India (from 3.3% to 9.4%). Major declines in communist strength occurred in Austria (from 5.4% to 3%), Belgium (12.7% to 9%), Denmark (12.5% to 1%), France (28.6% to 20.03%), West Germany (8.4% to 2.2%), Great Britain (0.41% to 0.22%), Netherlands (10.6% to 2.4%), and Norway (11.9% to 1%). In West Germany, the Communist party was outlawed in 1956; the figures in the table refer to the election of 1953, the last in which communists participated under their name. In the parliamentary elections of 1969, communists joined forces with various other groups under the name "Action for Democratic Progress," which polled 0.6% of the vote, but it is impossible to determine how many of this small number were communists.

that they must prove pragmatically, through actual accomplishments, the usefulness and practicality of public ownership in particular industries or services.

Concerning compensation, socialists share the general democratic conviction that no citizen may be deprived of his property without due process and compensation. Important as public ownership of the basic industries is to their plans, socialists consider public ownership not an end but a means to an end, and a means that does not justify the violation of property rights.

There is another vital difference with regard to public ownership. Communists seek to transfer *all* means of production, distribution, and exchange to the state, because according to communist doctrine publicly owned property is always preferable to private enterprise.

By contrast, socialists seek to work out a set of empirical principles that will indicate in a *particular* instance whether a specific *industry or service* is to be transferred to public ownership and control. The socialists' criterion may be that the industry under examination is a monopoly (such as gas and light, telephone, and other utilities tend to become); or that the industry is sick (as the British coal industry was before its nationalization); or that the industry, although neither inefficient nor monopolistic, is of such vital importance to the national economy that it seems socially undesirable to leave its operation in private hands (the British iron and steel industry was nationalized on these grounds).

The British Conservatives are in substantial agreement with Labor on the first two criteria; on the third the two parties are in partial disagreement. Clearly, the irreconcilable difference of viewpoint with regard to private property is not between conservatives and socialists, but between democrats (conservatives, liberals, or socialists) and totalitarians (fascists or communists).

Philosophically and politically, the difference between communists and socialists goes to the root of things. As we saw earlier, Lenin's theory of the professional revolutionary is based on the assumption that the majority of the people (or the working class) are unable to think for themselves; that a minority, the Communist party, has the job of leading the proletariat; and that within the minority a small group of men, the professional revolutionaries, are to formulate policies and assume leadership. Thus, in Leninist theory (and in communist practice), a small minority within a minority is the ruling elite.

This elite concept is totally rejected by socialists, who believe in democracy and majority rule within their own party as much as in their own nation. Clement Attlee, British prime minister from 1945–1951 and leader of the Labour party from 1935 to 1955, writes in his book *The Labour Party in Perspective* (1937) that his party's strength depends, "not on the brilliance of individuals, but on the quality of the rank and file." Attlee's own career confirms this diagnosis; brilliance was not his forte, and he lacked the dynamic leadership qualities of a Churchill or a Roosevelt. Harold Wilson, too, is no Churchill or Roosevelt, but a solid party man who inspires confidence rather than enthusiasm.

Contrary to the communists, socialists believe in peaceful persuasion as the only method of promoting their program. Communists feel that it is useless to seek change by persuasion because all means of communication, education, and propaganda are biased in favor of the capitalist status quo and that freedom of the press amounts to little if one lacks the necessary funds to start a newspaper. For this reason the communists were stunned when the British Labour party polled its electoral victory in 1945 and again in 1950, 1964, and 1966.

According to orthodox Marxism-Leninism, such victories were impossible. Since the British press was overwhelmingly in favor of the Conservative party, how could the voters, who presumably had been reading the pro-conservative papers daily for years, vote Labour? According to Lenin, workers under capitalism are mentally enslaved to capitalist ideology and cannot therefore be peacefully converted to socialist thinking until there has been a change in the economic structure of society. Only *after* capitalism has been destroyed, Lenin argues, will the workers be able to think along anticapitalist lines, because (as Marx said) it is the conditions of man's life that determine his thinking.

To the communist, every capitalist system, whether democratic, authoritarian, or fascist, is a bourgeois dictatorship; specifically, democratic institutions in a capitalist system are considered so much façade and hypocrisy which do not make the capitalist system any less dictatorial. Once capitalism—even liberal capitalism—is identified with dictatorship, the communist insistence on violence as the sole means of change is a logical conclusion.

Socialists, on the other hand, draw a fundamental distinction between two types of capitalist system, the political dictatorship and the liberal democracy. In a liberal democracy socialists believe in playing according to the rules of the game—provided, of course, the other side does the same.

Finally, *socialists reject the communist thesis that the choice in a democracy is between full capitalism and full collectivism.* Democratic parties do not concern themselves with bringing about the millennium at a certain date but seek to tackle issues that are comparatively manageable and to avoid definitive solutions that are irrevocable.

Socialists therefore envisage the transition from a predominantly capitalist economy (a purely capitalist economy exists and has existed only in the minds of the extreme right and the extreme left) to a predominantly socialist economy, not as a result of a sudden revolutionary coup that makes the return to private enterprise impossible, but as the result of gradual measures, none of which by itself irrevocably alters the nature of the whole economy.

Whereas the communists think in terms of three absolutes—capitalism, revolution, communist dictatorship—socialists think in terms of three *relative* concepts: a predominantly capitalist economy as the starting point, a long period of gradual change, and finally a predominantly socialized economy.

ELEMENTS OF SOCIALIST THOUGHT AND POLICY

Totalitarians of all shades have authoritative statements of doctrine, such as the *Communist Manifesto* or Hitler's *Mein Kampf.* Socialism, on the other hand, like many other liberal movements and ideas, has no bible, probably because liberals generally cannot agree on their beliefs and doctrines and are better at criticizing bibles than at writing them. Moreover, socialism has developed in different countries in accordance with different national traditions, and there has never been any central authority to lay down a socialist party line.

Despite the absence of such authoritative statements of socialist doctrine, it is not too difficult to cull from socialist writings, and from the policies of socialist parties, the outlines of socialist thought and policy. What emerges, however, is not a consistent body of ideas and policies. It has been the main strength—and weakness—of socialism that it has had no clear-cut body of doctrine and that it has fed on contradictory sources, sources that reflect the contradictions of the societies in which socialism has developed.

The complex, and frequently self-contradictory, elements of socialist thought and policy can best be illustrated from the British socialist movement, the most influential in the world. The elements that stand out in the British movement are:

1. Religion
2. Ethical and aesthetic idealism
3. Fabian empiricism
4. Liberalism

1. In *The Labour Party in Perspective*, Attlee writes that

the first place in the influences that built up the Socialist movement must be given to religion. England in the nineteenth century was still a nation of Bible readers. To put the Bible into the hands of an Englishman is to do a very dangerous thing. He will find there material which may send him out as a preacher of some religious, social, or economic doctrine. The large number of religious sects in this country, and the various tenets that many of them hold, illustrates this.

The *Christian Socialist movement*, headed by two clergymen, Frederick Maurice and Charles Kingsley, reached its peak in the middle of the nineteenth century and was an important source for the later development of working-class and socialist organizations. The Christian Socialists had as their guiding principle the concept that *socialism must be Christianized, and Christianity socialized.*

George Lansbury, Attlee's predecessor as the leader of the Labour party, writes in *My England* (1934):

Socialism, which means love, cooperation, and brotherhood in every department of human affairs, is the only outward expression of a Christian's faith. I am firmly convinced that whether they know it or not, all who approve and accept competition and struggle against each other as the means whereby we gain our daily bread, do indeed betray and make of no effect the "will of God."

The late Archbishop of Canterbury, William Temple, came very close to socialism in his *Christianity and the Social Order* (1942). Temple holds that every economic system is, for good or ill, an immense educative influence and that therefore the church must be concerned with it. The church is thus bound to ask "whether that influence is one tending to develop Christian character, and if the answer is partly or wholly negative the church must do its utmost to secure a change in the economic system so that it may find in that system an ally and not an enemy."

This practical concern of Christianity was particularly strong in Victorian England, throughout the whole second half of the nineteenth century. A sense of moral seriousness and dedicated disinterestedness characterized the Victorian period, and Victorian religion, while conceding that grace and faith were essential to salvation, nevertheless emphasized conduct and *salvation by works*. Many socialist leaders of the older generation who (like Attlee and Cripps) came from upper-class homes were steeped in an atmosphere in which religion was taken seriously.

Another religious influence of profound importance in Britain was the tradition of religious dissent, of *nonconformity*. In other European states, Protestantism had resulted in freedom *of* the church in relation to Rome, but not necessarily in freedom *within* the church in matters of doctrine and church government. To the nonconformist, Protestantism meant freedom of individual conscience and the freedom to organize voluntarily in associations of like-minded believers. This principle of *voluntary association* was later translated from religion into politics, where it became the life principle of the democratic society.

It was in the village chapels of the eighteenth and nineteenth centuries that many local leaders of working-class organizations learned to think for themselves, as well as to conduct public meetings and administer finances. *Wherever nonconformity was strong, labor unions and cooperatives were strong;* in fact, the trade unions have been aptly called the present-day descendants of the earlier nonconformist congregations. Nonconformity supplied more than a particular religious outlook: it was also the source, in the labor movement, of the idealism, the moral dedication, and the seriousness that have characterized the movement and its leaders.

If one studies the internal organization of some nonconformist churches, one is struck by its similarity to the organization of trade unions: both are loosely federated unions of voluntary bodies freely associating with each other. The Labour party today is also a federal union, made up of three main bodies—trade unions, cooperatives, and local constituency organizations—each of which is in turn made up of loosely federated organizations. Because the Labour party has this federal character, its internal structure resembles more the American federal system than the much simpler and more streamlined political system of Britain itself.

The complexity of the religious root of modern British socialism becomes apparent in the fact that *nonreligious, rational humanism* has also played a vital role in the evolution of socialist thought and action. Robert Owen was a rationalist and, among more modern socialist leaders in Britain, Sidney and Beatrice Webb, Harold J. Laski, G. D. H. Cole, and Hugh Gaitskell, to mention but a few, have not been much inspired by formal religious beliefs. It remains, however, of some interest that the political leaders of the labor movement, men like George Lansbury, Clement Attlee, and Sir Stafford Cripps, have more often been profoundly religious, whereas the principal intellectual figures, the men who formulate ideas rather than policies, tend to represent the *rationalist* root of socialism. Prime Minister Harold Wilson, a professional economist, comes from a background of strong religious nonconformity, and religion means a good deal to him. Although he is reluctant to express his religious feelings in public, he has often preached in nonconformist churches. His type of socialism has been called by a fellow Labourite "Methodism, not Marxism."

In the United States too, religion has played an important part in the cooperative and communal settlements established in the eighteenth and nineteenth centuries as well as in more recent socialist activities of a political and propagandistic nature. In the twentieth century, democratic socialism in the United States has been symbolized above all by Norman Thomas, who was a minister of religion before he took up the cause of socialism as his life's mission.

In contrast, religion has played a much smaller part in continental European and Latin American socialism. In England religious dissent was the bridge between religious and political unorthodoxy; in the virtual absence of nonconformity outside the English-speaking world, however, dissent from the established social and political order has generally also included dissent from the established church or from religion itself.

Before World War I, Russian radical and socialist movements were notably free of any religious influence or inspiration. In his monumental study, *The Spirit of Russia* (1913), Thomas Garrigue Masaryk, a renowned philosopher and later the first president of Czechoslovakia, observed that "Christian socialism is practically unknown in Russia" (*The Spirit of Russia*, new ed., 1955, II, 356). Masaryk's analysis in 1913 was later confirmed by the victorious rise of Leninist communism. In France and Germany, there were small groups of religious socialists, but, on the whole, socialists tended to be anticlerical or at least indifferent toward religion since most churches in continental Europe openly supported the political and economic status quo. During World War II, the heroic struggle of many priests and ministers against Nazi-fascist oppression brought about a closer understanding between churches and most socialist parties. Since then, the churches have become less committed to one particular set of social and economic theories, and the socialists have abandoned much of their earlier anticlericalism. Also, British socialism has proved to many socialists in other lands that socialism and religion do mix, provided the mixture is accomplished in the right spirit.

2. *Ethical and aesthetic idealism* is another source of British socialism, although its impact cannot be measured in votes and membership cards. Expressed by poets like John Ruskin and William Morris, ethical idealism was not a political or economic program, but a revolt against the squalor, drabness, and poverty of life under industrial capitalism. Developing first in England, cap-

italism probably produced more ugliness there than anywhere else, because English industrialists had no way of imagining what it would do to clean air and water and to the beauty of the English countryside, no way of foreseeing the rapid disfigurement of lovely old towns and villages by slums and factory centers.

Whereas Marx approached industrial capitalism in terms of cosmic laws—the development of world history according to inevitable social laws, philosophical materialism, the law of the falling profit rate, to name but a few—Morris kept his gaze closer to the ground. He saw around him ugly household goods and furnishings, and men and women who lacked joy and beauty in their daily lives. Once, when asked in a public meeting what he thought of Marx, Morris said, "I am asked if I believe in Marx's theory of value. To speak quite frankly, I do not know what Marx's theory of value is, and I'm damned if I want to know." What Morris cared about was human beings, not this or that "system." He felt intensely that the arts must be brought back into everyday life and that people's creative impulses should be given expression in their daily life and work.

The influence of Ruskin and Morris was more negative than positive. They showed what was wrong with a civilization—physically and morally—that was built on strife and squalor, but they did not formulate any specific program to improve the conditions to which they objected. Nevertheless, this aesthetic and ethical revolt was important in preparing the intellectual environment in which socialism could later find a sympathetic response.

Ruskin and Morris were read mainly by the more educated class, which absorbed from them—as well as from Charles Dickens, Thomas Carlyle, and other writers—a groping understanding of what industrial civilization does to man, not only as a worker, but as a human being. The aesthetic and ethical rebels of Victorian England undermined the self-confidence that then prevailed and fostered self-criticism; out of that doubt and self-criticism more positive socialist ideas could later be developed step by step.

In one particular field—town and country planning—the Labour party reflects directly and explicitly the message of Ruskin and Morris. The whole concept of community planning—which is more than tearing down slums and building neat little row houses of uniform size and style—owes much to the outlook of the early pioneers of socialist thought, for whom problems of industry merged with more general problems of creating a community in which each member would have access to the means of civilized enjoyment.

3. *Fabian empiricism* is perhaps the most characteristically *British* aspect of the British labor movement. The Fabian Society, founded in 1884, was named after a Roman general, Quintus Fabius Maximus Cunctator—the "delayer." The early motto of the society was: "For the right moment you must wait, as Fabius did; but when the right moment comes you must strike hard, or your waiting will have been vain and fruitless."

The founders and early members of the Fabian society included George Bernard Shaw, Sidney and Beatrice Webb, H. G. Wells, and Graham Wallas. It was noteworthy that none of them came from the poorer classes and that there was a sizable proportion of writers in the group.

In Sidney Webb's historical survey of the basis of socialism, included in the *Fabian Essays* (1889), we find what is still the basic philosophy of Fabianism and, more generally, of British socialism. Webb looked upon socialism (eleven years before the foundation of the Labour party) as an inevitable outcome of the full fruition of democracy, but he insisted that his "inevitability of gradualness" was sharply different from the Marxian inevitability of revolutionary, catastrophic change.

Webb emphasized in the *Fabian Essays* that social organization can come only bit by bit and that important "organic changes" can take place, in England at least, only under four conditions: first, such changes must be *democratic,* acceptable to a popular majority, and "prepared for in the minds of all"; second, they must be *gradual,* causing no dislocation; third, they must *not* be regarded as *immoral* by the people; fourth, they must be *constitutional and peaceful.*

Marxians on the Continent and elsewhere aimed their propaganda at the proletariat. As to the middle and upper classes, the job at hand was to liquidate them, not to convert them to socialism. Because the propaganda was thus aimed exclusively at the proletariat, it tended to be highly emotional and sloganized, taking into consideration not only the educational level of the workers, but also the fact that they were expected to be half-converted before they were ever exposed to Marxist agitation.

The Fabian Society started from the assumption that there could be *no progress toward a just social order in Britain unless the middle and upper classes could be shown the reasonableness and equity of the basic claims of socialist thought and policy.* Since government in Britain was by persuasion and consent, and since the governing classes of Britain were largely recruited from the middle and upper classes, there could be no change of policy in Britain without the preliminary consent of those classes. It was fortunate for the Fabians that they spoke the same language—literally and metaphorically—as did the governing classes and knew how to *permeate* the latter in ways that would have been closed to formal propaganda from persons outside the same class.

The Fabian technique of permeation was based on the premise that you do not change a reasonable person through a single brilliant argument, lecture, or emotional appeal. It was the Fabian policy to work on the minds and feelings of their hearers in a slow, gradual process rather than in one sudden act of conversion, and preferably on social, informal occasions rather than on formal, official ones.

An emotional appeal to a high British civil servant, telling him that according to the Marxian dialectic the capitalist system is doomed, and that such doom will be followed by the classless proletarian society, was likely to have less effect than a casual reference at luncheon to a new government report, written by a fellow bureaucrat, on the incidence of disease and crime in slum areas. Similarly, serious discussion of a recent book by a reputable and scholarly economist on changes in the distribution of income among various social and economic groups was likely to have more effect on a conservative political leader than the shorter appeals of "Down with Capitalism" and "Long Live Proletarian Solidarity."

Permeation had also another side. The Fabians did not consider it their job to pass resolutions, make appeals to kings and parliaments, or address themselves to the masses of the people. They were interested in convincing a small group of persons, regardless of party affiliation, as long as they had two qualifications: first, they had to be persons of *continuous* influence in public life, so that the long process of permeation, if successful, would pay off; second, such persons would have to be *reasonable*, by which the Fabians meant not partisan extremists. Since such persons could be found in all political parties, the Fabians cultivated conservatives who met their qualifications as well as liberals.

This sort of Fabianism assumes a *Fabianism in reverse*, or else it would not stand a chance of success. For example, Fabians and other socialists in England religiously read *The Times*, not because they agree with its editorial viewpoint (generally conservative), but because it is "a good paper." In many other countries socialists consider the local substitute for *The Times* a source of bourgeois contamination from which they should steer clear.

The difference between the Fabian and Marxian-communist approaches can best be seen by contrasting the writings of the two groups. Marx was little interested in the minutiae of life; his magnum opus, *Das Kapital*, is an attempt to give meaning to history as a whole, and much of his thought was devoted to fundamentals of economics and philosophy. Lenin wrote volumes and volumes on such subjects as *Materialism and Empirio-Criticism*. In contrast, more than 95 percent of all Fabian publications have been pamphlets rather than heavy tomes, and pamphlets lend themselves more to small subjects like *Municipal Milk and Public Health* (Fabian Tract No. 122) than to the future of Western civilization. The Fabian Society is rarely to be found in high intellectual altitudes, sniffing the thin air surrounding the metaphysical peaks; it is more often found "nosing about in the drains," seeking to remedy some immediate and *specific* condition.

Early in the history of the Fabian Society, Fabian Tract No. 70 (written by George Bernard Shaw) made it plain that Fabianism was no rival to existing philosophies trying to explain the whole cosmos and that it had "no distinctive opinion on the Marriage Question, Religion, Art, abstract Economics, historic Evolution, Currency, or any other subject than its own special business of practical Democracy and Socialism." This sense of practicality and concreteness is indicated by typical titles of Fabian tracts and other pamphlets: *Liquor Licensing at Home and Abroad*; *Life in the Laundry*; *Public Control of Electrical Power and Transit*; *The Case for School Nurseries*; *The Endowment of Motherhood*; *The*

Reform of the House of Lords; and *The British Cabinet: A Study of Its Personnel, 1909–1924.*

Two Fabian pamphlets, *Metropolitan Borough Councils: Their Constitution, Powers, and Duties,* and *Borough Councils: Their Constitution, Powers, and Duties,* were written by Clement R. Attlee in the spring of 1920, when Lenin was busy, not with the reform of borough councils, but with the destruction of states and empires.

The Fabian approach can perhaps best be shown in a simple illustration: if a slum clearance project is debated in terms of fundamental issues—such as socialism versus capitalism—agreement between advocates of the project and their opponents is unlikely. However, if the pertinent facts can be clearly brought out—the cost (in dollars and cents) of a slum area in terms of disease, crime protection, fire hazards, compared with the cost of building new houses with public assistance—the original gap has been considerably narrowed, and agreement will be likelier than it was when the argument centered on issues of apparently irreconcilable ultimate values.

The successes of Fabianism have probably stemmed chiefly from this concern with *reducing questions of principle to questions of fact.* Fabians gambled on the notion that facts do matter and that the impact of facts ultimately determines how people will think and act.

In his autobiography, *Power and Influence* (1953), Lord Beveridge has an interesting sidelight on the Fabian faith in facts. One of the greatest contributions of Sidney and Beatrice Webb was the creation of the London School of Economics and Political Science in 1895, in order to provide an adequate opportunity for the study of economics and allied subjects. The Webbs themselves chose the first four directors of the London School. Of the four, Beveridge tells us, the first two became Conservative Members of Parliament, the third had socialist sympathies, and the fourth (Beveridge himself) was a Liberal. The Webbs, Beveridge says, "believed that the impartial study of society would further the Socialism which was their practical aim, but they were prepared to take the risk of being wrong in that belief."

The Fabian technique of trying to reduce apparently irreconcilable differences of principle to negotiable disagreements over facts is no invention or novelty but is implicit in the very nature of the democratic society. We have peace in a free society to the extent that people are willing to keep to themselves conflicting fundamentals in religion, morals, and philosophy. Separation of state and church in the United States was effected and has been maintained not because Americans are indifferent to religion, but because the framers of the Constitution thought it wise to keep a fundamental issue like religion out of politics and to concentrate on issues in which people of all religions can cooperate without injury to their religious belief.

Fabianism has frequently been described as reform without resentment, social reconstruction without class war, political empiricism without dogma or fanaticism. Despite its small size (its membership never exceeded a few thousand), the Fabian Society has had an enormous impact. In the 1945 election, which led to the first Labour government based on a substantial parliamentary majority, 229 of the 394 Labour Members of Parliament were Fabians, and more than half of the government, including Attlee (prime minister from 1945–1951), was Fabian. Hugh Gaitskell, who succeeded Attlee as leader of the Labour party, was also a Fabian of long standing, as is Gaitskell's successor, Prime Minister Harold Wilson.

4. *Liberalism* has become an increasingly important source of socialism, particularly since Liberal parties have dwindled to insignificance in many countries. In England, the Liberal party has virtually disappeared and the Labour party seems to have inherited about one-third of the estate. Temperamentally, many Liberals do not find it easy to join a socialist movement; the passion for individual liberty and individual difference is still the most distinguishing trait of the Liberal.

Apart from the tendency toward red tape and regulation for the sake of regulation, there is also in socialism a tendency toward the state, the mass, and collectivity. Both tendencies are repugnant to the true Liberal, the man who occasionally still likes to be himself and not just a number in the National Register. Yet, during the last forty years, more and more Liberals have joined the Labour Party. Why?

In the first place, the weakness of the British Liberal party is due to the fact, not that it has failed, but that *its success has made it unnecessary*. Both the Conservative party and the Labour party are now thoroughly committed to Liberal principles of respect for individual freedom of worship, thought, speech, and association. Liberalism as a protest against clericalism is no longer a live issue in England (or in most other countries).

Free trade, another great ideal of nineteenth-century British Liberalism, no longer arouses passionate political interest. Both Conservatives and Labourites are committed to some form of tariff protection, and even the Liberals realize that free trade no longer has the importance it once had.

In the 1960's, the issue of free trade reappeared in the controversy over British membership in the Common Market. The division of public opinion was *within*, rather than between, the two major political parties. Liberal ideology played a less important part than the estimates of economic benefits expected from British membership.

In the question of empire too, the Liberal approach of the nineteenth century is no longer relevant, since nearly all of the empire is gone. The liquidation of the empire after World War II occurred under both Labour and Conservative governments.

The specific issues gone, many Liberals have joined the Labour party, or vote Labour, or think of themselves as vaguely socialist. Liberalism has generally been to the left of the Conservatives, and in a country with a two-party system, like Britain, if one wishes to stand to the left of Conservatism, the Labour party is now the only platform to stand on.

On issues of public ownership, the Liberal elements in the Labour party are opposed to doctrinaire policies of nationalizing for the sake of nationalizing—i.e., the Liberals in the Labour party are generally on its right wing, just as the Liberals in the Conservative party are on its left wing. The right-wing Labourite is so close to the left-wing Conservative in mentality, outlook, temperament, and policies that it takes a pencil of electronic sharpness to draw the line of demarcation between the two.

Liberalism has contributed much that is lasting in British socialism. Because of the Liberal influence, socialist leaders are more moderate and less doctrinaire than they might otherwise have been, and they have a deeper respect for individual liberty. Liberalism has turned the Labour party into a national party rather than one based on class, and it has bequeathed to the Labour party the Liberal message that there can be reform without bitterness and hatred.

SOCIAL-ECONOMIC CHANGES AND REFORMS

The victory of the Western nations in World War I provided a strong stimulus for the growth of socialist parties throughout the world. The war had been fought in defense of democracy against the authoritarian militarism of Germany and her allies, and during the war promises were made to the peoples of the major democratic belligerents that military victory would be followed by the establishment of a new social order based on greater opportunity and equality.

In England, the Labour party reflected in its growth and development the protest against the old social order. Founded in 1900, the party polled only two seats in the Parliamentary elections of that year. By 1910 forty Labourites sat in the House of Commons, and the party had ceased to be a negligible factor. In 1918 the parliamentary representation rose to 57, and in 1922 the Labour Party obtained 142 seats out of 615, replacing the fading Liberal party as the second strongest party in the country. In 1924, the Labour party, though still a minority, formed a government with the tacit support of the Liberal party, but the experiment lasted only ten months, because the Liberals finally decided that they could not go along with a socialist program.

In 1929, the Labour party became for the first time in its history the largest single party in Britain, obtaining in the general election 288 out of 615 seats in Parliament. Although lacking an absolute majority in the House of Commons, the party formed a government that lasted until the summer of 1931. The coming of the world depression in 1929 weakened Britain economically, and the Labour government, being unable to follow socialist policies to cure the depression and unwilling to adopt conservative remedies, resigned in the summer of 1931. In the ensuing election the parliamentary representation of the Labour party dropped to 52 out of 615, but by

1935, the last election before World War II, its strength in the House of Commons had risen again to 154. As long as the shadow of Nazi-fascist aggression hung over Britain, however, there was little chance for embarking upon a major experiment of social and economic reform.

Between 1935 and the end of the war in Europe there was no general election. In the first postwar general elections, held on July 5, 1945, the Labour party obtained 394 out of 640 seats, with the result that for the first time in British history a Labour government was formed with a clear majority in the House of Commons. In 1950, the Labour majority fell to a bare 315 out of 625 seats, and because of the narrow margin and the resulting instability of government, a new election was held in 1951. The Labour party lost it, as it lost the next two general elections in 1955 and 1959. In 1964, Labour staged a comeback and won the election by a narrow margin. But since its majority of three in the House of Commons proved insufficient for a stable government, Prime Minister Harold Wilson called for a new election in 1966. This time Labour won with a decisive majority of 97 Members of Parliament—not the triumphant victory of 1945, when Labour had a majority of 148 in the House of Commons, but still a clear mandate from the people to be governed by Labour for a full term of five years.

Between 1900 and 1918, the Labour party was not officially committed to socialism, although it included many individual socialists. In 1918, when the party adopted socialism in its program, its commitment to the nationalization of industry was just about complete. But as the party learned the facts of life it changed its outlook drastically and urged nationalization only where it had been proved pragmatically that public ownership would do more for the welfare of the nation than private ownership. In the election of 1945, for example, the Labour party did *not* enter the campaign with a program of "socialism" in the abstract but promised to nationalize specifically listed industries and services if elected to office.

In each case, it explained why nationalization was necessary. For gas and light, water, telephone and telegraph, and other utilities, the criterion of nationalization was the existence of a *natural monopoly*. On the coal industry, there was general agreement in Britain, regardless of party, that the industry was so sick and inefficient that it

Drawing by Illingworth, © Punch, *London*

ROUND THE CORNER

could not be put on its feet except through nationalization. The iron and steel industries were declared to be so *vital to the nation* that their management could not safely be subject to the decisions of private persons. The nationalization of all inland transportation, by rail, road, and air, was proposed on the ground that *wasteful competition* could best be avoided by a *coordinated scheme* of transportation owned and managed by public authorities. The Bank of

England was also proposed for nationalization on the ground that its purpose was so obviously public. Finally, the election program of 1945 also promised the setting up of a National Health Service, so that the best possible health and medical facilities might be available to every person without regard to his ability to pay.

After the electoral triumph of 1945, the Labour party methodically carried out its program. With one exception, there was little argument over nationalization. On the exception, iron and steel, the Conservatives argued that the industry was highly efficient and that the needs of the national welfare could be accommodated without nationalization.

The attitude of the British toward nationalization was generally one of indifference. The exception was, and is, the National Health Service, because of its direct effect on the everyday life of the individual citizen. Although no one was compelled to join the National Health Service, 97 percent of the population and 96 percent of the doctors are in it. At first the administrative and technical difficulties in setting up the necessary machinery caused considerable delay and confusion. As the program began to hit its stride, however, adverse criticism largely died down. Now the National Health Service has established itself as a part of British life. The Conservative party, like the Labour party, is fully committed to the program. The medical profession, while not enthusiastic about it, has nevertheless publicly accepted it as essentially "sound." As to the British public, public opinion polls have found that about 90 percent of those questioned are on the whole satisfied with the National Health Service. Discussion in Britain is no longer about the basic issue of a national health insurance program, but about ways of improving its practical operation. One serious problem has arisen in recent years that was not anticipated when the program was set up. In the middle and late 1960's, several hundred doctors have left Britain annually, mostly for the United States, and the low income of physicians in Britain was generally considered to be the main reason for that brain drain.

The Labour government elected in 1945 also set up a comprehensive cradle-to-grave scheme of *social security*. The system provides protection against sickness, unemployment, and old age, supplemented by maternity grants, widows' pensions, and family allowances. Social security as set up by the Labour government was no

invention of the Labour party, but the culmination of several decades of social legislation enacted by Conservative and Liberal governments. A fully integrated system of social security was first
proposed during World War II in the *Beveridge Report* (1942);
in the middle of the war, both the Conservative party and the
Labour party pledged themselves, if elected to office after the war,
to introduce a comprehensive system of social security.

A further policy of the Labour government in the years 1945–
1951 aimed at greater *social equality*. The setting up of the basic
institutions of the welfare state in itself contributed to greater social
equality by bringing within the reach of large sections of the population many facilities and services that hitherto had not been available to them. *Educational opportunities* on the secondary and university levels, for example, were made available to children of lower-
income families. In addition, several new colleges and universities
were founded in an attempt to combine British educational features
with the American goal of providing higher education for the many
rather than for the select few.

In 1965, the Labour government began to tackle one of the keys
to social equality—the secondary school. In Britain—as in most
other countries—there are two main types of secondary school: an
academic, for a small minority, that leads to college; and a vocational, for the mass of the people, that ends at age 15. The main disadvantage of such a system is that the decision about going to college must be made at age 10 or 11 on entering a specific type of secondary school; an additional disadvantage is that the system segre-
gates the members of different social classes at a very early age. For
these reasons, the Labour government started, from 1965 onward,
to adapt the British system of secondary education to the American
pattern, in which most high schools combine academic with vocational education. Interestingly, Labour spokesmen for this reform
often refer to the American experience; as in so many other instances,
what socialists in other countries call the socialist ideal of equality is
accepted in the United States, in theory at least, as the noncontro-
versial American concept of equality of opportunity.

Taxation was the greatest leveler. Thus, in 1910 a person with an
income of £100,000 retained, after payment of taxes, about £94,000.
In 1969, the net income on £100,000 after payment of taxes had

shrunk to about £15,000. Inheritance taxes took about 50 percent of larger fortunes in 1938, and up to 80 percent in 1969. In 1938, the last normal prewar year, there were 6,600 persons in Britain whose income was over £6,000 after payment of taxes. The number of persons in that group had dwindled to 60 by 1949 but rose again to 3,000 in 1960 and to 17,700 in 1963. However, the total after-tax income of the 6,600 persons with incomes over £6,000 in 1938 was £62.2 million, or about £10,000 of average income in that group. In 1963, the total after-tax income of the 17,700 persons with incomes over £6,000 was £129.5 million, or about £8,000 of average income in that group. It should be remembered that the value of

Drawing by Acanthus, © Punch, London

"IT FOUGHT FOR YEARS AGAINST RISING TAXATION, BUT AT LAST IT SURRENDERED."

the pound was cut to one-third of its prewar purchasing power, so that the *average real income in the top group* in terms of purchasing power was only *about one-quarter* in 1963 of what it had been in 1938.

While the share of high incomes in terms of the national income has declined in Britain, there has been a sharp increase of the middle-income groups, particularly skilled workers. The trend toward more social equality can also be seen in the fact that the proportion of the national income paid in wages and salaries increased from 60 percent in 1938 to 70 percent in 1965, whereas the income from dividends and interest declined considerably during the same period. All these policies have by no means brought about absolute equality, but they have gone a long way toward eliminating extremes of inequality.

Dropping much of the traditional socialist belief in nationalization, the Labour party has come close to the Conservative party, which in turn no longer opposes the basic principles of the welfare state. Inasmuch as both parties seem to be united on kindred principles of social policy, and because so much of the British economy depends upon factors external to it (such as its ability to compete with other countries in foreign markets), there is little room left for such differences in principle as characterized the classic nineteenth-century struggles between the Whigs and the Tories.

In the 1960's, British politics thus gave the impression of ideological peace and near-uniformity. The Labour party, in particular, is in search of a new program and set of principles that can inspire the country, for the *impulse of early socialism*—nationalization plus social security—*has been largely spent.* The very acceptance of the welfare state by all political parties has thus become the main source of socialist hesitation and stagnation.

Moreover, the basic issue of the welfare state—how to distribute the national product—is overshadowed by a much bigger problem: how to increase the productivity of the British economy and make it more competitive in world markets. In the 1950's and 1960's, as we saw in Chapter One, the growth rate of the British economy was considerably below that of the Soviet Union and the major non-communist economies (Japan, West Germany, Italy, France, and the United States). Comparing the performance of the British economy with western European economies, we find that in 1958–1968 output per man-hour in manufacturing rose by 45 percent in Britain, by 64 percent in France, by 78 percent in West Germany, and by 112 percent in Italy. Per capita gross national product in 1958–1967 rose by 58 percent in Britain, but by 97 percent in the Common Market countries. The discrepancy in the rise of incomes of wage and salary earners was even greater: their average income rose by 61 percent in Britain in 1958–1967, but by 106 percent in the Common Market countries.

One of the effects of the unimpressive record of the British economy has been the growing pressure on the pound. After the Wilson cabinet committed itself to defending the pound at all cost, it finally devalued it by almost 15 percent (from £1 = $2.80 to £1 = $2.40) in November 1967. This new value of the pound was not easy to defend, and in pursuing its goal of financial stability the Labour government has followed orthodox financial policies of sacrificing full employment and welfare expenditures to the defense of the currency. Ironically, a Labour government can carry out such an orthodox and restrictionist policy, including antistrike legislation, more effectively than a Conservative government, which can be more easily subjected to the charge that its financial orthodoxy merely reflects the views of bankers.

The persistent weakness of the pound is directly related to the unfavorable balance of payments, or the difference between what a country earns from exports, tourism, and income from foreign investments, shipping, insurance and what it spends on imports, foreign travel, capital movements abroad in a given period of time. Since a high proportion of the British national product depends on transactions with other countries, the balance of payments is particularly important. From the inception of the Wilson government in 1964, Britain's balance of payments was consistently unfavorable, and even the devaluation of the pound in 1967—making exports cheaper and imports dearer—had no immediate effects. The first half of 1969 brought the first glimmer of hope; in that period Britain was able, for the first time under the Wilson government, to chalk up a small payment surplus of $115 million.

The Labour government is aware that in the elections in the 1970's the issue of Britain's balance of payments will be the key one. In working for a more favorable balance of payments the Labour government in the late 1960's cut welfare expenditures at home and reduced military expenditures abroad, but so far it has not been able to come up with a socialist solution—or with any solution—to the problem. In the eyes of most British voters, the issue of socialism versus capitalism is irrelevant to the issue of Britain's international economic position, her ability to pay for what she receives from other countries in goods and services.

In addition, every British government will be judged by the effects of its economic policy on the standard of living of the people. In 1950, British levels of consumption held fourth place in the world. By the late 1960's, they had dropped to fifteenth place, a considerable decline in the relative standing of the British economy. In absolute terms, British levels of consumption are high and rising, but the rate of increase is much slower than that in numerous other countries, both noncommunist and communist.

On the Continent, the Scandinavian countries have had the most impressive record of social reform, both in the interwar years and after World War II. From the early 1930's onward, the Scandinavian countries have been generally governed by socialist administrations based on parliamentary majorities, and as a result communism has been kept down to minor proportions in all three countries (Norway, Denmark, Sweden). The Scandinavian socialist movements have emphasized economic development and social security rather than nationalization, and their economic policies have been centered on fiscal measures (such as cheap money) and taxation rather than on public ownership. Full employment is a major point in Scandinavian (as in British) socialism.

One of the important lessons of the social and economic reform in Scandinavia in the last thirty years is the emphasis on *socialization rather than nationalization*. One of the most serious political weaknesses of the British program of economic change has been the tendency to substitute *state* ownership and management for private ownership, thus increasing the tendency toward governmental centralization. In contrast, the Scandinavian reform programs have experimented with other types of social ownership in lieu of private ownership.

The most significant contribution of Scandinavia to social reform is the use of the *cooperative movement* rather than the state as the agent of social and economic reform. Whereas in Britain, as in most other countries, the cooperative movement has been largely confined to retail and wholesale trading in a selected group of articles, the Scandinavians have set up cooperatives for slum clearance, health insurance, and industrial production. This Scandinavian *middle way* seeks to avoid the evils of unbridled capitalism and, at the same time, the dangers of statism.

PROBLEMS OF NATIONALIZATION

Socialist theory and practice have undergone drastic changes on the issue of nationalization in the last fifty years. When the British Labour party adopted a socialist platform in 1918, it demanded (in Clause IV of its revised constitution) "the common ownership of the means of production, distribution, and exchange." At that time, this formula expressed the prevailing socialist orthodoxy.

Today, not a single socialist party in the world, nor a single socialist leader of repute and responsibility, still adheres to the old formula of nationalizing *all* the means of production, distribution, and exchange. In July 1951 the Socialist International, speaking for more than 30 Socialist parties throughout the world, adopted a program that specifically rejected the older doctrine of total nationalization and conceded that socialist planning is compatible with private ownership in agriculture, handicrafts, retail trade, and small and medium-sized industries.

In 1959, the German Social Democratic party, the largest democratic socialist party on the European Continent, adopted a new program in which freedom, justice, and respect for the individual are declared to be its highest values. As for nationalization, the program specifically states that "efficient small and medium-sized enterprises are to be strengthened to enable them to prevail in competition with large-scale enterprises." Only where, for natural or technical reasons, competition is impossible, does public ownership become a necessity. The following two general principles are included in the program: "Private ownership of the means of production is no longer identical with the control of power"; and "Every concentration of economic power, even in the hands of the state, harbors dangers."

In 1964, the Social Democratic party adopted a series of new resolutions spelling out its domestic and foreign policies in detail. This time, the word "nationalization" did not even appear, so dead an issue had it become since 1959. The economic policy was summarized as follows: "Only a combination of the market economy and monetary and fiscal over-all control and welfare policy can be the solution suited for our time." In its "Government Program" of 1969, the Social Democratic party spelled out its economic and social programs in detail, but again there was no mention or discussion of "nationalization." The usual welfare and labor union policies were advocated: secure employment, technological progress, regional planning, and tax reforms in favor of low-income groups.

The leader of American socialism over four decades, Norman Thomas, wrote in *Democratic Socialism: A New Appraisal* (1953) that "the state under the most democratic theory and practice will become too huge, too cumbersome, if it seeks to control directly all economic activity." Ten years later, in *Socialism Re-Examined* (1963), Thomas states again: "American socialists nowadays generally accept, as they should, a mixed economy, controlled by the overall concept that production should be for the good of all. For the state, under any system, to try to own and operate everything, would deprive us of some of the important values of private initiative and responsibility." Thomas speaks of the dangers of statism inherent in total nationalization, and like many other socialists he stresses that the alternative to capitalism is *socialization, not nationalization.*

Individual freedom is inextricably linked to the diffusion of power. This truism has always been admitted by socialists to apply to political government. They are now coming around to the idea that in the economic realm, too, there can be no individual freedom unless there is diffusion of economic power.

The concept of socialization implies the diffusion of publicly owned property. Property is owned and managed not by the state but by producer or consumer cooperatives, labor unions, churches, educational institutions, hospitals, and other organizations, and these organizations derive their powers from voluntary association rather than from the sovereign authority of the state.

This approach has been successfully tried in Scandinavia as well as in Israel. In Scandinavia, most public housing has been built not by the state, but by corporations that combine individual ownership and management with financial assistance from housing cooperatives and municipal agencies. In Scandinavia too, as mentioned earlier, cooperatives are not confined—as they are in many countries—to the retail business, but are common in the fields of manufacturing and wholesaling. In Israel, the Federation of Labor is the largest employer in the nation; it has a considerable share in the ownership and control of such basic industries as highway transportation, navigation, aviation, banking, building, heavy machinery, cement, glass, and rubber. A sizable proportion of Israel's agricultural production is in cooperative farm communities. In all, the "workers' sector" in the economy accounts for almost one-quarter of Israel's national product.

None of these solutions is final, and mistakes are constantly made, but these forms of socialization do seem to their advocates to avoid the worst evils of nationalization—monopoly and the resulting concentration of economic and political power. In a capitalist democracy, the economic power of private monopolies can at least be opposed by the political power of the state. *When the monopolist is the state itself, who will protect the citizen against the state?*

Today, then, no socialist party advocates any longer that *all* industries be collectivized; nationalization is recommended only for *some* industries. How many is some? There is no clear-cut answer, but there seems to be universal acceptance among socialists of the idea that natural monopolies in the public utilities field should be publicly owned and managed. The concept of the "sick industry" (e.g., the British coal industry) and the criterion of the "key industry" (e.g., the British steel industry) have also been accepted as standards upon which nationalization may be based.

It appears that *nationalization lends itself best to industries or services that are highly standardized—that is,* where *uniform rules of administration* can be easily applied (this is the thesis of "gas and water socialism"). On the other hand, in industries that demand high adaptability to changing conditions, for example, industries that produce largely for export or industries that operate with a considerable element of risk, the case against nationalization or socialization is strong. The tendency of a bureaucratically run enterprise to put security above adventure and risk is incompatible with rapid industrial expansion. The automobile industry a generation ago and the photocopying industry today are the products not of pre-existing giant enterprises, but of relatively small corporations that were willing to put capital into new and risky products.

It remains to be proved that this same spirit of adventure, risk, and experimentation can be shown by publicly owned enterprises. After all, it is one thing to risk, and speculate with, one's own money; it is quite another thing to use the public treasury for questionable, though potentially very profitable, ventures. Similarly, it has been argued that, under public ownership, declining industries (such as coal and railroads) are being artificially propped up by the government when, for economic reasons, they should be allowed to decline. "This has been a great shock," a former high British official writes, "especially for the workers in these industries, as it has always been assumed that the workers were to be the main beneficiaries of state ownership. They naturally demand, therefore, that the Government should take the strongest measures to arrest this decline—regardless of the effects on the national economy" (R. Kelf-Cohen, *Twenty Years of Nationalisation: The British Experience,* 1969, pp. 315–16).

The traditional concern of socialists has always been with *distribution* rather than *production.* The most creative contribution of socialism has, therefore, been its revision of the internal social structure of nations in the direction of equality. Many countries with strong socialist parties exhibit internal cohesion and unity, the direct result, according to socialist leaders, of a high degree of social justice based on the concept of "fair shares for all." In contrast, these leaders point out, where socialism has recently been weak, as in France and Italy, the people are torn and disunited, and there is a general feeling of alienation and resentment.

It has not been shown so far that publicly owned enterprise is any more efficient in production than private enterprise or that it has materially increased the people's standard of living. C.A.R. Crosland, a leading British economist and member of the Wilson cabinet, makes important concessions on both points. First, he admits that the performance of nationalized industries in Britain has not been conspicuously better than that of private enterprise and that nationalized industries have been plagued by "bureaucratic centralization." Speaking of living standards, he also argues that further nationalization "cannot be said to be necessary to full employment and prosperity, for these exist already" (*The New Leader*, February 29, 1960).

From the very beginning, public enterprise has found that three specific difficulties hamper its overall performance. First is the *managerial problem* of administering vast public enterprises with flexibility and initiative and at a low cost. The excessive tendency toward centralization and playing it safe is a serious matter. Moreover, it is not certain that the managerial situation will improve as nationalization continues. In the first phase of public ownership, the public corporation can draw upon managerial talent which has been trained in the tough environment of private competition, but if nationalization goes on, management of public enterprises will have to draw its top personnel from among its own ranks. It will then be seen whether persons trained and bred in the secure, sheltered atmosphere of bureaucratic monopoly will possess as great a capacity to operate large undertakings as is shown by graduates of the hard school of private, competitive business.

If the American experience can serve as a guide to managerial performance, the outlook for nationalized enterprise is uncertain. In American corporate business, industries that are near the bottom of the executive pay scale (and presumably attract less able executives) include regulated industries like insurance, savings and loan associations, banking, air transport, railroads, and public utilities. These industries are either monopolies (as in the case of the public utilities) or enjoy relatively little competition since their very existence generally depends on a governmentally granted franchise. There is relatively little product innovation in such industries, operations are often highly routinized, and seniority is a determining factor in promotions. By contrast, the industries near the top of the executive pay scale (automotive, chemical, metals manufacturing, electronics, department stores) are characterized by creativity and product innovation under the pressure of substantial competition.

Promotion is less influenced by seniority, outside executive talent is more frequently brought in, and there is therefore a greater turnover of executive personnel.

In nationalized industries producing standardized goods or services (such as public utilities) the management problem may not be too serious. But in competitive industries, where flexibility and innovation are essential, nationalized industries will find it more difficult to attract top quality executives for two reasons. First, as an industry becomes nationalized, it automatically becomes monopolistic and routinized and allows for less creativity and executive initiative than are demanded under conditions of private, competitive enterprise. Second, nationalized industries—like regulated industries in a nonsocialist economy—pay lower executive salaries, and able executives prefer more challenging positions that offer better pay to more routinized work at lower pay. In 1969, a government agency, the Prices and Income Board, investigated the salary gap between the private sector and nationalized industries; it found that in private companies of comparable size, top salaries (for vice-presidents and up) averaged one-third to one-half more than those in nationalized industries. In some cases, large private companies paid top salaries that were three, four, and five times as high. Top salaries in nationalized industries in 1969 averaged only $25,300—small not only by American standards but also by western European standards. Since Britain is likely to remain a predominantly private economy for a long time to come, outstanding managerial talent will continue to move into the high-paying private, competitive sector.

The steel industry may well become a testing ground. During its six years of office in 1945–1951, the Labour government hesitated to nationalize the steel industry, although it had committed itself to doing so, because there was little public support for the measure outside of a doctrinaire, left-wing element in the Labour party. Before leaving office in 1951, the Labour government laid the groundwork for the nationalization of steel, but before the scheme could be put into full operation, the Conservatives came into office in 1951. They immediately returned steel to private ownership but set up a national Iron and Steel Board to protect the national interest in the industry.

When Labour returned to office in 1964, the Wilson cabinet did not immediately propose renationalization of steel, since the Labour majority in Parliament was only three or four, and the government preferred to play it safe. However, after Labour was returned to office in 1966 with a substantial majority of 97, it proceeded to renationalize steel. In the opinion of independent observers, this was not done for economic reasons, but in order to placate the left-wing group in the Labour party, which insisted on nationalized steel.

The problem of management in nationalized industries is closely connected with a second major problem. In private business, the *system of profits and losses* operates in a crude but effective way to keep efficiency at a relatively high level, and the threat of bankruptcy is always real. In a public enterprise, this system no longer operates to the same extent; if there are losses, no one goes bankrupt, and the losses of one division can be passed on to the whole enterprise. Even if the whole enterprise or industry is in the red, management can, because it has a monopoly, either increase prices or receive cheap credits or subsidies from the government.

Third, there is the *political difficulty*. How are public corporations to be related to the elected respresentatives of the people? If the public corporation is too closely supervised by parliament or congress, its management may become demoralized and lose efficiency. If parliamentary control is relaxed, on the other hand, up goes the cry that there is not much difference between the old and the new systems (since if management can do more or less as it pleases, what has nationalization changed?). After two decades of nationalization, experience has shown that whatever political control over nationalized industries is exercised, it is done by the executive branch, not by the legislators. A former undersecretary at the Ministry of Fuel and Power who observed the problem of democratic control of nationalized industries from the inside for many years, concludes that "public ownership and parliamentary procedure do not go well together" (R. Kelf-Cohen, *Twenty Years of Nationalisation: The British Experience,* 1969, p. 177).

Because of all these difficulties and complexities, many leading socialists are increasingly reconciling themselves to the virtually complete elimination of nationalization from the socialist program, emphasizing the concepts of equality and welfare instead. In a Fabian tract on *Socialism and Nationalization* (1956), Hugh Gaitskell,

Drawing by Anton, © Punch, London

**"I WAS THE CHAIRMAN OF THE BOARD UNTIL I FOUND OUT
ABOUT THE RATES FOR OVERTIME."**

the late leader of the British Labour party, concludes that "the most vital question is how far greater social and economic equality can be achieved without more nationalization and public ownership." After the electoral defeat of 1959. Gaitskell went even further by publicly advocating that the Labour party eliminate from its constitution Clause IV, which calls for common ownership of the means of production, distribution, and exchange.

A prominent spokesman of the right wing in the Labour party and minister of defense in the Wilson cabinet, Denis Healey, goes even beyond Gaitskell. A generation ago, American writers like A. A. Berle said that in the American capitalist enterprise the real power is in the hands of professional managers rather than of the shareholders who legally own it. This viewpoint is now increasingly recognized by socialists as being equally applicable to publicly owned enterprise. "Industrial power in every large, developed economy now rests with a managerial class which is responsible to no one. The form of ownership is irrelevant. State control over nationalized industries is as difficult as share-holder control over private firms" (Denis Healey, *The New Leader*, August 17, 1957). For a high-ranking socialist to say that the form of ownership is irrelevant marks a basic change of outlook.

More important than what socialist leaders and thinkers have said is the fact that most voters have clearly and repeatedly expressed their opposition to further nationalization. In the 1950's and 1960's, numerous polls were taken on this question, some by independent polling organizations and others by Labour organizations. In every instance, from 65 to 80 percent of the voters have opposed further nationalization; more seriously, even among Labour party supporters the number of those who favor further nationalization is generally only one-third to one-half of those who oppose it.

In the elections of 1964 and 1966, the Labour campaign therefore barely mentioned public ownership and concentrated on the topic of economic growth as Britain's No. 1 problem. Taking his cue from the successful Kennedy campaign in 1960, Harold Wilson stressed the need for Britain to "move forward," to get out of the lethargy and stagnation which, according to him, were the result of thirteen years of Conservative rule. In particular, Wilson promised that a Labour government would increase and strengthen higher education and scientific research and that the new opportunities in research would stop the "brain drain," the emigration of British scientists to other countries, mainly to the United States. In his devotion to scientific growth Wilson went even so far as to say that "if there was one word I would use to identify modern Socialism it was 'science'" (*The Relevance of British Socialism*, 1964, p. 41). While Wilson also promised social welfare improvements in the campaigns of 1964 and 1966, the emphasis clearly shifted from accelerated social justice to accelerated economic growth. Because the rate of British economic growth since the 1950's has fallen way behind that of the other major economies, nationalization, whether commercially a success or a failure, has had little impact on the problem of British economic growth. By staking its future, at least for the next decade or two, on this issue rather than on the side issue of nationalization, the Labour party is aware of the fact that it will be judged by the people in the light of its record on restoring Britain to a position of economic excellence and leadership.

More recently, surveys in various parts of the world (including western Europe and Britain) have shown that about two-thirds of those polled reject both capitalism, if capitalism means the exploitation of the many by the wealthy few, and socialism, if socialism means government ownership of the economy. Two-thirds of the interviewees favored social welfare and private property. More specifically, 70 percent of those polled stated that socialism meant to them "social welfare" rather than "government ownership" (Ralph K. White, *Foreign Affairs*, January 1966, p. 225).

A leader of the Labour party, Douglas Jay, has succinctly stated the reason democratic socialist movements have swung away from nationalization toward the welfare state, economic security, and social justice: "Modern experience has proved that although governments are not always very efficient at producing goods, they are highly efficient at redistributing income and wealth" ("The Future of British Socialism," *New Politics*, Winter 1963, p. 97).

THE IMPASSE
OF SOCIALISM TODAY

Socialists today find themselves bewildered and uncertain of the future. For more than a half-century, the socialist movement was almost entirely devoted to propaganda and organization outside the framework of governmental responsibility. Now that so much of the socialist program has been realized, however, socialism faces a fate similar to that of organized political Liberalism.

Just as political Liberalism has passed away largely because some of the causes it championed have died a natural death while others have been solved by conservatives and socialists along liberal lines, socialism too may gradually pass away, as far as its original program is concerned, even though political parties with the socialist label may continue for a long time.

In the field of international affairs, governmental responsibilities have modified the traditional socialist outlook. As long as socialist parties were in opposition and had to confine their political activities to propaganda and electioneering, they could more steadfastly adhere to the classical socialist doctrine that capitalism was the root of all international tensions. From experience with both fascist and communist imperialism, socialists have learned that international affairs are much more complex and that the forces of imperialism can be tied to any system of economic organization. Moreover, once socialist parties assume governmental responsibilities in foreign policy, they tend to follow established national interests on the one hand and economic realities on the other. At times, the requirements of national economic planning under socialist governments have given socialist foreign policies an element of isolationism, which is in sharp contrast with the traditional doctrinal commitment to internationalism.

Thus the foreign policy of the Labour government during the years 1945–1951 was discouraging to all those, in Europe and America, who believed that Britain would be the natural leader in a movement for a united Europe. In fairness to the Labour government, however, it should be noted that the Conservative government that followed it vacillated for years on the issue of joining the Common Market. Britain finally applied but was turned down by the opposition of France led by de Gaulle. Yet this French attitude in 1963 would have been ineffective if Britain's commitment to European unity had been less half-hearted and less hedged with ifs and buts. The division of public opinion in Britain on the Common Market was not based on party. Although the Conservative party, as a whole, was a little more receptive to the idea of European integration than was the Labour party, the main line of division was within each of the two major parties. It is, therefore, at least conceivable that when British public opinion more vigorously embraces the idea of European unity, a Labour government may well lead Britain into the Common Market. The Wilson government tried in 1967 to do so but failed because of de Gaulle's opposition. After de Gaulle's resignation in 1969, the outlook for British entry into the Common Market has greatly improved, and either a Labour or a Conservative government is likely to associate Britain with the Common Market in the early 1970's. Having liquidated its far-flung empire, Britain is getting adjusted to the fact that it is now basically a European, and not a world, power. Both the Conservative and Labour parties are resigned to this new status, although the Conservatives find it somewhat harder to give up abruptly the memories of Britain as a Great Power with worldwide interests.

National interest is also the primary factor in determining the foreign policies of other socialist governments. Norway, always looking out toward the Atlantic rather than to the European continent, has strongly favored the alliance with the NATO countries. By contrast, Sweden's socialist governments have followed a policy of maintaining strict neutrality and avoiding alliances, but keeping Sweden fully armed with the most modern weapons and ready for self-defense in case of attack. This Swedish policy is based not on socialist isolationism, but on the traditional Swedish policy—a policy that has worked for a century and a half—of keeping Sweden out of alliances and wars. In the Middle East, the socialist-dominated government of Israel is strongly associated with the United States, but India's government, though strongly pro-socialist, is pursuing a policy of nonalignment between East and West. All these policies have little to do with socialism and are based primarily on national interests, attitudes, and traditions. Looking at the picture as a whole, it can be said that the foreign policies of socialist government have been no better and no worse than those of nonsocialist governments in the same countries. The quality of a particular government depended on how intelligent and farsighted that government was, rather than on whether it was socialist, liberal, or conservative.

In July 1951, the Socialist International was reestablished. At its first congress, more than 30 Socialist parties committed themselves to support the rearmament of their countries for collective defense against the threat of communist aggression. Meeting again in June 1962 in Oslo, the Socialist International rejected the idea that the democratic nations should disarm unilaterally. As to the causes of the cold war, the Socialist International stated that the "East-West rivalry has largely been imposed upon an unwilling world by the communist leaders." These resolutions are primarily of interest as they reflect a marked change of socialist outlook on the nature of war.

The present difficulties of the economic program of socialism are not likely to be resolved so soon. One great objective of socialism, the *welfare state*—that is, the responsibility of the community for a minimum standard of social and economic security for every person—*is no longer a monopoly of socialist parties.* All other parties in democratic nations, with the exception of ultraconservative diehards, are also in favor of the welfare state. Some parties are more warmly for it than others, and some parties recommend more benefits than others; but, as a general principle, the welfare state (in the minimum sense) is accepted by reasonable persons in all parties and is no longer a matter of partisan controversy.

The concept of the welfare state no longer requires a separate political party. In fact, much of the welfare state in England was historically the work of the Conservative party, and the limits of the welfare state are increasingly set by the ability to pay for its benefits rather than by differences of ideology. Thus, the Labour government in 1968 and 1969 introduced 30-cent charges for prescriptions and fees of $10 for glasses and $15 for teeth, thus breaching the principle of universal medicine without fees. It also overhauled the old-age pension system, so that contributions and benefits will be more closely correlated to earnings. The principle of universality, under which the same benefits are given to everybody regardless of need or income, has been mainly defended by socialists on the ground that means tests are thereby avoided. Yet the experience of the welfare state has taught the Labour party that under this principle of universality the needy do not receive enough benefits, and that in 1969 there were still one million persons in Britain living below the poverty level. As a result, the principle of "selectivity" has been increasingly debated in Britain, with more zeal by Conservatives than by Labourites. Under the principle of selectivity, more benefits are provided for those who need them than for those who do not, but a welfare system using the selectivity principle cannot do without some form of means test. In the context of British social history, the very term "means test" evokes for many British reformers, socialist as well as nonsocialist, a long chain of abhorrent memories going back to the operation of Elizabethan poorhouses. Pragmatically, the Labour party is unlikely to switch from universality to selectivity in a wholesale manner, but the current thinking and policies are groping in the direction of more selectivity, since the British economy does not produce enough—not yet, at least—to provide universal benefits on a level which is so high that the needy will receive enough for an adequate standard of living. In the period of 1964–1969, welfare expenditures nearly doubled, but the total output of goods and services increased by only 20 percent.

The very fact that after two generations of socialist propaganda and accomplishment the main principles of the welfare state have been accepted by all parties in democratic states has created a real dilemma for the future of socialism. If it keeps on trying to convert the converted, it will lose the old fire and enthusiasm that made it a distinctive movement in the Western world in the last three generations. If its leaders are unable to formulate a new program, adapted to the needs of the last third of the twentieth century, the party may simply settle down to a fixed position slightly to the left of the conservative parties, separated from the latter not by a basically different economic or political philosophy, but simply by its own concentration on translating the conception of the welfare state into a reality at the earliest possible moment.

SOCIALISM IN DEVELOPING COUNTRIES

The distinction between socialism and communism is of particular importance in the developing countries. The overriding political fact in poor nations is the desire to attain rapid economic growth. Without such economic progress, the newly emerging nations feel, there can be no genuine political independence or international leadership. Domestically, rapid economic growth is the only means of satisfying the yearning of the people for better living standards, health, and education.

The history of the last two centuries has shown two methods of rapid economic development; first is that of the most advanced Western nations (northwestern and central Europe, North America, and Australia and New Zealand), in which the free market was the main instrument of producing rapid economic growth. While it is true that government greatly aided this process (tariffs for infant industries; land grants for railways and educational institutions; legislatures, executives, and courts favoring the employer rather than the employee), it is still true that private initiative and capital were primarily responsible for the economic progress of the Western nations in the last two centuries. Without any government-sponsored five- or ten-year plans, private individuals decided how available resources—labor, capital, land, raw materials—were to be used, and individual consumers decided how much of their income was to be consumed and how much saved.

Economic growth in these Western nations was greatly favored by factors that are largely absent in developing nations today: a stable government, a fairly efficient civil service, relatively high levels of education, means of transportation and communication (highways, canals), and—perhaps most important of all—a considerable level of technological and entrepreneurial skill and initiative. Some nations—such as Great Britain, the Scandinavian countries, or the United States—had developed democratic political institutions before rapid economic expansion took place. As Alexis de Tocqueville noted in his *Democracy in America* (1835), "democracy is favorable to the growth of manufacturing, and it increases without limit the numbers of the manufacturing classes."

The second historically proved method of rapid economic growth has been communism. In this method, the state owns the means of production and sets an overall goal—such as a five-year plan—of what is to be produced and how the available resources of labor, land, and capital are to be employed. The freedom of the consumer, worker, and producer is replaced by the dictate of the state. Because the communist state possesses totalitarian power, it can generally ensure that the plan is translated into reality. This may take a few decades, and millions of people may pay with their lives, but eventually a modern industrial economy does develop at a rapid pace. It is important to note that no nation has so far freely chosen the path of communist economic development: communism has either been imposed by internal revolution or civil war (Russia, China, Yugoslavia, Cuba) or by external armed force (the communist states in eastern Europe, and Tibet and North Korea in the Far East).

In facing the issue of economic modernization, developing nations today generally do not wish to imitate either the Western capitalist process of development or the communist path of complete state planning and ownership based on political repression. Nearly every developing nation likes to think that its economic and social problems can be solved through methods which are different from both Western capitalism and Soviet or Chinese communism. The label which is attached to this "third way" is that of socialism. In the context of underdeveloped countries socialism means many things to those who profess it.

First, socialism in the developing world stands for the ideal of social justice. In developing countries, the differences between the rich and the poor are proportionately greater than in the wealthier countries. Socialism, then, stands for the commitment to raise the poor masses to a higher level and to narrow the gap between the thin upper class of the privileged and the vast mass of the dispossessed. Socialism means more welfare services for the poor, more schools for the uneducated, and more human dignity for the traditionally underprivileged. Where tribal organization of society is still alive, socialism is but a new term for traditional tribal loyalty and solidarity. Thus, African socialism is defined by a leading Tanzanian statesman:

The foundation, and the objective, of African Socialism is the Extended Family. The true African Socialist does not look on one class of men as his brethren and another as his natural enemies. He does not form an alliance with the 'brethren' for the extermination of the 'non-brethren.' He rather regards all men as his brethren—as members of his ever extending Family" (Julius K. Nyerere, *"Ujamaa": The Basis of African Socialism,* 1962, p. 8).

When attacked for betraying socialism by encouraging private foreign investments in India's fertilized industry, essential to its increased production of food, Prime Minister Indira Gandhi affirmed her government's commitment to both socialism and democracy in a nationwide address on April 24, 1966. Then she gave her definition of socialism: "What we all want is a better life, with more food, employment, and opportunity in conditions of economic justice, equality, and with individual freedom."

Second, the term socialism in developing countries often stands for the ideal of human brotherhood and world peace through law. As a result, socialists in developing nations frequently advocate nonalignment between the two sides in the cold war. Even where, as in India, the reality of Chinese invasion has made nonalignment difficult, socialists still cling to it as a hope for the future. In Africa, the view is held that the world is divided, not between capitalist and communist countries, but between rich and poor countries, and the poor countries "should be very careful not to allow themselves to be used as the 'tools' of any of the rich countries of the world," whether such rich countries are capitalist or communist (Paul E. Sigmund, ed., *The Ideologies of the Developing Nations*, 1963, p. 208).

The third meaning of socialism in developing countries is the commitment to planning. Because developing countries look upon economic growth with a sense of urgency, they feel that the functioning of the free market may not ensure the kind of rapid economic expansion and growth that are called for. Some basic elements of a modern economy—highways, means of transportation, hospitals, low-cost housing, schools—cannot, in the very nature of things, attract private enterprise, since they are the framework within which private enterprise and profits can be generated but which in themselves usually do not create such profits. Also, there is the kind of basic enterprise, such as the manufacture of steel, for which there is either not enough private capital available or which cannot hope to compete with foreign established enterprises. Only the state can build the foundations of a modern economy (highways and the like), and only the state can assume the risks of profitless enterprise over a number of years, if such enterprise is necessary for the economy as a whole. In 1963, for example, India had five steel plants, of which three were state-owned. With a population of over 460 million, India produced only 5.6 million tons of steel in 1962, as compared with nearly 100 million tons produced in the United States. Yet even at her low level of development, India needed in 1963 at least ten million tons of steel. As a step toward this goal, she asked American aid for the building of a sixth steel plant, to be state-owned, which would eventually produce about four million tons of steel. After several years of negotiation, the United States finally turned India down, largely because the projected plant would be state-owned. Indian businessmen, opposed to socialism as a general principle, publicly regretted the American position, because, in the words of the Indian Chamber of Commerce, the American refusal "could also hurt the private sector of Indian industry, which is badly in need of more steel" (*New York Times*, September 8, 1963).

Shortly after India was turned down by the United States, Russia offered to build the needed steel mill—one of the great Soviet propaganda triumphs of the decade. Although India is anticommunist in her domestic policy and has a predominantly private property economy, the Soviet Union was able to overcome dogmatic ideological inhibitions more effectively than was the United States. Yet the ideological gulf between India and the Soviet Union is much wider than that between India and the United States.

The need for planning, to which all developing countries are committed, does not imply overall or even large-scale nationalization of the means of production. Here, India again provides a good illustration, as she is committed to the general idea of socialism. India has much public enterprise in heavy industry, coal, electric power, rail and air transportation, chemicals, and life insurance. In 1969, the Indian government also nationalized the fourteen biggest banks so as to gain a controlling financial leverage over the whole economy, particularly in foreign trade and over investment priorities. Since the late fifties the Indian government has sought to strengthen the public sector of the economy by allocating two dollars for its development for every one dollar in the private sector. Yet, even after the nationalization of the banks only about 14 percent of the economy was in the public sector, and the government seeks to increase the proportion of public enterprise by creating new productive facilities rather than by nationalizing existing ones. As a result, public and private companies often compete in the same industry. Where the competition is with foreign companies—as in the case of Air India—public companies do well. Where the competition of public enterprise is with domestic Indian companies, public enterprise does less well, and where it has a monopoly its performance has been least impressive and vigorously criticized in India itself.

Indian economic policies follow a pragmatic course rather than a rigid ideology of public enterprise for the sake of public enterprise. The differences between Indian economic policies and those of advanced Western nations are due to the different stages of economic development rather than to abstract theory. Where rapid development was necessary in the United States—as recently, for example, in atomic energy, jet aircraft, supersonic planes, space technology—the planning and financing have come almost entirely from the government, since in each of these areas the initial job was too big, too costly, and too profitless for private enterprise or initiative. What atomic energy or space technology in their beginning stages are for the United States, steel or railroads may be for India or any other developing country.

In the economic field, socialism in developing countries thus means an economic structure in which some industries are completely private (such as farming, handicrafts, small business), in which others have both a private and a public sector (as in heavy industry), and finally, in which the public sector dominates (transportation, public utilities). While this is the general meaning of socialism in the economic sphere in developing areas, the practical application varies in different countries. In general, it can be said that nationalization has gone furthest where political democracy is weak or nonexistent, as in Egypt, Algeria, or Burma. Where constitutional government is a reality (as in the Philippines, India, Israel, Chile), private enterprise is encouraged or at least tolerated.

Thus, we see that the meaning of socialism in developing countries differs from that in the wealthier countries, because the historical situation is different. In the West, socialism has meant, not how to industrialize an undeveloped country, but how to distribute the fruits of a wealthy society in a more equitable way. As a result, the concept of the welfare state has virtually absorbed the idea of socialism. By contrast, socialism in developing countries is confronted with the task, not so much of distributing the fruits of an industrial economy which hardly exists, but to build an industrial economy, so as to raise the economic and educational level of the masses of the people. For the same reason, while socialism in Western countries has generally developed best within a framework of established constitutional government (as in Britain or Scandinavia), socialism in developing countries frequently develops within a tradition in which authoritarian rule by foreign imperialists or by native power-holders has been the rule. It is therefore to be expected that socialism in some developing countries will show a greater tolerance for authoritarian practices than has generally been true of Western socialism.

Yet, in the final analysis, socialism in the developing countries tries to imitate neither the Western capitalist pattern in toto nor the communist totalitarian pattern. From communism, the developing nations (regardless of their commitment to socialism) have borrowed the idea that economic development can be planned, and in some cases must be planned, by the state. However, most developing countries have decided that they want planning without the police state of communism. As to the capitalist West, the developing countries, and especially the socialist elements in them, greatly admire its technological efficiency. Nonetheless, the great disparities of wealth as produced by the relatively freely functioning capitalist economies of the West seem a less worthy object of imitation in developing countries. The most important aspect of Western nations that appeals to developing nations is political democracy based on the rule of law. Whether the developing nations will be able to merge, under their concept of socialism, the Western political idea of liberty with the economic concept of planning, largely borrowed from the practice of communism, still remains to be seen. If the developing nations should fail in their attempted synthesis of constitutional government and economic planning (including partial government ownership of industry), there is the possibility that they (or some, at least) may consider constitutional government expendable, but not rapid economic development through full-fledged planning and public ownership of industry.

FOR FURTHER READING

Attlee, Clement R. *As It Happened.* New York: Viking, 1954.

Buber, Martin. *Paths in Utopia.* "Beacon Paperbacks." Boston: Beacon Press, 1960.

Caute, David. *The Left in Europe Since 1789.* New York: McGraw-Hill, 1966.

Cole, G. D. H. *A History of Socialist Thought.* 5 vols. New York: St. Martin's Press, 1953–1960.

Cole, Margaret. *The Story of Fabian Socialism.* "Stanford Paperbacks." Stanford: Stanford University Press, 1969.

Crosland, C. A. R. *The Future of Socialism.* New York: Macmillan, 1957.
―――. *The Conservative Enemy: A Program of Radical Reform for the 1960s.* New York: Schocken Books, 1962.

Crossman, R. H. S. *The Politics of Socialism.* New York: Atheneum, 1965.

Dean, Vera Micheles. *New Patterns of Democracy in India.* 2nd ed. Cambridge, Mass.: Harvard University Press, 1969.

Ebenstein, William. *Great Political Thinkers.* 4th ed. New York: Holt, Rinehart & Winston, 1969. Chapter 24.

Fleisher, Frederic. *The New Sweden: The Challenge of a Disciplined Democracy.* New York: McKay, 1967.

Foot, Paul. *The Politics of Harold Wilson.* Harmondsworth: Penguin Books, 1968.

Fried, Albert, and Ronald Sanders (eds.). "Anchor Books." *Socialist Thought: A Documentary History.* Garden City, N.Y.: Doubleday, 1964.

Friedland, William H., and Carl G. Rosberg (eds.). *African Socialism.* Stanford: Stanford University Press, 1964.

Gaitskell, Hugh. *Socialism and Nationalisation.* London: Fabian Society, 1956.

Goldthorpe, John, and others. *The Affluent Worker: Political Attitudes and Behaviour.* Cambridge: Cambridge University Press, 1968.

Hayek, Friedrich A. *The Road to Serfdom.* "Phoenix Books." Chicago: University of Chicago Press, 1960.

Heilbroner, Robert L. *The Great Ascent: The Struggle for Economic Development in Our Time.* "Harper Torchbooks." New York: Harper & Row, 1963.

Jenkins, Roy. *Essays and Speeches.* New York: Chilmark Press, 1968.

Kaldor, Nicholas. *Causes of the Slow Rate of Economic Growth of the United Kingdom.* Cambridge: Cambridge University Press, 1966.

Kelf-Cohen, R. *Twenty Years of Nationalisation: The British Experience.* New York: St. Martin's Press, 1969.

Lewis, W. Arthur. *Development Planning: The Essentials of Economic Policy.* New York: Harper & Row, 1966.

Lowenthal, Richard (ed.). *Issues in the Future of Asia: Communist and Non-Communist Alternatives.* New York: Praeger, 1969.

Mishan, E. J. *Welfare Economics.* 2nd ed. New York: Random House, 1968.

Mises, Ludwig von. *Socialism.* New Haven, Conn.: Yale University Press, 1951.

Morgan, H. Wayne (ed.). *American Socialism: 1900–1960.* Englewood Cliffs, N.J.: Prentice-Hall, 1964.

Morris, William D. *The Christian Origins of Social Revolt.* New York: Macmillan, 1959.

Myrdal, Gunnar. *Asian Drama: An Inquiry into the Poverty of Nations.* 3 vols. New York: Pantheon Books, 1968.

Nyerere, Julius K. *Freedom and Unity.* New York: Oxford University Press, 1966.

Papanek, Gustav F. (ed.). *Development Policy: Theory and Practice.* Cambridge, Mass.: Harvard University Press, 1968.

Pigou, A. C. *Socialism Versus Capitalism.* New York: Macmillan, 1937.

Schapiro, J. Salwyn. *Movements of Social Dissent in Modern Europe.* "Anvil Books." Princeton: Van Nostrand, 1962.

Schumpeter, Joseph A. *Capitalism, Socialism, and Democracy.* "Harper Torchbooks." New York: Harper & Row, 1962.

Sigmund, Paul E. (ed.). *The Ideologies of the Developing Nations.* Rev. ed. New York: Praeger, 1967.

Thomas, Norman. *Socialism Re-Examined.* New York: W. W. Norton, 1963.

Tinbergen, Jan. *Central Planning.* New Haven: Yale University Press, 1964.

Turvey, R. (ed.). *Public Enterprise.* Baltimore: Penguin Books, 1968.

Ward, Benjamin. *The Socialist Economy.* New York: Random House, 1967.

Wilson, Harold. *The Relevance of British Socialism.* London: Weidenfeld & Nicolson, 1964.

———. *Purpose and Power.* Boston: Houghton Mifflin, 1966.

Index